The Crowd Goes Wild for
MORE THAN A GAME

"This book is a marvelous dialogue between two friends. It reveals why Phil Jackson is the winningest coach in pro basketball today. It shows how he thinks about the game and his players. It offers us his roadway to greatness, full of clarity, modesty, and candor."

—Bill Bradley

"An unusual amalgam of biography, spiritualism, basketball technique, and journalism."

—*Library Journal*

"The technical details in this wonderful book will give any fan a better appreciation of the game."

—*Publishers Weekly*

"There's plenty here to attract a broad spectrum of fans, from celebrity talk to techno-hoop strategy, but underlying it all is a reverence for a game that, when played well, can be a transcendent personal experience and a joy to watch."

—*Booklist*

PHIL JACKSON
AND CHARLEY ROSEN

MORE
THAN
A
GAME

A FIRESIDE BOOK
PUBLISHED BY SIMON & SCHUSTER
NEW YORK   LONDON   TORONTO   SYDNEY   SINGAPORE

FIRESIDE
Rockefeller Center
1230 Avenue of the Americas
New York, NY 10020

Introduction © Copyright 2002 Phil Jackson
Copyright © 2001 by Phil Jackson and Charley Rosen
All rights reserved, including the right of reproduction
in whole or in part in any form.

First Fireside Edition 2002

The hardcover edition of *More Than a Game* is published by
Seven Stories Press. This edition is published by arrangement
with Seven Stories Press.

FIRESIDE and colophon are registered trademarks
of Simon & Schuster, Inc.

Designed by Cindy La Breacht

Manufactured in the United States of America

10 9 8 7 6 5 4 3 2 1

ISBN 0-7434-4411-6

For information regarding special discounts for bulk purchases,
please contact Simon & Schuster Special Sales at 1-800-456-6798 or
business@simonandschuster.com

In remembrance of RED HOLZMAN,
my mentor and coach, who always said,
Basketball isn't rocket science;
it's about putting the ball in at one end
and about defending the basket at the other;
and it's about people playing together.
—PHIL

To DAIA, whose courage and honesty
inspire me to be truthful about myself.
—CHARLEY

CONTENTS

Introduction   IX

I . GETTING THERE

One: PHIL D. BASKET   11

Two: LEARNING THE GAME COUNTRY-STYLE   19

Three: LEARNING THE GAME CITY-STYLE   31

Four: WELCOME TO THE NBA   39

Five: ONE ON ONE   67

Six: PUERTO RICAN SUMMER AND THE BULLS   71

Seven: THE COCKROACH BB ASS.   85

Eight: TRIANGULATION   103

II . BEING THERE

Nine: T FOR TWO (TEX AND THE TRIANGLE)   119

Ten: THE ROAD TO LOS ANGELES   137

Eleven: POINT TAKEN   153

Twelve: THE LAKERS' SEASON   163

III . BEYOND WINNING

Thirteen: ON THE SCENE   221

Fourteen: THE "SECOND SEASON"   235

Fifteen: WHO'S GOT NEXT?   285

Glossary   293

Diagrams   299

Index   306

INTRODUCTION

My second season in L.A. was barely a week old when I realized this was going to be a very different season from any other. The 2000–01 Lakers would experience more unusual twists and turns than any championship team I had ever coached. Yet by the time the playoffs began, the Lakers were the most dominant championship team ever, something they proved in the playoffs. What held the Lakers together? What had been bad chemistry in January had become 24-karat gold in June. But the question remains: How did it happen?

In mid-November 2000, with the season less than ten days old, I asked Kobe Bryant to meet me for breakfast to discuss whatever was on his mind. We met before practice at 8 A.M., at a deli in the Marina, not far from our practice facility. I passed on the food, watched Kobe eat, and tried to get him to talk about his change of attitude and game.

The previous year, my first with the team, Kobe had been injured in the first preseason game. He didn't play for six weeks and joined the team in the first week of December. It was a team already fifteen games into the year, and he had to fit into the groove that was already established. On top of that, I had him come off the bench for a couple of games to help ease him into the mix. Before long, his trademark enthusiasm provided a spark for his teammates.

But this year, as early as preseason training I had noticed his lack of interest in the finer points of the game. He told me he had worked all summer, taking a thousand shots a day, and he *had* his game down pat. But I could see he wasn't enjoying the game of basketball, and Kobe loves playing b-ball.

"It's boring," he had said to me during a practice. We were taking a water break and I had just asked him why he was so blue on the court.

"What's boring?" I asked, knowing what was coming.

"The Triangle offense doesn't do anything for me—it's too simple."

I explained to him that the whole purpose of the offense was to keep it logical and simple. We wanted to line up the defense, read our opponents, and explore what they gave us. We cut short our talk to keep the practice flowing, but I kept in mind our exchange of views.

Our talk over breakfast wasn't going to be father-to-son or mentor-to-mentored. This was a young man wanting the liberty to explore the opportunities his career offered him. He knew that he was in his fifth season and he was averaging only fifteen or sixteen points per game. Kobe also knew he could do a lot more if he pressed his foot to the pedal.

I was trying to keep the game plan the same as the previous year and play a deliberate style of ball that featured Shaq as the anchor of the Triangle. Kobe felt that we needed to break it out and run the ball into the open field, where he could beat the defense before they got set. My argument was that Shaq wasn't ready to play the up-and-down game and it was going to upset the structure. An up-tempo pace wasn't my idea of how we needed to play to win, and that was my job—making the Lakers play to the best of their collective ability.

"Hey, PJ, I got to be true to myself," Kobe repeated for the third time.

"'You have to do what you have to do, and so do I.' What does that mean?" I asked him. "Do you want to be traded? Really think about this. Do you want to go somewhere else and play for another team?"

The words were spoken. Kobe stopped, swallowed, and began to review our conversation, redefining what he felt was his license as a player. He had worked hard during the off-season. He was in great shape. He wanted to be the best ever to play. He had this driving desire to be the best he could be.

"Hold it!" I interjected. "Do you know who was the best there can be in basketball?" and without waiting for an answer I said, "Bill Russell." I explained to him that Bill had won eleven championships and had never even averaged twenty points a game. That's what it's about: winning. And I added that he, Kobe, had a chance to be up there with the best if he played the game the right way.

Kobe grinned and said, "I'll always be a winner."

I could see our conversation was going around in circles. I told him that he wasn't playmaking from his guard position, so I was going to move him into the small forward spot to try to get us going—we were struggling to win early on. He said fine, that would give him less responsibility to run the offense and an open field to score. Hmmm, I left with a furrowed brow. Nothing had been resolved. I had just paid for breakfast with my young gun and he was on a mission—one that seemed counter to our best interests as a team.

This omen was something that would play itself out over the next two months as we struggled during the early season. We did okay, but we weren't cruising through the league like we had the previous year. We just couldn't get a winning streak going. The relationship between Kobe and me was becoming an issue. I tweaked him during film sessions—reran portions of game video when he would take on three or four guys and lose the ball, or when he might pull up and shoot when just one or two of his teammates were in the picture and the defense might be compromised, or Shaq wasn't across half-court. We were playing one-on-five a lot of the time.

December came, and I had a talk with Shaq about his free-throw shooting ineptitude. I had a variety of options to propose to him, including hypnosis, if he was interested. He told me that he had hired a guy and was taking extra practice. Now all I had to do was get Kobe under control and get back to the style of game that had made us champs the year before.

"What's so hard about playing ball with your head—logically?" he asked.

Hmm, I couldn't argue with that, but I needed time to convince Kobe that he was losing the trust of his teammates.

Then, while we were in the middle of a slump, *ESPN Magazine* came out with an article about Kobe. It wasn't that the article was so wrong, or that Kobe was so self-centered. It was just that Kobe hadn't taken into account how sensitive Shaq might be to some of his comments, how Kobe saw the Lakers as a team, and how he had to take over at the end of game play because Shaq wasn't a good free-throw shooter, etc.

Those comments didn't go over very well. We had been losing close games and it wasn't anyone's fault. Both Kobe and Shaq had not been successful at finishing games. The real reason, as I saw it, was that the rest of the team was being held hostage to the stardom of those two players, instead of fleshing out the total team play that is necessary to be a championship team.

Perhaps the best thing I did during this period of time was to encourage the other twelve guys on the team to let it go—not to take sides.

The press creates half of the problem. Remember, we had overcome a similar situation the previous year, but without all the distraction of the press. The papers were vying with each other to make headlines out of new accusations or insinuations by Shaq, Kobe, or me. I surely didn't want to be a moving target for the press, and I didn't want that for the team, either.

We were having a hard enough time beating teams we had beaten the year before. Shaq put it best on January 15 after an overtime win over Vancouver when he said to the press, "Hey, check it out for yourself; last year at this time we were 30 and 7, this year we're 25-12."

We weren't firing on all cylinders, but that is what makes coaching interesting and challenging. My continual mantra to the team was, "I believe in you—you believe in yourselves. Let all those naysayers have their critical comments now, because when the real season begins with the playoffs, we are going to make them eat their words."

But it seemed like we were never going to get on a roll. In late January, Shaq suffered a sprained arch and missed the last five games before the All-Star break. We just didn't have enough size to compete without him in a couple of those games, and we came into the February break with a 32-17 won-lost record. That's nothing to sneeze at, to be sure. But we needed to break away from the pack with an eight-to-ten-game winning streak, and we just couldn't find that kind of momentum.

Going into the All-Star weekend, I asked the players to take that five-day break and get some resolve—to come back dedicated to doing whatever it takes individually to bring the best out of our team. At the All-Star Game, by the way, Kobe was terrific—up until the last play. He turned over the ball and the East won behind Allen Iverson's play, and the "Lil' Rascal" was named MVP. Shaq had gone to the game and been Kobe's biggest cheerleader.

Our team room in L.A. has a dry-erase porcelain board. On the board, I write a variety of things, i.e., the upcoming week's schedule, our practice/game format, and what I expect out of the next four to five games—short-term goals. At the top of the board is a line—a continuum—that we call our "wellness" quotient. It has a positive/negative valence sign at each end of the line and a midpoint. I slide a bar up and down the line to signify where we are as a group in terms of our overall wellness.

We had been above mid-point almost the whole of the 1999–2000 season—good energy abounded—but this year we just couldn't get into our rhythm. We were below the midpoint for the first two months of the season. It seemed like one thing after another was going to make our season a depressing experience. Whenever we did get a second wind, or resolve and confidence in each other, an incident or injury would stymie us.

After the All-Star break, we reconvened in New Jersey. It was mid-February, time to face the challenge ahead of us. We won our first game versus the Nets, but lost guard Ronnie Harper to a knee injury that would eventually need to be 'scoped. He would miss the rest of the season and some of the playoffs. This especially hurt because Ronnie acted as my on-court conscience. If the team went up and down the floor a couple of times without running the offense, or Kobe or Shaq were too dominant during the game and we needed more group participation, Harp was the one who calmed down the team, organized the offense, and got us back in the groove.

This six-game road trip, ending in Texas, was our longest. We didn't seem to have gained the strides I had hoped for; we still couldn't get any momentum—a win in New Jersey, a loss in Philly, a win in Charlotte, and an ugly loss in Indiana, 110–109, after failing to finish a game we had led most of the way. To make matters worse, Kobe took a forced shot at the end of the game and hurt his ankle.

During the last game of the road trip, in Dallas, Kobe landed on Shaq's size 22 shoe, and really injured his ankle. We still won. The next night, in San Antonio, we won for the first time in my tenure without Kobe. Kobe would be gimpy on that foot for almost two months.

At the beginning of March, we got to twenty wins over .500, which is normally a benchmark figure for a team, but not for the champion Lakers. It's great to be twenty over .500 in January and thirty over by the All-Star break. But we expected more of ourselves, and so did our fans—and don't forget the press. One bright spot in a season where we lost a total of 277 player games due to injuries was to happen in mid-March. It would be the keynote to our season.

Derek Fisher came back after recovering from an operation for a stress fracture in his foot. We really needed some fresh legs, and Derek provided them. He scored a career-high twenty-five points after sitting out 62 games of the season. Derek, a career five-point-per-game scorer, would average over eleven points per game for the rest of the season and be a spark plug for our team during the playoffs.

However, our team spirit was not totally healed, and I would inadvertently contribute to another bout of doubt during a road trip in March. During our day off in Milwaukee, I was working the inter-view market, talking about this book with a writer from Chicago, Rick Telander. Rick is an old friend. He was talking about *More Than a Game*, my interest in giving books to players, and literacy in general. The conversation wandered, and we talked about some of the books I had given athletes. He asked me a familiar question—what books had I given to Kobe and Shaq and why?

I told him about giving Shaq Herman Hesse's book *Siddhartha*, and what he had said when he read it: "I know why you gave me that book. It's about a man with lotsa riches and women, who seeks enlightenment." He was right on!

Kobe's book embodied a different idea. I gave Kobe *Corelli's Mandolin*, a book about two cultures, the Italian occupiers and the Greeks during WWII. Kobe was raised partly in Italy and enjoys Italian culture. The book describes the subtle political power play by the Greeks, who are trying to outmaneuver their Italian occupiers who want to control their lives.

When Rick asked me why I chose that book, I talked about the Kobe of the year past and his growth as a player and his intensely competitive nature. The book was about how one can live a life regardless of the restrictions and controls. Rick wanted to know more, and I expanded on Kobe's competitive desire to win games, against all odds.

I said, in effect, that Kobe's desire to win had even allowed him the luxury in high school of toying with games to make them more competitive. Because the games were so uncompetitive for him, he had to find challenges to make them interesting. This was all hearsay from a secondhand source, but one that I considered credible.

Little did I know that Rick would use the sensationalism of this off-the-record sidebar of our interview for a publicity advantage. In effect, I had accused Kobe of playing with the score to make the games a challenge, so he could dramatize the game.

During the Milwaukee game, Kobe injured his ankle again for the third time in about three weeks and had to come out of the game. From a 16-point lead in the first half, we squandered our advantage and ended up with another demoralizing loss, as well as losing Kobe to injury. Immediately after the game, our director of publicity, John Black, had news of the article published that day by Telander, and made me aware that it was going to raise a stink.

We flew back to L.A. that night and I got to Kobe and told him about the article, which I hadn't yet read. I hadn't intended to demean him—or even for the remarks to be published. Little did I imagine how far the accusations would go, as the sports radio commentators really jumped on it.

There were defenders of Kobe that wanted me to resign and quit. Sonny Vacarro, a "sneaker squeaker" for Adidas, vilified me, as would a number of press people that had rallied earlier around the theory that I had pushed Jerry West out of his job. Two camps formed again, and instead of being the peacemaker easing the tension, I was the one with my back to the wall. Mitch Kupchak, who had succeeded West as general manager of the team, was caught in the middle, trying to defend me and calm the camp that was after my head.

On one of those mid-March days when games seem to begin almost before the previous one ends, I called a team meeting in our media room. I stood before the team and told them I was the culprit, and even though I hadn't meant any harm—there it was! Now we could rally as a team, or get into a funk about it.

Kobe was injured and we didn't know how long it would be before he would be able to play. He started intensive therapy to heal and strengthen his ankle and foot, a lot of it off-site at the Kerlan-Jobe Orthopaedic Clinic. He would miss almost three weeks and eleven games until April 10. After five games out, he tried to play against New York on April 1. It took just a few minutes for him to know he wasn't ready. Ironically, that would be our last loss for more than two months.

The next week, we went on a four-games-in-six-nights road trip to the East, finishing up in Minnesota. Kobe hinted that he would like to stay behind and get therapy on his foot and ankle. I asked him to join us instead, and bring his personal therapist along. We just had to keep our team together. I asked Ron Harper, who was doing therapy on his knee, to go along, too, even though he wouldn't play. It was important that we keep the energy positive and continue to grow as a team. That trip was what changed our year.

We started to play basketball very logically and efficiently. Brian Shaw, who replaced Harper, and then Kobe, showed a steady hand, and with the advent of Derek Fisher we had a different attack and a solid defense. We won four games on the road and then went home and finished up the season with five outstanding games, all wins.

Kobe rejoined the team and fit in seamlessly. What went on during this stretch was something that I wish I could bottle and sell. It was as if a light had dawned on all the Lakers at the same moment in time and they were enlightened. But the reality was that a core group of players—Rick Fox, Robert Horry, Brian Shaw, Ron Harper, Horace Grant, Tyronn Lue, Devean George, Mark Madsen, and a rejuvenated Derek Fisher—had kept their confidence and resolve high until the seed of togetherness had germinated in the group. I always tell my players that I believe in prayer. The Lakers' internal prayers for the melding of their talents were fruitful and timely, because no team I have ever coached has dominated the playoffs like the 2000–2001 Lakers.

Everybody seemed to have a shining moment in the playoffs, as the Lakers played basketball like a team. Shaq told the world that Kobe was the best player on this, or any, planet. He was during the San Antonio series, when he had the dominant advantage, but he was more than willing to give the ball to the Big Aristotle, Shaq, in the finals versus Philadelphia. Fisher was tenacious and timely with his 3-point shots. Horace Grant nullified Chris Webber in the Sacramento series. Fox played defense like a Tasmanian devil. Robert Horry dropped in some timely 3-point shots and played defense like an octopus. Tyronn Lue came through in the finals, played Iverson very well, and sparked our effort. Brian Shaw masterfully launched some Shaw-Shaq redemptive passes and some 3-point shots. Ron Harper came back for the last two series and gave us experience and poise down the stretch in two of the finals games against Philly. We were a complete team. The Lakers had melded their talents.

I can only hope the trials and successes of last year bode well for the Lakers this season. We think we are going to be very good, but we know winning three consecutive championships takes a very special team effort. The hunt is on.

As I write this preface, we have just completed the first month with a 15 win and 1 loss record. Have we learned the lessons the hard way—through experience—and are we now reaping the benefits of those lessons?

- **Lesson 1:** No matter how tough the challenge, believe in yourself and your teammates.
- **Lesson 2:** Don't criticize or gossip about your coworkers. The disorder it creates takes a lot of mending and binding of wounds.
- **Lesson 3:** Stay the course—don't give up. Pick yourself up no matter how hard or how often you fall. It's all about how many times you're willing to get up and give it a go the next time.
- **Lesson 4:** No matter how great the player, or players, it takes a team to win. Everyone must be willing to sacrifice and give of themselves to be the champions.

I think, yes!

MORE THAN A GAME

I. GETTING THERE

ONE

PHIL D. BASKET

CHARLEY

When he coached the Chicago Bulls, Phil Jackson's game plan was to create a secure yet open environment that could develop the character and chemistry of his players. Finding a workable balance between freedom and discipline was not an easy task, especially when dealing with mega-stars and their mega-egos. Part of Phil's method is always to set goals that are higher than the ones required by the situation at hand, so that anybody traveling along with him can sense a greater journey beyond the immediate concerns of winning ball games.

Over time, Phil's efforts to discover that environment took on the qualities of a search for the Holy Grail. Eventually, he hooked up with Tex Winter, who had the magic playbook in his hand. With Tex acting as Merlin to Phil's Galahad, miracles were wrought.

The latest miracle was Phil's ability to motivate a young and immature team like the Lakers to accept an unselfish philosophy and thereby win a championship—and do it all in his very first season in Los Angeles.

But I've been traveling along with Phil for nearly thirty years, and one of the things I've learned from him is to always expect the unexpected.

I first met PJ at a postgame party in the spring of 1973 in his loft on West Nineteenth Street, brought there by a mutual friend, Stan Love, a six-foot-nine well-credentialed hippie and part-time powerless forward for the Baltimore Bullets. Having been *Sport* magazine's pro basketball beat writer for a year or two, I'd encountered numerous NBA super-duper-stars and found most of them to be totally self-involved. Even the wondrously humble Julius Erving had been three hours late for an appointment. But Phil was obviously of a different breed.

For starters, instead of being a deluxe townhouse or duplex penthouse apartment, Phil's loft was situated above a Great Bear auto-body shop. (As I would soon discover, the noise and fumes rising through the floorboards severely limited the livable sections of the loft during business hours.) I was the only celebrant at the party whom Phil did not know, yet he was very solicitous in his attentions, and sincerely curious about me.

Coincidentally, my current assignment for *Sport* was an article called "The Soul Brothers," which was an exploration of three of the NBA's most insistent individualists—Stan, of course, the quintessential Laguna Beach Love child; Billy Paultz, a beer-chugging native New York party mammal extraordinaire; and John Hummer, an authentic Princetonian and putative Chaucerian scholar. A sudden impulse moved me to ask Phil if he might be interested in being included in my story. "That would be interesting," he said.

In part, this is how Phil's section came out:

> *"Playing basketball is just like everything else:*
> *They own your body and they try to own your head.*
> *—Phil Jackson, player, New York Knicks*

Jackson's body and head co-exist in a loft on New York's lower West Side. There's a hammock suspended from the ceiling of the living room, a dart board with Spiro Agnew's face serving as the target, and on the far wall a photograph taken by Phil of a Colorado mountain.

Phil was throwing a party to celebrate Saturday night and the dozen or so guests seemed to be very comfortable with each other. A bag of walnuts lay casually torn open on the living room table, a bottle of wine occasionally made the rounds, and someone was melodiously banging on the piano in the corner.

But the most revealing thing in the room was Jackson's record collection—a dust-covered stack which included the likes of Andy Williams and Frank Sinatra, and then the active stack—the Grateful Dead, the Allman Brothers, et al.

"My taste in people has changed also," Phil said. "None of my friends are basketball people. Aside from Bill Bradley, I never really had a friend on the Knicks. Because of the pressure, the inconvenience, and the competition, you have to stop at a certain level. With your teammates, you get down to everything but your personal lives."

Jackson has started maybe twenty games in his tenure with the Knicks, but his bed-spring hair, his mustache and his Ichabod Crane body are as well-known to every basketball fan as Jerry West's nose.

"It's like living in a smaller world," Jackson continued, "a complete world but just a lot smaller. And, in a way, professional sports is just like the real world—a lot of people have invested a lot of money and that leads to politicking and pressure situations. Kids come into the league and get big money right off the bat, and the guys getting the bread have to play, even if someone else is better."

When Jackson was a rookie out of the University of North Dakota in 1968, he was a second round draft choice and signed a one-year contract for $13,500.

"Bill Bradley turned pro basketball around," Phil said. "In 1968, he got $400,000 for four years, which was an incredible sum then. After his first game at the Garden I couldn't find a seat in the locker room because there were fifty reporters around. I mean people from *Time* and *Life*. Bradley was a public figure to the nth degree. He had the romantic Princeton-Rhodes Scholar thing going for him, but mainly, he was the latest white hope. Pro basketball is dominated by black players, but the people who own the sport, pay to see it live, sponsor it on TV and write about it are white. So they all focused on Bradley."

Phil's boots and dirty socks were leaning against the sofa, but nobody seemed to mind. A few people were on the roof, pressing their faces against the skylight, and a young woman was working on a floor-to-ceiling crossword puzzle hanging next to the dart board.

"Ballplayers have to wear suits on most teams in the NBA," Phil was saying as he wiped his hands on his pants. "The Knicks happen to be the only club where you can wear jeans. If it wasn't for the fact that I'm a Knick, I couldn't dress and act the way I do and still stay in the league."

But Phil's life-style does cause some unique problems. He's the Knicks' media hippie, and it has gotten to the point where the counter-culture community expects him to trip for every game and to attend an obligatory number of rock concerts.

"Sometimes I feel like an amoeba on a slide," Phil said. "But I just try to ignore all these extraneous things as best I can—they're all so totally absurd. It's fun for people to have their superstars, but you can't take the cross off their backs and put it on yours."

Phil keeps his perspective by going camping during the off-season, surrounding himself with friends who will still be there the day after he is finished as a ballplayer, and puffing on a good cigar. He is capable of discussing offense as "a very civilized breaking down of a team's defense," and of shilling for a hair spray. It's all part of the game and Phil is careful to keep certain things from getting too close to him.

"In *The Hobbit*," Phil said, "the Grand Wizard can blow smoke rings in all different colors. He just sits there and blows them to the ceiling. I can only aspire to that."

Yet beneath his peaceful hippie smile, Phil was a relentless competitor (a characteristic that would eventually endear him to Michael Jordan). At the same time, he was never possessed by the Vince Lombardi ethic that equated losing with dying.

After his playing days were defunct, Phil had a turn as assistant coach with the New Jersey Nets under head coach Kevin Loughery—but when Loughery left, so did Phil. Eventually, Phil wound up as head coach of the Albany Patroons in the Continental Basketball Association. Among the league's hard-bitten veterans, the CBA was also known as "Come Back Again" or the "Crazy Basketball Association." Nevertheless, Phil took every advantage of his tenure there. And since PJ and I had a similar vision of the game and I lived in Woodstock, a mere sixty miles south of Albany, I was recruited to become Phil's assistant coach.

During our three-year partnership in Albany, what most impressed me about Phil's approach to the game was his ability to make coaching adjustments. After we'd gotten whipped by twenty points by a particular team, I would despair of ever beating that ball club. However, even back then Phil was able to identify and isolate an opponent's weak points, and by changing the angle of a certain pick, or perhaps forcing a certain player to his right instead of his left, he'd enable the Patroons to turn the score around in the rematch. Phil's special gift was being able to find the "is-ness" of a play, a player, a team, and/or a game. And he gave me a lifetime's worth of insights into the strategies and philosophies of the sacred hoop.

Among other things, I learned:

➤ The game will always reveal the players, and the coaches as well.

➤ Ballplayers *always* know when their coach is lying to them, and vice versa.

➤ Referees are a necessary evil. They spend so many hours in darkened rooms watching game tapes and concentrating entirely on locating mistakes—three-second violations and illegal defenses, extra steps, fouls called and uncalled—that the beauty of the game eludes them.

➤ Ball games are won or lost in practice sessions.

➤ A player's character is more important than his talent.

➤ There's no substitute for experience, and most players aren't really capable of understanding the game until they're twenty-six or so.

➤ Role players are (almost) as important as All-Stars.

➤ How a team fares in the first five minutes of the third quarter is a function of the adjustments made (or not made) by the coaching staff at halftime.

➤ More important than how many points a player scores is when he scores them.

➤ Coaching basketball can be dangerous to one's mental, physical, and psychological health.

➤ Pro basketball requires a discriminating brutality from even the most marginal players.

➤ The perfect game doesn't match the good guys against the bad guys, but features ten players playing one ball game.

➤ And, yes, life is indeed a metaphor for basketball.

After two seasons with the Patroons, Phil and I were becoming dissatisfied with the flex offense—its graceless movements, limited entry passes, and vulnerability to freely switching defenses. Phil had added a "box" offense to the Patroons' repertoire, but it was too jammed, too physical, and too mindless.

We certainly knew the "right" way to play the game: the picks, the cuts, the set-up passes that never registered in a box score. Filling a lane on a fast break to create a space for a teammate. Hitting the open man. Playing balls-out defense, rotating, boxing out. All the wordless communications and small unselfishnesses that made the game so much fun. But these ingredients only seemed to come together accidentally—when the "right" players matched with the "right" coach in the "right" place at the "right" time.

We also knew that despite our collective and individual successes— the championships won in the NBA and CBA, the collegiate games where we'd each notched forty-plus points and twenty-plus rebounds—we were both missing something. Our glimpses of hoop-time nirvana were too fleeting, too agonizingly suggestive of another reality where the flow was the norm, where the game transcended the clock, the scoreboard, and the individual players. We could sometimes hear the heartbeat, but we couldn't see the heart. What we sought, what we *needed*, was a means of systematizing the "right" way to play.

The quest so consumed us both that when Phil and I discovered that Bobby Knight, the irascible coach of Indiana University, would be conducting a weekend clinic in Poughkeepsie, New York (only forty-five minutes southeast of Woodstock), we readily convinced the Patroons' bigwigs to pick up the tab for the two of us to go.

Phil and I had always been interested in Knight's half-court offense, a seamless unfolding of timber-shivering picks, slashing cuts, and cleverly angled passes that created unopposed jumpers, backdoor layups, and plenty of space for the big men to roam in the lane. We were eager to discover the whys and wherefores of Knight's system, and if he'd also throw in a few words about his zone press, we'd be doubly grateful. Sure, we knew beforehand that Knight could be overbearing and opinionated, but he was also a highly accomplished technician, and he'd surely teach us something we could use. The workshop convened one Saturday morning at a public high school. The worn and scratched gymnasium floor was filled with several rows of slat-backed wooden folding chairs facing a stage that was bare except for a stray basketball and a podium. The chairs were mostly filled with fresh-eyed coachlings, some of them decked out in sports jackets and neckties, others wearing brand-name sweat suits or neatly pressed trousers and short-sleeved knit shirts that were patched above their hearts with the names and logos of their own sponsoring institutions: Goshen High School, Orange County C.C., Pine Bush Boys Club. And they all stared adoringly at Knight as he mounted the stage, eased his paunch behind the podium, and adjusted the microphone.

Knight was clad in nattily creased chino pants and his trademark blood-red Indiana U. sweater. With his gray hair so neatly clipped that it resembled a gleaming war bonnet, and his stone-colored eyes staring above and beyond his worshipful audience (perhaps at the backboard and basket suspended above the far-off baseline?), the General launched into a full-blown attack.

"Sportswriters," he snorted. "They think they're experts because they watch so many ball games, but in reality they don't know shit from Shinola."

While Phil and I sat expectantly with our pens poised above our blank notebooks, the young coaches laughed to beat the band.

"Recruiting sucks," quoth Knight. "I hate it when my entire day is ruined by a seventeen-year-old."

This was followed by another round of sidesplitting, knee-pounding laughter. The General sure is a pistol, ain't he?

And then Knight started talking about drugs. Heroin, cocaine, uppers, downers, crack, marijuana—they were all the same. Destroying the moral fiber of America. Turning our young people into feeble-minded, undisciplined wimps. Why, if Knight were president (his suggestive fantasy was here interrupted by cries of "Hear! Hear!" "Yeah!" and even a "Right on!"), he'd make a phone call to whoever the hell was in charge of the one country, Colombia, that exported the largest amount of drugs to our otherwise blessed shores. And he'd say, "Hey, señor. This is the president of the United States of America, the greatest nation in the history of the world, and I'm giving you an absolute ultimatum and I'm only going to say it once, so you'd better listen good. *Comprende?* You know alla those poppy fields and pot fields you got set up down there? Well, if those fields ain't burned to ashes by twelve noon in exactly three days, I'm gonna send a fleet of planes to bomb your goddamned country from here to hell and back again so it won't be good for nothing except to pave it and turn it into the world's largest parking lot!" Then he'd hang up the goddamned telephone and tell his flyboys to start their engines!

Yahoo! The morning session ended with a standing ovation.

Phil and I sat in stunned silence while the gym emptied. What an exhibition of reckless self-indulgence, of irresponsible leadership run amok. Then Phil flashed me one of his characteristic wry grins and said this: "It's been a long day, Charley, so let's make the best of it. There's a ball up on the stage, and if we clear the last few rows, we'll have enough room to play some one-on-one."

So we played, shirtless and sweating, fouling each other and laughing out loud, hitting miraculous shots, missing easy ones, and never keeping score. We played until our fellow participants began to reenter the gym. Then we pulled on our shirts, left the ball for dead on the foul line, and made a quick exit stage left.

With our notebooks still unmarked, we headed back to Albany, and back to our search for the truly righteous system that would enable both players and coach to access the secret heart of the game.

TWO

LEARNING THE GAME COUNTRY-STYLE

PHIL

I'm convinced that every successful coach has been profoundly influenced, for better or worse, by every coach or teacher he (or she) has ever played for. The development of my own coaching style has been culled from the personalities and methodologies of numerous dedicated and talented men at various levels of the game.

My first teacher was my father, Charles, who along with my mother, Elizabeth, was a Pentecostal minister. Dad always fit well into any kind of group and he respected everybody. Instead of delegating whatever work had to be done, he always took on part of the load himself. I can remember my dad in overalls along with the rest of the work crew cleaning up the church grounds every spring. He worked right alongside the others and pulled his weight, even though he was the leader of the church. Leadership manifests in a variety of forms and Dad had a physical carriage that inspired other people to understand that he was a trustworthy and responsible man. As I grew up, I naturally took on some of my dad's characteristics, not the least of which was his physical carriage.

My basketball education began when I was in the fifth grade in Great Falls, Montana. Basketball was an intra-school sport, and my first coach and mentor was "Babe" (a very popular name for coaches and players in those days). Fortunately, he was able to see something in me—some glimmer of athletic potential and competitiveness—that I couldn't see myself. After our very first practice, Babe spent fifteen minutes teaching me how to shoot a step hook, which subsequently became my best offensive weapon.

Like every other kid my age, I played whatever sport was in season. In the fifties, baseball was the only sport that kids thought about playing professionally, and I was no different. But all sports came naturally to me. I played pitcher and first base in baseball, quarterback in football, and as I continued to grow, I played every position on the basketball court. I also competed in track and field (running the 440 and 880, and high-jumping five feet six inches in the fifth grade), and I even played ice hockey in grade school and junior high. I don't think I was a particularly gifted athlete, it was just that I was good under stress, understood gamesmanship, and *loved* competition. But when I was a seventh grader, I began to develop a special interest in basketball.

This came about when a 4-H agent named Don Hotchkiss started-ed a league that included teams in six neighboring counties in Montana and North Dakota (where my parents had recently relocated). The four H's are *Health, Hands, Heart* and *Hearth*. It was a federally sponsored agricultural outreach program that truly emphasized all that was wholesome in rural communities. The official 4-H motto, "Learning to do by doing," foreshadowed my later interest in Zen. Whereas the junior high school basketball team only played a measly ten-game schedule, the 4-H'ers played an additional twelve to fourteen games. Hotchkiss confined his coaching efforts to making sure each of the players got an equal amount of court time, while also insuring that the best players were in the game in the fourth quarter.

Our normal Saturday-morning road trips packed ten players plus

Don into two station wagons for two-hour excursions in severe wintry weather to small towns in Montana like Medicine Lake, Sidney, and Scobey, as well as places like Watford City and Crosby in North Dakota. And if the referees were agreeable, we'd gladly play a double-header.

Two of our road games were on Indian reservations—their style was to fast break and press from the opening tip to the final buzzer, and it was great fun. Both teams would end up with seventy to eighty points, which was quite a feat for a thirty-two-minute ball game. But as much as I enjoyed the helter-skelter pace, by the time I was a freshman in high school, I was ready to be reined in and taught the fundamentals of basketball.

My experience at Williston High School was both excruciating and exhilarating. The painful aspects were a ten-inch growth spurt during my freshman and sophomore years, and the routine hazing I experienced at the hands of the upperclassmen—finding my tighty whiteys floating in a toilet bowl after practice, or "oops, too late" discovering that my jockstrap had been smeared with analgesic balm.

I made the varsity team as a tenth grader, but even though I was six foot one, as tall as any of my teammates, the team was dominated by seniors, so I played a limited role. My coach, Bob Pederson, ran a lot of screen-and-rolls for our sharpshooting wings and guards. I was more of a driver-slasher looking to launch my hook at every opportunity, and I had to create most of my scoring opportunities on my own. My biggest advantage was being left-handed. I got to play, and I even lettered, but most of all I was beginning to see much deeper into the game.

Up until then, I'd been mystified by the complex movements of the offense and the defense. But as the season progressed, I began to recognize the logic behind every cut, every screen, every defensive adjustment. Before long I was able to anticipate the immediate possibilities and make advantageous moves or counter-moves. My vision and my timing were a step ahead of the other players, so I could react to situations before the defense was ready. It was a lot of fun to be able to force my defender to move in a certain way and then counteract his movement. I was still a neophyte player, yet I'd already identified my comfort zones where my hook shot was virtually automatic. I was also very quick to the ball for someone my size, and my hands were sure. And above all I wanted to win—I *needed* to win.

On a more technical level, that was the year when I learned the limitations of an offense based on jump shooting. We had to work too hard for every shot, we rarely got layups, and our post-up opportunities were limited.

Being an underclassman, my life off the court was much more complicated. Because I was so skinny, my nickname around the school was "Bones," and all I heard were jokes about my physique. "Bones was caught cheating in biology—he was counting his ribs," they'd say. I became so self-conscious that I never went swimming without wearing a t-shirt.

At the same time that I felt humiliated by all of the jokes at my expense, I also loved being the center of attention. It was a very confusing time for me, moving between the two extreme poles of popularity and being made fun of for being skinny and awkward.

During my sophomore year I understood that my popularity was due to my increasing effectiveness on the basketball court, but this felt wrong to me. Since both of my parents were Pentecostal ministers, my days began with Bible readings and family prayers, and ended in church (four or five times every week) with evening vespers and prayers. We subscribed to the local newspaper and the *Reader's Digest*, but the rest of our lives revolved around the Gospel's "Good News" and spreading it to the world. My parents strictly adhered to St. Paul's teachings that you can't be popular "in the world" and still be a good Christian because eventually you'll serve "Mammon" instead of God. I was supposed to be a living example of a Christian youth who was sanctified by grace. While I was certain that I didn't want to serve Mammon (whoever/whatever that was), I also liked having a life that was separate from the sacred life. "The World" didn't seem like such a bad place after all. In fact, all of the praying and churchgoing seemed to be boring, almost meaningless, and suitable only for elderly people. Of course, I had to keep my true feelings to myself and go through the motions of adhering to my parents' lifestyle. And I did believe in having a personal relationship with

God. But I was pulled in conflicting directions and my life became a balancing act worthy of the Flying Walendas.

So I started finding excuses to avoid going to church. I was in every play and social event that the school provided. I built floats, I was in the science club, the lettermen's club, and even the school's radio broadcasting club, Coyote on the Air. I went on to play Horse in the junior play and Moose in the senior play; my biggest part was the role of King Neptune in the Coyote Capers. I sang a song that went, "I'm Neptune, King of the Sea, and I welcome you all to my Kingdom." Everybody agreed that comedy was my specialty.

Things became serious on the basketball court during my junior year. I started along with four seniors who'd just finished a championship football season. Even though they were small, they all had tremendous foot speed, strength, and athleticism. They were also fierce competitors who didn't tolerate losing. To suit the abilities of this group, Coach Pederson discarded our previous offense and instituted a speed game.

I was now a slim six-five center, who rolled across the lane looking to shoot my hook shot. Very seldom was I allowed to roam more than ten feet away from the basket. We grew as a team as the season progressed, winning twelve of our last thirteen games.

Coach Pederson was a mild-mannered man, a deacon in his church, who never said anything more severe than "Confound it." If we played a lousy game, he'd never berate us. "Well, boys, that's too bad," he'd say. Then he'd tell us exactly which part of our game we needed to work on. He made sure that practice was fun, and he nurtured in us an appetite for basketball. Among many other things, Coach Pederson taught me that a good coach should fit his game plan to match the particular talents of his players.

I had opted not to play football during my junior year. I was a 165-pound rack of bones and I didn't think that I was strong enough or heavy enough to play the game aggressively. My buddy Bubby Carlson had developed into a much better quarterback than me, so I was also slated to change positions and become a *lineman*. Ouch! But I felt the odds were too short that I'd suffer a serious injury at either position. The previous season I'd seen a player get smacked in the head during a practice session and suffer a concussion. Immediately after the impact, he was so dazed that he couldn't talk, and he wound up having to wear a neck brace. But the football players were farm kids toughened up by the severe North Dakota winters that made everybody else crazy. As the unconscious player was carried off the field, his teammates had laughed at him and taunted him for being soft.

My basketball coach supported my decision to forgo football, and I lifted weights instead. But the football coach thought *he* was supposed to make the decisions about who would play and who wouldn't. Besides, every athlete who was deemed capable of making even the smallest contribution to any varsity team was expected to give his all. In my absence, the football team had won the state championship, and I was a pariah.

The football season ended just after Thanksgiving and that's when many of the players joined the basketball team, including Pete Porinsh, who was the captain of the football team and sure put me to the test. I was trying to fit in with them, but there was a lingering question about my toughness.

What most annoyed Porinsh was my habitual complaining about referees' bad calls. During a time-out in the fifth game of the season, Pete finally unloaded on me. "Grow up, Jackson," he barked. "You complain like a little baby every time you're fouled. All you do is get us in trouble with the referees and change the game so we get the short end of the stick. Just shut up and play!"

I was shaken by Pete's outburst, but I knew that I *had* to gain his respect. And I did. I buckled down, started playing much better, kept my complaints to myself, and ended up averaging about twenty points per game.

We had a wonderful season, and reached the final game of the state tournament, where we faced off against the Rugby High School Panthers. All of us Coyotes were so nervous that just before the opening tip-off our starting forward threw up on the court. I had a good game, scoring twenty-seven points, but Rugby's balanced attack turned the game in their favor.

Despite my success on the basketball court, my junior year was a difficult one. My older sister, Joan, got married, and my two older brothers, Joe and Chuck, were away at college. Suddenly I was alone in the house with my parents and, as is normal with teenagers, I didn't quite know what to say to them. Also, I had grown out of all of my hand-me-downs, so none of my clothing fit me properly. I was basically lost and confused, and looked it. I lived to read, but I was into stuff I couldn't fully understand: Somerset Maugham, Fyodor Dostoyevsky, and Boris Pasternak. My parents bought me a World Book Encyclopedia set and I ate that up quickly too. Reading was the only way I could find out what was outside my limited scope of experience.

I had friends in Williston, but because my parents were ministers I found I was held to a different standard than other people. If I accidentally said "Shit," everybody would jump all over me. "Uh-oh," they'd say. "Phil swore. You're going to go to hell, Phil." I went out with girls, but it was usually on their initiative. It wasn't that I was afraid or shy, I just didn't have many social graces. I had an old 1950 Chevy that my dad and I had bought for seventy-five dollars, so I had a way to take dates out. There was some kissing and necking in the car, but I was still a virgin, and technically faithful to my parents' religious principles.

By my senior season, I'd grown to six feet six inches and 180 pounds, and I was hitting my stride. Coach Pederson instituted a 2-3 shuffle offense that emphasized my pivot play. Because I was now so much bigger and stronger, I was a better rebounder and shot-blocker and had much more of an influence on the game. I was also able to dunk the ball in competition for the first time.

We had an outstanding season and our game against Grand Fork Central was the first state championship game ever televised throughout North Dakota. In the first half I snuck up behind Central's point guard, stole the ball, and dribbled the rest of the way for a dunk. Because of the telecast, "The Dunk" became a memorable event for North Dakota basketball fans. The Coyotes had an easy time and I scored forty points, my career high.

After the game I had barely showered and dressed when I was suddenly faced with still another situation I was not prepared to handle: being recruited by college basketball coaches.

Since the state finals were held at the University of North Dakota's field house, Bill Fitch, the newly appointed coach, had seen me at my best and had the first crack at me. He was a curly-haired, chubby-cheeked man, extremely personable and quick to relate to everybody. He showed up in the locker room right after the championship game and asked Coach Pederson if he could drive me over to the Bronze Boot Cafe, where a celebration had been arranged by several of Williston's most prominent businessmen. When I met him in the parking lot, Bill noticed that I didn't have a winter coat. "Nothing fits me in a top coat," I shrugged, "so I just wear my letter jacket in the wintertime." With that, Bill took off his coat and insisted that I wear it. I was impressed. On the way over to the restaurant, Bill made his pitch. He said there was a place for me at UND if I wanted to stay within the state. He also emphasized that there'd be no illegal handouts or payment for phony jobs.

His low-key approach was welcome and turned out to be quite a contrast to some of the other coaches' recruiting tactics—from a brief but majestic audience with John Kundla, coach at the University of Minnesota (and former Lakers' coach), to North Dakota State, which offered me a hundred dollars a month to hang around every Saturday morning with some alumni athletic booster. It all seemed like prostitution and only made me appreciate Bill Fitch's moral integrity all the more.

Even so, making a decision was a lonely and stressful process. I had scholarship offers from seventy colleges, but neither of my parents could offer much guidance since they had limited understanding of the secular world and absolutely no grasp of the world of intercollegiate athletics. My mom, however, expressed a desire for me to say close to home. Even though she had never seen me play in high school, she wanted me nearby so that I could easily come home for the holidays.

When the recruiting process began, I'd been leaning toward the University of Minnesota, but I was put off by Kundla's attitude, the distance (500 miles) from Williston, and the huge (40,000) student body. Ultimately I did choose the University of North Dakota, mostly on the basis of Bill's personality. He promised that he'd put UND on the map as a small-college basketball power and I believed him.

The frosh coach was Louie Brogan, and because of our abbreviated schedule I can't remember his system of Xs and Os. I do recall, however, that his term for what I later called a "backdoor step" was "a dog leg," which was a much more visual description of a certain cutting route.

That year was little more than a waiting period for me—waiting to play varsity ball, learning the intricacies of on-campus life, and learning how to shave around pimples. I scored more than twenty-four points per game for the frosh team, but I was also in a kind of limbo—not a varsity player and not quite a civilian either.

My life shifted into overdrive when I became eligible for varsity ball as a sophomore. Bill Fitch's preseason training was notorious (even more so when he moved on to the NBA); for six weeks he worked us like we were hard-nut marines. We would run line drills until we were dizzy, and then do push-ups in between. But we were big, quick, motivated to play defense, and our superior conditioning made us tough to beat.

My teammates called me "The Mop" because I spent so much time on the floor, but it was better than being called Bones. I managed to average nearly twelve points and an equal number of rebounds per game, but Paul Pederson was the star—a third-team, small-college All-American. We went undefeated (12-0) in the North Central Intercollegiate Athletic Conference, and qualified to compete in what was then called the NCAA Small College Division Tournament—different from the major college tournament only in that our centers were smaller. We reached the quarter-finals, where we were smoked (97-64) by a Southern Illinois team that featured Walt Frazier, an All-American guard who would later be a teammate of mine with the New York Knicks.

During the summer I played semi-pro baseball in the Basin League with a team located in Mobridge, South Dakota. This was an NCAA-approved outlet for college baseball players in the days before professional teams were allowed to pay undergraduates to play minor league ball without forfeiting their eligibility in other sports. I'd been away at Boys State (a leadership camp sponsored by the American Legion) back in North Dakota, so I arrived in

Mobridge after the season was under way, and consequently I was not in the pitching rotation. Mobridge was a hot prairie town and I earned my living expenses by pumping gas in a local service station. At the time, I had high hopes of being a professional baseball player—I had once pitched a one-hitter for the UND team, and the highlight of my hitting career had been a line-drive double off the center field wall against Satchel Paige (who was only sixty at the time) during an exhibition game. But in Mobridge I was used mostly in a mop-up role. After conferring with the coach, I became convinced that a career in major league baseball was nothing but a dream for me. From then on I devoted myself full-time to basketball.

My numbers were up during my junior year (21.8 ppg) and once again we qualified for the NCAA postseason tourney. For the second consecutive year we reached the quarter-finals and faced Southern Illinois—the primary difference being that Frazier was academically ineligible. We trailed for most of the game, but the outcome was up for grabs until the last few minutes. I made a bad pass and we lost by four points.

Spurred by another disappointing loss, I spent the entire summer preparing for my senior season and my last shot at a championship.

Bill Fitch always drove his players to achieve their peak performance. Before my senior season he told me that if I played up to my potential, I'd probably be getting an offer from an AAU team—the Phillips 66 Oilers, and the Akron Goodyears were the best known, and best paying, of these outfits. I wasn't sold on AAU ball, only because I felt that I had an outside chance of playing in the NBA, but I knew it was important for me to have a good year. In addition, since I would be the only returning starter, I was expected to be the team leader.

I'd always assumed that the guards were the natural leaders of a basketball team since they distributed the ball and were primarily responsible for implementing the coach's system. I worked out with some of the underclassmen before the season started, but I didn't know what else I could (or should) be doing as the team's leader. I just tried to score, rebound, and defend like I always did.

In my junior season UND had been ranked number two nationally, but prior to my senior season we were unranked nationally and only rated third in our conference. We struggled early in the season because our talent level was down, but also because Fitch had instituted a new offense to take advantage of my abilities. It was a 1–4 set that was never really identified by any name. I knew that I enjoyed playing the offense because there always seemed to be a lot of usable spaces, and also because most of the movement was toward either the basket or the unguarded areas. Anyway, the offense was definitely intriguing. Twenty years later I happened to see a tape of one of our games and I was astounded to see that we were running the Triangle! There I was working the post on the strong side and the pinch post on the weak side. It seems that Bill had attended one of Tex's clinics and was incorporating some of Tex's ideas.

For me, the turning point of my final year at UND came after an early-season loss to DePaul in Chicago. The game had turned sour when our unseasoned guards lost their poise under DePaul's trapping defense. After the game I went out to John Barleycorn's, a tavern on the Northside, with a former UND cheerleader. I was a big-shot senior, this was my third trip to Chicago, and I was convinced that I knew my way around. But a snowstorm blew up and I couldn't get back to the hotel in time for the midnight curfew. Fitch and his assistant coach, Jimmy Rodgers, were waiting for me and Bill cut me up pretty good. Fitch said that I had abdicated my responsibilities, and until I proved myself to be a true leader of this raw group of players, I was no longer the team captain.

A leader must adhere to the same rules as those that apply to the lowest scrub on the team. I knew that I was the team's leader on the court, but the curfew incident helped me get serious about my off-court leadership. Bill certainly knew the right string to pull.

I was embarrassed and angry, and I played with increased intensity for the rest of the season. I had a lust to score, and averaged over twenty-seven points per game.

Once again we qualified for the postseason tournament, but this time we didn't get past the regionals, where we lost to a Louisiana Tech team coached by Scotty Robertson (who would later coach the Detroit Pistons). Because of early foul trouble, I barely lasted twenty minutes in the only college game Red Holzman (the Knicks' scout and future coach) ever saw me play. The game was played at the state college in Normal, Illinois, and the next night I scored 51 points in the consolation game. My total was the field house record there, a record eyed by Illinois State's best player, Doug Collins (who would eventually become my boss with the Chicago Bulls). Doug told me that the record haunted him until he finally broke it in his senior year (1974).

The season may have seemed like a great personal success for me. But more than accumulating impressive numbers, my experience that year revolved around learning the importance of staying focused on team goals, of not giving up on my teammates, of showing them the way on and off the court. These lessons would last much longer than my playing career.

THREE

LEARNING THE GAME CITY-STYLE

CHARLEY

During the late 1940s, the seasonal sports on Fulton Avenue in the West Bronx were baseball, punchball, stickball, two-hand-touch football, off-the-bench, -stoop, -curb, or -wall, kick-the-can, and tie-a-little-kid-to-a-tree-in-the-park-and-leave-him-there. Our version of basketball featured a small rubber "Spaldeen" and the vertical lower square of a fire escape ladder, which served as the goal.

All through my childhood my father was acutely ill—his tubercular left lung had been surgically excised back in 1937 in a primitive attempt to prevent the disease from spreading. He couldn't take ten steps without having to halt and catch his breath in small gasping doses, and he spent most of his time in bed, within easy reach of a gray torpedo of oxygen, moaning his anguished mantra, "God, what did I ever do to deserve this?"

Plagued by a confusing jumble of fear, pity, anger, and shame, I took every opportunity to absent myself from the apartment and played every sport with a fierce energy that often outpaced my meager skills.

I first started to take basketball seriously when I was thirteen: during one of my long, brooding, solitary walks, I followed the sound of the bouncing ball and came upon a "steady run" in the wintertime locker room of a public swimming pool in a Negro neighborhood not far from Fulton Avenue. It was a full-court game played between portable baskets on a cold stone floor. Wandering in out of sheer curiosity, I was instantly welcomed. "Lace 'em up, big fella. You got next with me."

The game was presided over by Bill, rumored to have been a Harlem Globetrotter in his distant youth. It was a ferocious and honorable game in which the shooter was the only player who'd ever dare admit to being fouled, and everybody else rebounded like gangbusters. Cowardly hoopers were denounced as "bitches" and worse.

I loved the company of those joyful warriors who played with such sheer aggression and passion. Smelling from booze on Saturday mornings. Laughing away everybody's mistakes. "Keep on shooting, Mister Charley," Bill would urge me. "You throw enough shit against the wall, some of it's bound to stick." But at the time I couldn't master the fine art of shooting a basketball—it seemed to squirt out of my hands like a gigantic watermelon seed. "Young Mister Charley," Bill would exclaim with a laugh, "even if you was standing on the beach, I don't believe you could piss in the ocean." Yet Bill also encouraged me ("big as you are and bigger as you gonna be…") to persevere.

My first formal game was in a ninth-grade tournament at Junior High School No. 44, where my class (9-2) was trounced by class 9-14, a team composed of unruly young men who'd been left back several times and who shaved every day. My only memory is of playing in a cold, windy schoolyard wearing long pants and shirttails, of getting razzed for being so clumsy as to trip over a foul line, and of then getting beaten by my father for tearing my pants.

Even so, I was recruited to play with my classmates in a local community center league. And whenever we dared to defeat the Jabones, another team of tough guys and troublemakers, we had to fast-break all the way home.

After long, lonesome sessions in the playground I ultimately developed an awkward, but adequate, corkscrew jumper to complement an old-timey Larry Faustian "pivot shot" (which was a forerunner of the jump hook). At the tender age of fifteen I was a senior at Roosevelt High School, and having grown to six-foot-six and 210 pounds, I easily made the varsity basketball team. The coach was a math teacher named Howard McManus, who was smart enough to let our All-City guard, Jackie Thompson, run the team. Coach McManus's only advice for the rest of us was this: "Bend your knees, boys. Bend your knees." My career high for the Rough Riders was five points against the sissies of Grace Dodge Vocational High School.

Meanwhile my father's condition deteriorated. Every three months or so he'd experience a crisis and be rushed off to the hospital. "This is it," my mother would sob. "This time…"

The varsity coach at Hunter College, a tuition-free institution in the Bronx, was a childhood chum of my uncle Richard, and somehow, despite my inferior high school grades, I was encouraged to matriculate there. The freshman coach was Tony Russo, who stressed toughness and grit. I was bigger (six-eight) and stronger (230 pounds) than any of my teammates, and I compensated for my basic shyness and confusion by being mindlessly aggressive. Coach Russo employed some kind of high-post offense that I was spectacularly unsuited for. I averaged eight points per game with the frosh and went scoreless against archrival CCNY the night before my father died.

My father was forty-six going on a hundred when he finally succumbed to an attack of something quick and painful. I accompanied my mother in the last ambulance ride, and just before we reached the hospital, Daddy roused himself. I remember that his blue eyes were tightly clenched and staring at a space just above my head. The last words he ever said to me were, "Hi, kid."

The day after the funeral, my mother packed all of his clothing into two large suitcases—underwear, shoes, two of his three suits, shirts, ties, his overcoat, galoshes, socks, and his hats. I was then instructed to lug the suitcases over to Mr. Schneiderman's used clothing store on Washington Avenue. "Tell him it's one price for everything except the suitcases," my mother told me. "Take whatever he offers. Don't argue. Don't bicker."

Like my father, Schneiderman was a card-carrying member of the Communist Party. Schneiderman frequently visited my father's sick bed to debate the pros and cons of Zionism, but that morning he was all business. He offered no condolences, no fond memories, and no sense that he'd ever seen me before. "These are out of style," he said, then offered me twenty-five dollars for the lot.

My mother never asked me for the money. I guess she figured it was my hard-earned inheritance.

Suddenly I felt free to be a child, and before long I also became the tallest player in the brief history of Hunter College varsity basketball. Coach Mike Fleischer had been a classmate and close friend of the infamous CCNY hoopers (who'd won both the NCAA and NIT championships back in 1950 before being exposed as dumpers and point shavers). One of Coach's best pals was Ed Roman, a hulking six-foot-six board-banger with a surprisingly deft shooting touch. Except for his corrupted dossier, Roman certainly possessed the smarts, the size, and the talent to have been an outstanding NBA player. From time to time Roman would show up at the Hunter gym and tutor me in the theories and practices of pivot play. Footwork. Balance. Boxing out. The works.

It was just a week before the varsity's preseason practice was set to convene when, during a three-on-three scrimmage, I tried to bully my way around Roman's wide body (as per his instructions) and attack the offensive boards. A quick bang to freeze him, then a half spin, and I thought I was there, when all at once the lights went out.

Out of nowhere, his elbow had blasted the middle of my face back into the abyss.

Coach Fleischer drove me to Fordham Hospital, where a doctor inserted two metal rods into my swollen nasal passages, and, with one blood-soaked and painful yank, realigned the broken bone into at least a semblance of its original position. According to Coach, the blood, the swelling, and even the subsequent black eyes, were all badges of honor. I was now a bona fide pivotman, theoretically unafraid to stick my face into the rebounding scrum in the shadow of the basket. Coach consoled me by saying that a busted nose was easily preferable to a sprained ankle, because the latter would prevent me from playing. "Don't worry," he added, "before you're through, you'll break a lot of other guys' noses!"

Once the season was under way, we played mostly 1-3-1 zone defense and a static offense that stationed me in the low post. Our game plan called for me to shoot first and never ask questions, effectively making spectators out of my teammates (who either had to find their own shots off the offensive boards, run out and shoot before I settled into the pivot, or launch quick shots when the defense sagged to deny me the ball). Assists didn't seem to matter, but we were all jealous of each other's shots and point totals. As friendly as we were off the court, once the lights were switched on, we were far from being a team. I wound up averaging seventeen points and twelve rebounds as the Hunter Hawks finished with a record of 9–10.

Yet there were two games that seemed much more significant than any others: The second game of the season was against Rider College, a win for us, but marked by my catching another elbow with my face—this one shattering a tooth. The incident cost us a timeout, during which Coach said to me, "Not to worry, Charley. You're not bleeding and you won't miss a minute."

The second unforgettable game was at Brooklyn College, where we were in the process of being soundly trounced late in the game when Coach officially surrendered by emptying the bench. The Brooklyn College coach quickly followed suit and everybody settled back to watch the scrubs try to make garbage time last forever. The only trouble was that one of the Brooklyn College subs (number 46) was out of control, throwing indiscriminate elbows, undercutting the legs of airborne jump-shooters, and even throwing a punch in a close-quarters rebounding melee. The referees, eager for the lopsided game to end, ignored Coach's protests, sucked on their whistles, and let the clock run down. Coach Fleischer was furious as he stood up and shouted down to his opposite number on the Brooklyn bench, "Hey, Coach! Why don't you get that jackass out of there before he hurts somebody?"

The other coach's rude reply was, "Fuck you, Fleischer! You coach your team and I'll coach mine."

With that, Coach walked over to where I was sitting comfortably on the pines and said this: "Go back into the game, Charley, and take that asshole out."

"What do you mean?"

"Elbows to the face are like Christmas presents," he said. "They're better to give than to receive."

Moments later I found myself side by side with number 46 along the foul lane while one of my teammates prepared to shoot a free throw. As the shot was released, number 46 leaned into me and assumed the proper "box out" position, thereby hindering me from rebounding a possible miss. I was expected to try to muscle him closer to the basket, but instead I cocked my right arm and aimed my elbow at the middle of his face. WHAM! I connected so solidly that several of his teeth were broken and a small fountain of blood splashed into the lane. In their haste to keep the clock in motion, neither referee noticed anything amiss. While the Brooklyn College coach screamed bloody murder, Coach just shrugged.

In the locker room I received Coach's congratulations. "Good job, Charley. The guy got exactly what he deserved."

I was flushed with the elation of my first kill. So that's how it felt! The power. The sense of reckoning. *Now* I was a man. Fuck with me or my teammates at your own peril.

But the flavor didn't last long enough. Even on the long subway ride back to the Bronx, I began to question the bloodthirsty imperatives of this strange game. I was confused, disappointed, and ashamed of myself. At the same time, there didn't seem to be an alternative. I was too slow to ride the crest of a fast break, too white to fly, and too unskilled to either razzle or dazzle. I was doomed to be a banger.

So, over the next two seasons, I mastered the sternum smash, and broke virtually every school scoring (24.2 ppg my junior year) and rebounding (16.0 per game as a senior) record as the Hawks barely managed to play .500 ball (a combined 31–28 during my tenure). I was moved by what Coach called "the competitive drive," which I interpreted as the urge to humiliate an opponent. Nail him on a blindside pick and bust his ass to the floor. Make him bleed. Roast him like a turkey. Annihilate his personality.

Every sequence of every game tested the value of who and what I was (or was supposed to be). Yes, I had fun in practice and in the schoolyard, but when the lights were switched on, I played with the desperate fear that I'd be exposed once and for all as a slow-footed, fumble-fingered klutz.

At the same time, I knew that I was missing something. What I was doing on the court didn't match what I felt. Truth, beauty, harmony—all of these seemed to exist just beyond the stretch of my peripheral vision. So I persevered.

After I graduated from Hunter, I would wistfully follow the bouncing ball: playing on the USA Basketball Team (along with Art Heyman and Larry Brown) at the Sixth Maccabiah Games in Israel, on the St. Anthony Eagles, the Rotolo Electricians, the Camden Bullets and Scranton Miners of the old Eastern League, the New York Bears, the Newburgh Hotels, Eat at Joe's, and Woodstock Joneses. Playing against the likes of Dolph Schayes, Oscar Robertson, Jerry Fleishman, Wilt Chamberlain, Connie Hawkins, Cazzie Russell, Rick Barry, Bill Bradley, a one-eyed high school All-American, murderers and cutthroats in various max joints (who all played with remarkable civility lest their precious hoop-time be revoked), plus assorted drunks, professional football players, and lunatics. Playing in Madison Square Garden, midnight runs in Harlem, interchangeable Y's, a home for the blind, on a parallelogram court in the Bronx, in the World Senior Games in Utah. Gradually, painfully, learning that the game wasn't all about *me*.

Whenever I remembered, I would pass, pick away, and moved without the ball. But too often, the insistent rhythms and sounds would slide my game back into my cluttered past. Missing shots, missing the point of it all, missing my life.

I'd go to graduate school, earning an M.A. in medieval studies, and dropping out of a Ph.D. program at St. John's when asked to revise my dissertation (a derivative puff of smoke concerning Christian allegory in Chaucer's "General Prologue" to *The

Canterbury Tales). And through two marriages, two divorces, and one knee surgery, I would keep playing.

Eventually, through a series of epiphanies forgotten, ignored, trivialized, then finally re-remembered, my view of the game would start to evolve. I watched Red Holzman's Knicks hit the open man. I hooped with PJ and Eddie Mast. Until I came to understand that every game was a chance for communion—with my teammates and opponents, with myself. And amid the squeak of sneakers on a polished wooden floor, amid grunting collisions and unexpected grace, I grabbed at the chance to be awash in the flow. The chance to celebrate the dribbling, leaping, dancing rites of salvation.

Along the way I would retire numerous times because of injuries or illness, once leaving me unexpectedly bedridden for several months with gout. Lying there with sleep my only escape from the excruciating pain, fearing for my life, cursing my unlucky stars, I found myself replicating my father's plight.

I would resume playing for several years after that, barely able to stumble from one foul line to the other, but remembering more than forgetting. Younger, stronger players would push me around as if I was made of straw. I played what I called "The Over 50 Defense"— if I could catch the player I was presumably defending, then I wouldn't let him go. My knees throbbed, my fingers were bent, and my left hip ached, but I enjoyed playing. Passing would be more satisfying than scoring. Setting weak-side picks created open shots for my teammates. Because of a lingering bursitis condition in my elbows, the sternum smash of yore would become too painful to even think about. Instead of playing bone-on-bone, instead of staking my ego on every possession, I came to joyfully dance through the games as best I could. I admired and vocally applauded good plays made by both teams. Just as happy to lose as to win, I was thrilled just to be playing. At long last, when I was too vulnerable to play with hatred anymore, I finally got it right.

FOUR

WELCOME TO THE NBA

PHIL

Looking back at my playing career, it's clear that Red Holzman was the one coach who most influenced what would become my own vision of the pro game. Red had seen me play only twenty minutes in the NCAA Small College Tournament, but something I was doing must have caught his eye. Following his recommendation, the Knicks selected me in the second round (the seventeenth pick overall) of the 1967 NBA draft.

There were two other North Dakota athletes who had received pro offers—a baseball player and a football player—so all three of us signed with the same agency. My instructions were: meet with the Knicks' general manager, Eddie Donovan, in New York but don't sign anything.

I was supposed to be met at the airport by Red Holzman, whom I had never seen before. All I knew about Red was that he had once played pro basketball, so I expected him to be rather tall. Instead I found a stocky, balding five-foot-nine individual who looked about as tough as I imagined anyone forty-seven years old could look.

"Go get your luggage," Red told me in a gruff voice, "and I'll drive you to your hotel." I later discovered that this straightforward manner was typical of Red. I followed him to a brand-new 1967 Chevy convertible, and we chatted politely as we drove into the city.

We were traveling down the Brooklyn-Queens Expressway when we happened to approach a pedestrian bridge. I looked up and saw a couple of teenagers leaning over and laughing. As we passed underneath, one of them threw a rock at the car and smashed the front windshield.

"Welcome to New York City," Red said. "If you can take that, you'll do just fine here."

I sat there in amazement and didn't know what to think.

Red dropped me off at a hotel located directly across the street from Madison Square Garden, and the next day I went over to talk to Mr. Donovan. He asked me if I had ever seen a game of professional basketball. I told him that we didn't have a television set at home, but while I was away at school I had seen a couple of play-off games on TV. I had never seen a game live. Mr. Donovan seemed to be rather frank and sharp, but not unkind. In any case, we weren't totally at ease with each other. He had never seen me play, and I had no familiarity with NBA basketball, so we didn't have a common frame of reference. We finally got around to talking dollars and cents. Following the advice of my agent, I said that I would rather not sign any contract right then. Mr. Donovan expressed disappointment, but I was insistent.

On our way upstairs, Red took me past the arena where the circus was performing. I'd never seen a full-blown circus before, so I was fascinated. I could see spotlights shining on trapeze artists, I could hear children shrilling with delight, and I could smell the musty odors of the circus animals.

Red then took me to say hello to Ned Irish, the president of Madison Square Garden. We chatted for about two minutes, and then I was ushered back out into the street.

I was still in a bit of a daze, so I spent the rest of the day in the hotel. It was the Memorial Day weekend, and I watched the parade on TV. There were veterans of the armed forces, cops, and firemen—over 500,000 people marching in support of the Vietnam War. To me, New York City was the epitome of the liberal East, so I was surprised by the prowar sentiment.

I didn't leave my room until I went downstairs to the coffee shop for a late-afternoon snack. The spectacle of two waitresses battling over which one was entitled to the tip I had left made me retreat immediately to my room, where I waited for Neil Johnson to come get me.

Since Neil was a Knick player and a native New Yorker, arrangements had been made for him to take me out for a Saturday night on the town. But I could see that the six-foot-seven, 240-pound man with red hair and sloping shoulders wasn't too thrilled with the idea of chaperoning me. He took me to a fancy restaurant, and we talked a little about his college days and where he lived in the city. Then he looked at his watch and said, "Look, Phil. I've got other things to do, and I'd just as soon split. The Barnum and Bailey Circus is playing over at the Garden, and you can go see it if you want to. What if we call it a night?" That was fine with me. Then he slipped me a twenty-dollar bill and took off.

I decided I would spend the rest of the evening walking around Times Square. The first thing I saw was some ponytailed guy on a soapbox shouting about the Vietnam War and pacifism. There were about twenty people standing around listening, but the other passersby completely ignored him. Nobody seemed to notice all the blind people rattling their tin cups either, and it looked like every third person I passed was talking to himself. I cruised around for a few blocks with my hand glued to my wallet before I realized that I really couldn't stand the tension in the air. So I turned around and went back to the hotel, where I called the airline and changed my flight out to the earliest one I could get—a 7:00 a.m. plane back to North Dakota.

But New York wasn't finished with me yet. I had to take a cab to the airport, and all I had left was a ten-dollar bill. The cabby took one look at me, heard me say, "Howdy," and then took off on the

Great Circle route. The fare came to $9.50, and as I finally boarded the plane, I still heard the cabby's curses ringing in my ears for giving him only a fifty-cent tip.

Welcome to the big city, Phil.

My agent ultimately negotiated a deal with the Knicks and arranged for Red to come out to North Dakota with the contract for me to sign. Red would also be bringing some kind of game film for me to borrow until I reported to training camp.

When he showed up, Red just did his job and didn't try to impress me by talking about New York glamour or cars or money. We got into a short discussion about my future, and I told him that I wasn't sure how much I wanted to play professional basketball. Red replied with total respect for my feelings: "One thing that basketball can provide you with is the time to look at what you eventually want to do and the time to prepare yourself for it." I got a good feeling from that.

After Red took the signed contract and left, I bought a keg of beer and invited all my UND teammates over to watch the film he'd left with me. "This is the team I'm going to be playing for," I announced, and we settled back to see what kind of basketball I would be expected to play.

The game we saw was originally played on October 28, 1966, and it involved the Knicks and the Los Angeles Lakers. All it appeared to be was a bunch of guys running around and freelancing. Once in a while there was a pick. Pretty soon we started to laugh. We prided ourselves on the intelligent style of ball our coach, Bill Fitch, had taught us, and we could see nothing but a lot of physical contact and very poor shot selection. There were no patterns, no plays, nothing that I could do out there. Everything was sheer strength.

The Lakers had the superior talent and were just outgunning the Knicks, when all of a sudden there was a jump ball. It looked like the film stopped for a moment and the next thing we saw was the Knicks' Willis Reed being attacked by every Laker in sight. Willis was knocked to the floor and had all these guys hanging on him, when he seemed to get an infusion of energy and strength. He just stood up and shook everybody off. At that point it ceased to be a fight and became a massacre. Willis punched John Block in the nose, hit Henry Finkel in the head, and dumped Rudy LaRusso onto the floor. Another Knick, Emmette Bryant, was running around jumping on people's backs and kicking players in the head, but I couldn't take my eyes off Willis. He was a huge, barrel-chested man who weighed at least 250 pounds, and he was shrugging 230-pounders off him like a bear shaking off the rain. We ran the entire episode back and forth about five times in total disbelief. This was the guy I would be guarding every day in training camp? I had never seen anybody that strong in my life.

The film was Red's way of welcoming me to the NBA.

Somehow I managed to stay out of harm's way even while Willis worked me over in training camp, but I continued to be disappointed with the freewheeling style of the pro game. My new teammate, Walt Frazier (who had been the Knicks' top draft pick), felt the same way, and we'd complain to each other about how the pros didn't play basketball as concisely as college teams did.

To compound the problem, Dickie McGuire, the Knicks' current head coach, put a very loose hand on the team. The Knicks had responded relatively well the previous season (barely making the play-offs with a 36–45 record), but by the time I arrived in training camp in September 1967, several of the players were taking advantage of Dickie's laissez-faire attitude. It was clear that the ball club was more of an ungainly collection of individual players than it was a team. Players were routinely late for practice and team buses, and some players would smoke cigarettes and/or eat hot dogs at halftime. McGuire never said a word.

Where was the discipline? Where was the teamwork? Where was the heart of the pro game?

The biggest source of friction was at the small forward position, where Dick Van Ardsdale was competing for playing time with Cazzie Russell. Because our two big men were slow afoot (Walt Bellamy at center and Willis Reed at the power forward slot), Van Ardsdale's speed and defense was desperately needed. Cazzie meanwhile was a weak defender whose strength was his ability to be an explosive scorer.

In reality, Cazzie was most effective coming off the bench at certain crucial stages where he could often turn a ball game around. The trouble was that because Cazzie was a fan favorite and also the second-highest-paid player on the team, he couldn't accept playing behind Van Arsdale. (When Van Arsdale was eventually taken in an expansion draft by Phoenix, Cazzie was again shunted to the bench after Bill Bradley joined the team in December 1967. Four years later Cazzie wound up getting traded to San Francisco for Jerry Lucas.) Meanwhile, some of the players were advocates for Van Arsdale and some for Cazzie, and the controversy was extremely divisive.

The Knicks' backcourt was another awkward situation: Dick Barnett was a creative point-maker at the two-guard, while the point guard was Butch Komives, who was also a scorer. In addition, Walt Bellamy was not a very coachable player, and Willis was unhappy with the fact that Bells didn't always play hard. Also, several players didn't have total confidence in the way Dickie McGuire ran the team. The result was that the ball club lacked any sense of teamwork.

Another result was that just about midway through the season, Eddie Donovan fired Dickie and replaced him with Red Holzman. The first day of practice under the new regime, Red fined everybody who came in late, something that McGuire had never done. All the guys started bitching because Red laid ten-dollar fines on them, but nobody ever came late again.

Red also instituted a procedure that I later incorporated into my own coaching methodology: holding closed practices. The idea was to allow players to make their mistakes in private and without any more pressure than was generated by the team itself. Practice time became our *sanctum sanctorum* and helped create the sense of team unity that we had notably lacked.

If Red was able to provide us with the overall guidance we needed, he also dramatically changed our game plan by using two distinct units. I was grouped with Walt Frazier, Emmette Bryant, and Van Arsdale, with Nate Bowman at center, and our job was to full-court-press on defense. This tactic suited my abilities perfectly, and I played so well in the second half of the season that I was named to the All-Rookie team. I was so impressed with the tactical advantages of employing a speed unit that I eagerly came to accept Red as my unofficial mentor.

Above all else, Red was a master at managing people. He could accurately gauge the intelligence and temperament of his players and determine how each one of them should be treated. Some guys needed a pat on the back, some needed a kick in the pants. He was always brief and to the point with the media, always willing to stay in the background. Red was fair, impartial, and if sometimes he strategically failed to tell us the whole truth, he nonetheless never lied to his players.

But Red was also flexible: NBA players were permitted to satisfy their military obligations by spending one weekend a month in either the National Guard or a Reserve unit back in their respective hometowns. Bill Bradley, Cazzie Russell, Howard Komives, and Dick Van Arsdale would leave the team after a Friday-night game, serve a stint that usually began at six or seven o'clock in the morning, finish up by four in the afternoon, then rendezvous with the team in whichever city we happened to be playing. If the Knicks were on the West Coast, they wouldn't miss any game time. But if we were somewhere near the eastern seaboard, they'd usually arrive midway through the first quarter. To save time, the guys would change into their uniforms on their way to the arenas. It was all kind of helter-skelter, and Red was able to go with the flow.

With so many key players continuously coming and going, Red didn't always put a lot of pressure on the players to be here or there at a certain time. Shootarounds the morning of a ball game were strictly optional, and five or six interested players would pile into a cab if a court was available. Especially on the road, Red gave us enough room so that we were comfortable and agreeable whenever he did have to assert more control. At the same time, we were responsible enough not to take advantage of whatever freedoms he allowed us.

I suffered a back injury in January 1968 that required a spinal fusion, and I missed the remainder of that season. The truth was that any players on a team's roster for the 1969–70 season would be eligible to be selected in the latest expansion draft, so the Knicks' front office deliberately had me sit out another full season, even though I probably could have played.

Even with Red at the helm, however, the surviving players still didn't blend well together. Red's solution was to trade Bellamy and Komives to Detroit for Dave DeBusschere (on December 19, 1968)—and that move signaled the rise of the Knickerbockers. In place of the lethargic, lead-footed Bellamy, DeBusschere was a tenacious and mobile power forward who always played as hard as he could. Gradually, Red altered our approach to the game until we became a full-court-pressing, fast-breaking, cohesive team. We came up short against the Celtics in the Eastern Division finals, but in the spring of 1970 the team won its first-ever NBA title.

I was allowed to travel with the team during our championship season, but players on the injured list were prohibited from sitting on the bench. Occasionally I also did color commentary for the telecasts. Being a civilian for a season and a half, I naturally became somewhat dislocated from the team, but Red made sure to talk basketball with me at every opportunity. By explaining what the team's game plan was night after night, he kept me focused and involved.

Being on the sidelines for so long, I also got a different view of Red's system. His basic offense was a two-guard set, with two wings on opposite sides of the court just above the foul line extended, and with the center in the low post. When the ball was dumped inside, the strong-side guard and wing ran a squeeze, which is essentially a pick-and-cut sequence. Except for the fact that the corner wasn't filled, Red's 2-3 formation was similar to some aspects of the Triangle. As a change-up, Red also ran a "2-1" offense, which was a high-post set. More than having a discernible system, however, Red ran certain plays out of certain formations and relied on the intelligence of his veteran players to get the job done.

I could also get a good perspective on the way Red used his personnel. Some coaches like to keep their players guessing as to who's going to be the first sub off the bench and when that's going to happen. I believed that this approach doesn't allow players to prepare themselves properly. When a player doesn't know when he's going into the game, he wastes a lot of energy trying to stay up-up-up.

Then just as he loses his focus and begins to fade, that's the time the coach usually calls his number.

With Red, the bench players had a good idea when they'd be used, so they could get themselves psyched. Dean Meminger, for example, usually went in with two minutes left in the first quarter. When I was ready to play again, my first rotation generally came after the first quarter break, so I had plenty of time to stretch and loosen up. I also knew that I'd be playing for ten to twelve minutes at a time, substituting for Bradley, then DeBusschere, and sometimes for Reed. Red's system kept the guys on the bench involved in the game and ready to play, and it's something that I brought with me when I became a coach.

I also liked the way Red used his time-outs. His primary concern was always defense. Then, instead of diagramming offensive plays, Red would ask the players what we wanted to run. Again, this is something that I still use. "Okay, guys. What's going on out there? Tell me what you think will work."

Red's ego always took a backseat whenever the team's welfare was concerned, and the players loved playing for him and with one another. There were such high levels of trust and unselfishness that every ball game became a celebration of the joys of basketball. Our five starting players could all handle the ball (including center Jerry Lucas), which made us extremely mobile and flexible. Dean Meminger, Hank Bibby, and I were the primary bench players, and our job was to up-tempo the game. The Knicks won another NBA title in 1973.

Even though leg injuries had limited Willis Reed's playing time, he was still the unquestioned leader of the team. It was his commanding presence that got everybody's respect. In a different way, Bill Bradley was another leader. Bill was on good terms with all of his teammates, and he became a leader by consensus.

Red also put me in a leadership role; my functions included being generally alert and also being enthusiastic about practices and games. In addition, Red made sure that all the new guys on the team roomed with me on the road so I could teach them our offense. Subtle though it might have been, I took my role seriously.

We reached the Eastern Conference finals in 1973–74, then things quickly fell apart. More and more, the media was having a negative effect on the game. Instead of emphasizing the highly competitive aspect of NBA action, games were valued as entertainment. Dunk shots were routinely highlighted on the evening sports news, and style became much more important than substance. When Jerry Lucas, Dave DeBusschere, and Willis Reed retired (all of them solid, unselfish players, who would eventually be voted into the Hall of Fame), they were replaced by a new breed of talented yet unlearned players. I was extremely critical of this almost instantaneous changing of the guard—to say nothing of the forward and the center.

In the spring of 1973 I met an interesting character named Charley Rosen, a player-cum-writer whose love of the game and off-center view of society mirrored my own. Charley had been a star player for Hunter College from 1959 to 1962, and after graduation he'd played briefly in the Eastern League, the father of the CBA. His first novel, *Have Jump Shot Will Travel*, was about that experience and established Charley as a serious writer. By the summer of 1974 Charley and I were conspiring on a book called *Maverick*, an as-told-to autobiography of my first thirty years, and in the process we spent many hours together. Our shared passion was the purity of basketball—something that characterized both the Knicks and later the Bulls—and our natural lament was how that purity inevitably gets tainted.

I can remember a scene that epitomized much of what Charley and I had in common in those days: Driving his old Volvo, "Foodini," named after a television puppet character, Charley picked me up at my loft in the Chelsea district of lower Manhattan, and aimed us toward the West Village for lunch. Charley, who was an avid Deadhead, was in the process of writing an article on the Grateful Dead for a short-lived magazine called *Crawdaddy*, and he was waxing enthusiastic about how their story was truly a "righteous" one. In their formative years, all the members of the band had lived together in a house in the Haight-Ashbury section of San Francisco and had shared their earnings. Sometimes their combined income totaled only fifty dollars a week, but their authentic sense of community produced a sound that was remarkable in its connectedness. Charley believed that in a perfect world that might be the way a professional basketball team should be organized, with all the players living together, sharing their wealth, and thereby creating a real atmosphere of teamwork. I think this says volumes about Charley and his idealism.

For him (and for me) basketball has an essence that is almost sacred, and to play the game right on any level, the players must live their lives with awareness and integrity. Only by doing this can they surrender themselves to the moment, and bring the game (and their lives) to the kind of victory that transcends whatever the scoreboard may report. So, too, are the karmic shortcomings of players' personalities revealed in the way they play.

Charley and I worked on *Maverick* for one year. It was published in 1975, during a season in which Walt Frazier, Earl Monroe, and Bill Bradley were the only holdover starters left from the Knicks' championship teams of the 1970s. John Gianelli, a young third-year center, and I, a perennial sixth man, filled out the new starting lineup. Because of an expansion draft that sent Dean Meminger to the Atlanta Hawks, even our bench strength was drastically diminished.

The Knicks began the season with a rush, winning seventeen of our initial twenty-two games, but our lack of power and size soon caught up with us; we finished just under .500, and it was no surprise when we lost to Houston in the first round of the play-offs.

By the end of the season Charley was well into his second novel, *A Mile above the Rim*, and with his wife, Susan, had decided to move upstate to Woodstock to begin a full-time career as a writer. Charley and I remained good friends. His son, Darrell, and my daughter, Chelsea, were born only three months apart, and the Jackson family often made the hundred-mile journey up to Woodstock to see how the natives lived and to experience the Catskill Mountains in winter. Charley hated winter and had to be cajoled into joining me on the long ice-spangled hikes I loved.

The Knicks failed to make the play-offs in 1976 and 1977 primarily because several personnel changes didn't pan out, and the roster

became so overloaded with scorers and short on good passers that
our offense got flat. Then, in 1977, Red Holzman retired and was
replaced by my old teammate, Willis Reed.

I was thirty-two years old and a ten-year veteran. I was also a free
agent, and since the Knicks were determined to make more drastic
changes, I felt I'd be better off with some other team. The idea of
playing out West was appealing, but since nobody was interested in
my services, I re-upped with New York.

During the mid-1970s, the NBA was going through a difficult
time. The league was so overexpanded that the fans couldn't quite
keep up with all the new teams and new players. There was also a lot
of fuss about the players' long hair and gold chains, and concern
about widespread cocaine abuse. Until Magic and Bird came into the
NBA in 1979, the league was out of favor with all except the most
die-hard basketball fans. So it was that during the summer of 1977,
in an attempt to save money and at the same time antagonize the
players' union, NBA teams reduced their active roster from twelve to
eleven players. Another reason for this move was that several ABA
teams had been admitted into the NBA, and these new teams were
struggling to make ends meet. In any case, I was certainly not a lock
to make the final squad.

One of Willis's innovations was to make the players run two miles
on an oval cinder track within a prescribed time period. I was in good
shape, but not running shape. Bob McAdoo ran the course in twenty-seven minutes, Ticky Burden did it in twenty-eight minutes, and
I kind of limped in just behind them.

Tom McMillen was also on that team, and he decided that running on the grass would be easier on his shins, but he wound up tearing his calf muscle.

I never really liked the idea of forcing basketball players to run
long distances. Basketball players are like quarter horses, with big,
solid hocks suitable for short, powerful bursts of speed. Long-dis-
tance runners are like Thoroughbreds, with slim thighs and hips.
There may be some benefit wind-wise and discipline-wise in having
basketball players run for so long. Otherwise there's not much corre-

lation between one kind of running and the other. And the result was that the team was seriously damaged when McMillen went down.

We did have several top-notch players who survived the run—Lonnie Shelton, Spencer Heywood, Bob McAdoo, Earl Monroe, and Butch Beard. Just before the season, Willis traded Walt Frazier to Cleveland for Jim Cleamons. The Knicks also had three promising rookies—Glen Gondrezick, Ray-Ray Williams, and Toby Knight. We certainly had sufficient firepower to be a force in the play-offs.

Even though McMillen's calf injury healed, the Knicks dealt him to Atlanta and kept me—neither decision being particularly astute. The Knicks would have been much better off with McMillen playing and me on the bench as an assistant coach. Anyway, there I was, playing with a bunch of highly talented athletes I had trouble relating to both on and off the court.

Still, the team was very frustrating for Willis to coach. Heywood and McAdoo were fantastic scorers, and Willis ran mostly high-post/low-post stuff for them. But when it came to defense, which once was the pride of the championship-era Knicks, this team didn't have a clue.

If we could get other teams to take wild shots and play up-tempo, we were likely to win. And we could out-talent the mediocre teams. But McAdoo could be corralled by teams whose priority was playing defense. Because Heywood was effective only in a certain limited space, good defensive teams could also put the squeeze on him.

Even though Willis tried instilling discipline, his players resisted. McAdoo simply didn't want to play defense and risk picking up personal fouls; he reasoned that he couldn't score while sitting on the bench. The trouble was that McAdoo was our center, and if a team's center isn't active on defense, then the basket is unprotected. Spencer wasn't all that crazy about playing defense either, but his excuse was lingering leg problems. Willis never had a real chance to succeed.

When Willis took over the Knicks, he was only three years removed from his playing career, not nearly enough time to learn the game from a coaching standpoint. He still had a player's mindset, and he relied too much on his assistants—Dickie McGuire and Nate Jackson.

I wasn't in the rotation, and my only function was to play some backup center. I only appeared in sixty-three games and played just over ten minutes per. My scoring average was a measly 2.4 ppg, by far the lowest of my career. It was clear to me that my playing days were over, so at the conclusion of the season I said my good-byes. But the Knicks and the Nets worked out a deal that sent me to New Jersey for a second-round draft pick.

I wasn't sure that I wanted to continue playing until the Nets' coach, Kevin Loughery, called me and said, "Phil, I know you're at the end of your career, but coming to New Jersey could be a bridge between playing and coaching. I need a veteran player with experience to teach some of my young guys a few tricks. We only won twenty-four games last year, and I need your help."

At that time, and despite Kevin's inducements, I had no desire ever to become a coach. The only reason I accepted the deal was that playing for the Nets would keep me in New York.

The Nets' training camp was held at Rutgers University in Piscataway on a court with a rock-hard floor. Kevin's favorite conditioning drill (which I later adopted) was an intense series of sequential three-man weaves called ten-and-twos that he ran at the beginning and then again at the conclusion of every practice. My feet were killing me, but I struggled through.

Kevin's offense consisted of several generic NBA plays—a single-double sequence, some high-post stuff, a Hawk series, and plenty of post-up isolations for our two best scorers, Bernard King and John Williamson. If Kevin's strategies weren't as sophisticated as Red's, Kevin was a much more animated coach. Getting his guys to play hard was Kevin's specialty, and he often valued effort more than precision.

My exposure to a "non-Knick coach" actually marked the beginning of my long search for the perfect offensive system—one that would allow a team to play hard and smart. One that would involve all five players. One that would allow freedom while still adhering to a structure.

One day toward the end of training camp, Kevin asked me to ride over to the gym with him. After some pitter-patterings about the camp and the younger players, Kevin turned to me and said, "I never thought I'd want to tell an NBA player to retire, Phil, but I think the time has come for you. What I'd like you to do is become one of my assistant coaches. This is a good situation for you, Phil. Your contract would be guaranteed, and you'd be able to play in case of an emergency. Hell, you might be playing again in a week. As you know, the ball club is committed to youth, and I think you could help us more on the bench than on the court." My mind said no, but my feet said yes. As soon as I retired, Don Nelson called to ask if I wanted to come play with the Milwaukee Bucks. June and I had two young children, and we'd set up house in Fort Lee, which was right across the George Washington Bridge and not far from her parents in Connecticut, so I opted to stay put. Then four games into the season, Bob Elliot tore up his knee, and I was activated.

I mostly played backup center behind George Johnson, and helped Kevin try to discipline the youngsters. The best of the lot was Bernard King, a second-year player and a super-duper talent. But Bernard also had his share of problems—Kevin was positive that he was an alcoholic.

It was always fascinating to watch how Kevin handled his players: one time during practice Kevin was absolutely punishing Bernard. Ten-and-twos had to be executed perfectly before the next sequence could begin. "That wasn't good enough," Kevin said after Bernard's threesome had finished their first run. "Do it again." No matter what they did, Kevin made Bernard's group run through the drill over and over. "You traveled, Bernard. Do it again. No good, Bernard. The ball hit the rim when you dunked. Again."

After practice I asked Kevin what was on his mind. "Bernard came to practice drunk," Kevin said.

"Get out of here."

"I know alcoholism," Kevin insisted. "I grew up with it in my family. I can tell a drunk a mile away. But Bernard was trying to prove to me that he was sober, so he wasn't going to quit, or bitch, or puke. And I've got to give Bernard credit for taking his punishment."

John Williamson was also quite a talent and quite a character. His self-styled nickname was Super John, and he wore a jacket with this printed on the back. John was so selfish that he wanted everything. After ball games the team provided several cans of soda and beer for the players, and John routinely put all of the beer into his own travel bag.

"John," I said, "what makes you think that you deserve all the beer?"

"Because of this," he said, and pointed to the nickname on the back of his jacket. But if John was capable of driving his coach to distraction, he was also lovable in his own way.

At center we had George Johnson, the last underhanded free-throw shooter in the NBA. George could pass some and set picks, but he earned his paycheck by blocking shots. Jan van Breda Kolff was the power forward, with Tim Basset behind him. Eric Money was a dynamic scorer off the bench.

All the guys loved playing for Kevin because he could "see" a game as well as anybody in the business. He could take quick advantage of any matchup that went in his favor. He could tell when players were tired, when their hot hand was turning cold, when to call a time-out and when not to call one. But the most notable aspect of Kevin's game plan was his intense dislike of referees at large. This attitude coupled with his fiery temper got him kicked out of fourteen games that season.

For a while, another assistant named Dave Wohl and I kind of battled with each other to see who was going to take over the team when Kevin got booted. Kevin sometimes designated me to replace him and sometimes he was too pissed at the refs to offer any guidance when he made his exit. Anyway, I just fell into the role, and all the players seemed to accept the appropriateness of my being Kevin's backup.

Besides filling in for Loughery and playing a few minutes from time to time, my duties were mostly restricted to the practice sessions. After our ten-and-two routine, I would take charge of the big men, Dave Wohl took the guards and, following Kevin's orders, we'd each run suitable drills. I'd emphasize elementary defensive slides, various rebounding and tip exercises, and post-up drills. Wohl would conduct two-on-two, one-on-one, and other breakdown drills. These procedures would eventually form the backbone of the skill drills that I'd incorporate into my own practice routines when I started coaching in the CBA.

More significantly, however, Kevin taught me that extremism in the pursuit of victory was not a vice. He was the first coach I'd ever seen who would double-team an opponents' half-court inbounder. He'd have me and six-foot-eleven George Johnson jumping around and waving our arms to obliterate the inbounder's vision. Meanwhile, the other three defenders would play a zone. It was a gutsy tactic that proved to be consistently effective.

Through Kevin's eyes I also saw that referees tended to give the better teams the benefit of any doubtful calls. Teams that were middle-of-the-pack and worse could count on getting shafted. In an attempt to even out the playing field, Kevin was willing to bait the referees and volunteer for their spit list.

After a good beginning, the team really started to go bad in December. Super John was getting out of hand, and Bernard seemed to be distracted. Then Bernard got arrested and jailed when the police found him behind the wheel of his car and fast asleep at a stop sign. Upon further investigation, the police found some cocaine in Bernard's pocket, and a subsequent blood test also revealed that he was legally drunk.

At that point, Kevin was very agitated and ready to quit. "This is it," he said. "I can't take this team any farther. They don't have enough discipline, and they've stopped listening to me." Then, in the fury of the moment, Kevin told the general manager, Charlie Theokis, that I should be hired as the Nets' new coach. In reality, the Nets were a ragtag group of players, mavericks in every way—the type of team that only another maverick like Kevin could handle. Eventually Kevin let himself be talked out of quitting. But for the first time I was faced with the realization that someone whom I respected believed I was capable of being a head coach in the NBA.

The more I thought about the possibility, the more I decided that being a head coach wasn't something I really wanted to do. What bothered me was that the game had become more a matter of business than of pleasure. I saw how the young players came into the league all full of themselves and convinced that the team rules didn't apply to them. They had more physical talent than the veteran players, but not the awareness to play the game properly. Yet the owners were falling all over themselves trying to promote these immature players as bona fide stars.

Sure, I'd enjoyed the teaching aspects of being an assistant. I liked the way the team had grown, and I had every intention of coming back for the 1979–80 season as a full-time assistant coach. Yet as much as I expected to be asked back, I was also willing to get out of basketball altogether and get on with the rest of my life.

So I went back to Montana and resumed building my home. Working on the house with my brother Joe was a joyful experience. We did everything ourselves except the plumbing and the electrical wiring. And I longed to live a simple life centered around my family—a life that I had always idealized when I was on the road.

In August I called the Nets and was told that Loughery was coming back, that Bob MacKinnon had been signed as a full-time assistant coach, and that they did want me to return—as a player. (MacKinnon had had a long career as a college coach before surfacing in the NBA, assisting Jack Ramsey, Tates Locke, and Joe Mullaney in Buffalo, and then moving to Boston and working under Satch Sanders.) So I signed a player's contract for $100,000 and ground my way through training camp.

Bernard King had been traded to Utah for Rick Kelley, a short-armed seven-footer. John Williamson was dealt to Washington, and Eric Money was in Detroit. Our best scorers were Mike Newlin and Calvin Natt. Cliff Robinson and Winford Boynes were rookies, Jan van Breda Kolff was back, and Eddie Jordan was the point guard. The team wasn't nearly as talented, but was certainly less volatile than last season's squad.

Just a few days before the season opened, Kevin came to me with the same proposal as the previous season: He wanted me to retire and become an assistant coach. So I was cut from the active roster, waived through the league, and then offered a $25,000 contract to be

Loughery's second assistant. It was a huge pay cut, but June had given birth to twin boys (Charley and Ben) in late August, so I had to accept what was the only offer on the table.

As the season began, the team floundered. Every play, every game, was a struggle. We were about three players short of being a good team. In practice, I still did my half-court big-men drills, but MacKinnon had many more responsibilities than I had. That was fine with me—I had good relationships with Rick Kelley, Cliff Robinson, George Johnson, and the other big guys I was working with, so I was fairly comfortable in my niche.

Sitting on the bench in a suit instead of a uniform, knowing that my playing days were over, I was now able to fully appreciate Loughery's style of coaching. At the defensive end, his main objective was to keep the scorers from scoring, which he tried to accomplish by double-teaming. Hubie Brown had brought periodic double-teaming into the NBA in the mid-1970s, and Loughery made it a regular practice. On the flip side, Loughery was one of the first coaches to make isolation plays the bread-and-butter of his offense. He was always trying to find ways to circumvent the rules. If teams had to have at least three players on the strong side, then Loughery would move one of those players as far away from the action as was legally permissible and play two-on-two basketball. Above all, Loughery knew how to crank up his team and get them ready for big games.

Kevin's practice philosophy was a holdover from what had been the norm during his days as an active player: get in shape, get your shot together, get your offensive system down, understand what everybody's defensive responsibilities are, and let's scrimmage. The only skill training was limited to the half-court generic big-little drills done under supervision of the assistant coaches. Kevin was much better coaching in games than he was in practice.

With about twenty games left in the season, Kelley was traded to Phoenix, and I was activated as a player. I played sixteen games and averaged 4.1 ppg to finally finish up my playing career. The Nets had no more use for me on the court or on the bench, so I was thankful for my thirteen-year run, and I went on about my life.

I was focusing on finishing my house in Montana, and basketball was no longer in my personal equation. But during the summer I was contacted by a man named James West, who owned a CBA team in Billings, Montana, which was only about 450 miles from home, so I drove over to see what was going on. Billings had a nice arena and a pretty good practice facility. At the time, the CBA had franchises in Alaska; Hawaii; Great Falls, Montana; and Casper, Wyoming; plus several other teams in the East. I stayed in Billings for a couple of days getting to know everybody in the organization, and they seemed like top-notch people. The salary would be $25,000, which wasn't too bad. But after mulling over the idea I had to turn it down.

A few weeks later, I accepted an offer to do color for the Knicks radio broadcasts alongside Marv Albert. In addition, I did a few TV spots with ESPN (mostly a weekly review of college games), but they let me go, saying that the NCAA wouldn't allow an NBA broadcaster to work college games. Then Kevin Loughery called me in December to say, "We've got a ton of young players on the team, Phil. Even though I don't know how much longer I'm going to be here myself, I want you here with me in some capacity."

My job was to work with the big guys in practice, and to try to show the young kids how to go about being professional ballplayers. I was only there for about a month when Kevin quit and was replaced by Bob MacKinnon, who hired me as his assistant coach.

After coaching for many years at Canisius College, MacKinnon had a pretty good sense of structure. He introduced several full-court drills that had the guards and the wings working together. And I liked his skill drills, too. I did feel, however, that he failed to emphasize defense enough. Whatever attention MacKinnon gave to defense was more verbal than actual hands-on floor work.

MacKinnon was very disappointed when he realized that this was a team that would sometimes lie down and not play hard. They gave it a lick and a promise, but never delivered the goods. We suffered through a fifteen-game losing streak that the players seemed to accept all too easily; they were too young to care about anything but themselves. The Meadowlands arena was still under construction, and we played our home games at Piscataway in front of about five thousand fans. It was a stopgap franchise, and a far cry from what the NBA was supposed to be. At the same time, the Nets management was romancing Larry Brown, who was coaching at UCLA, so it was obvious that MacKinnon was an interim coach.

I'd always liked what I'd seen of Larry Brown's system when he coached the Denver ball clubs in both the ABA and the NBA. He was a teacher, and his teams played good defense. Late in the season, I did meet with Larry, who told me that he would be taking the Nets job, and that he'd already offered an assistant coach's position to Mike Schueler. At the time, Schueler was coaching at Rice and was deciding if he wanted to enter the pro game. The deal was that if Schueler turned him down, Larry would be happy to offer the job to me. Well, Schueler took Larry's offer, and I wound up trying my hand as a TV guy. I did color commentary on the Nets telecasts (with Steve Albert), and since the NCAA had relaxed the rule, also some college games for St. John's.

I collected a regular paycheck, but I felt lost behind a microphone. I was just another spectator, and totally disconnected from the action. The games were "out there," too far away to trigger any kind of emotional response. More than anything else, I felt like a parasite. As a result, my on-the-air comments tended to be flat and much too brief.

So I quit the Nets and moved the whole kit and caboodle out to Montana, where I got involved with Don Arthur in renovating the health club in Kalispell. But there was another job in the offing that could keep me in basketball. Flathead Valley Community College in Kalispell was attempting to revive their basketball program after a seven-year hiatus. They were on the lookout for a new coach, and expressed their interest in interviewing me. I knew that for many years the school had traditionally fielded some very good teams in competition with the likes of Treasure State C.C. and Northern Idaho C.C. One of my teammates in New Jersey, Tim Basset, had played junior college ball at Treasure State in Pocatello, Idaho, and he'd highly recommended the situation.

The previous coach had done much of his recruiting in Detroit and had brought several black ballplayers into the community. Kalispell was a very friendly town where nobody locked the front doors to their houses, and the keys to their cars were always under the foot mats—a very different atmosphere from what inner-city kids were used to. The subsequent outbreak of fights, petty thieving, and racial threats had forced the school's administration to shut down their basketball program.

Of course, the first question put to me in the interview was whether or not I'd be recruiting blacks. "Of course," I said. "Black kids are some of the best basketball players in the country. Even if this is a homogenous community, we should still try to bring in the best talent we can."

Well, the school's administration was liberal enough to go along with my plans, and it looked like I had a new job. But then I appeared at a public fund-raiser, and the issue of recruiting black players was brought up again. The community was so stirred up by my comments that the administration responded by backing out of their commitment to restart the basketball program, so there was no job to be had. Three years later they did resurrect the program, but on a much smaller scale.

Instead I devoted my time and energy to building up the health club, Second Wind, working twelve-hour days three days a week, and taking care of our four kids while June worked ten-hour days the other two days of the week. We all worked on Saturdays and Sundays. It was a real battle, and no matter how hard we all worked, there was no way the health club could ever support two families.

Then in January I got a call from another CBA team, the Albany Patroons, who were unhappy with their coach, Dean Meminger (an old teammate from the Knicks' heyday). The team had no chance of making the play-offs, but the Patroons owners wanted me to finish out the last six weeks of the season. Only after consulting with Dean, who concurred that the Patroons' season was a lost cause, did I agree to take the job. As expected, it was very awkward for me to replace Dean. In fact, he did make one request: he was only thirty-three years old and wanted the opportunity to try out for the team. Dean could still play the game, but the guys on the team had some scores to settle, and they simply unloaded on poor Deano, smacking him around and knocking him down at every chance.

I thought the team had some talented players, and I believed I could help them be a good team. We had Ralph McPherson, a tough rawhide Texan; Larry Spriggs, who eventually got picked up by the Lakers; Hollis Copeland, another ex-Knick. Also a player named John Leonard, who once refused to go on a road trip because he felt he hadn't played enough in the preceding game. Basically I ran Red Holzman's offense that Dean had already installed—some high- and low-post stuff, with some screen/rolls and weak-side screens.

Woodstock was just a scant fifty miles south of Albany, a straight shot up the New York State Thruway, so I asked Charley to come up and watch a game. Coincidentally, the game Charley saw was against the first-place team from Lancaster, Pennsylvania, which was coached by another Knicks ex-teammate of mine, Cazzie Russell. The Patroons lost the game after a rather sluggish second half, and afterward Charley and I analyzed the quality of ball played by these young men: the energy was there and the players were courageous, but for the most part their skills were not quite up to the level of "the Big Dance." Also, except for the point guards, the players seemed to be a position short, that is, power forwards playing center and guards playing the small forward spot.

In those days, the CBA All-Star game pitted a host team against the best players from all the other teams. In 1983 Albany was the host team, and the CBA All-Stars were coached by Cazzie Russell. The Patroons really responded to my efforts and came on to win the game. (It's interesting to note that only two host teams in CBA history have won All-Star games. And the other winning coach besides me? Charley Rosen on New Year's Eve 1988 with the Rockford Lightning.)

I enjoyed my first taste of the CBA, but I also thought I might get lost there and never find my way out. As expected, the Patroons missed the play-offs, and by the time I returned to Montana, the CBA's championship series was concluding in Great Falls, only 250 miles away. So I drove over to watch the deciding game. George Karl was coach of the Great Falls team, and for the occasion he wore a powder blue tuxedo. The game, and the championship, was won in overtime by the Detroit Spirits. Then, a few months later, Karl was named player personnel director of the Cleveland Cavaliers. This gave me some hope that there was indeed life after the CBA, so during the summer, when Albany pursued me for the 1983–84 season, I was ready to go. Because the Patroons were community owned, I didn't push them to increase their first offer—$18,000.

So my whole family loaded up a U-Haul trailer and hitched it to the back of our station wagon (a white Olds that Charley called "Vanilla Thunder"). Then, right before the Labor Day weekend, my wife, June, and our four children piled into the car and headed for Woodstock, where we had rented a house.

My first Patroons training camp opened the week before Thanksgiving Day and consisted of ten days of practice and one exhibition game. After dealing with several agents and eliciting scouting reports from my NBA connections, I invited twenty players to camp, all of them battling for a spot on the final ten-man roster. But I needed an assistant coach to help me condition and teach skills to this unwieldly number, and the best person I could think of was Charley. For the duration of the camp we roomed together at the Best Western Motel, right off Broadway in downtown Albany. I was amazed at the intensity and curiosity that Charley brought to coaching. We often broke the squad into two groups to work on warm-up skill drills, and then on guard and big-men drills. Charley was primarily responsible for the big men, and he was relentless.

He was always hanging around the big men, trading jump shots and outlandish opinions. According to Charley, every time a ballplayer fathered a child, he lost a step.

During my NBA playing days, all the players had roommates on the road. Along the way, I'd shared hotel rooms with Harthorne Wingo, Walt Frazier, Toby Knight, Eddie Mast, and Bill Bradley. What I wasn't prepared for was the obsessiveness with which Charley approached the game of basketball in general and in particular the prospective makeup of the Patroons. He could talk hoops all day long.

I imposed my own habitual routine of getting up early and planning the day ahead over breakfast. With one scheduled exhibition game and my decision to give the players a free Sunday, we still managed to cram seventeen practices into the ten-day period. Charley was fascinated by how meticulously the two-a-days had to be planned, and he loved the day-long intensity. The flex offense appealed to him, and he mastered its nuances in a short period of time. Physically both the coaches and the players suffered from the daily four to five hours of competitive activity, but there's no other way to teach the skills and the on-court awareness required for a frantic season that promised four, and sometimes five, games every week.

About a week into the preseason training camp, Charley began scheming how he could continue with the job of assisting me in coaching the team. I told him that I didn't know how much he could get paid, but he still thought the opportunity would be worthwhile. Anyway, the season started with a home game, and Charley sat on the bench wearing a sport coat and necktie, something quite out of character for him. Road games were a different story: to cut down on operating costs, the CBA by-laws permitted a team to dress only nine players away from home, and also prohibited assistant coaches from traveling with a team. The only exception was that an "accredited" trainer was permitted to sit on the bench during road games if the team was willing to pay the additional costs. In any case, after our first game, the Patroons went on a road trip, leaving behind one very unhappy player and an even sadder assistant coach. During the week we were away, Charley inquired of the CBA league office as to what specific credentials were required of an accredited trainer. And Charley figured out a way.

He'd been a physical education major at Hunter College, with enough anatomy and physiology courses to qualify for admission into a weekend Red Cross workshop that was periodically given in Albany. By mid-January, when Charley had completed the workshop, the CBA reluctantly allowed him to travel with the team. The Patroons squeezed out a meager salary plus the standard $15 per diem to pay Charley for the rest of the season.

But Charley had to satisfy one more qualification to sit on the team's bench—he also had to look like a trainer. That meant a medic's outfit, replete with white pants, a white shirt, and white shoes (although he received a special dispensation to wear sneakers). We

called him the "Good Humor man," yet Charley's basketball strategies were always taken seriously.

The rules of the CBA also stipulated that a team had to travel by
van on any trip under five hundred miles. This hardship served to
make road wins very scarce, and the constant proximity of coaches
and players severely tested everybody's patience and goodwill.
Becoming a unified team was a slow, agonizing process anyway, and
our progress was hampered by the fact that I was a headstrong rookie coach. It was Charley who helped soften my sharp edges and
enabled me to maintain a workable relationship with the players.
Even so, he was no medic, and several of the players chose to do their
own pregame taping.

It's my nature to trust that God will take care of everything in due
time, but Charley's way was to prod and press me to deal with issues
that had to be dealt with immediately. What about this possible
trade? Or that one? Shouldn't we give Lowes Moore some time at
the two-guard spot?

Something about Charley seemed to complement something about
me. I don't know whether it was the Communist Party background of
Charley's parents that helped balance my own conservative Christian
upbringing, or his radical hippie outlook that matched my own con-
trarian ways. Whatever it was, it brought about an unlikely exchange
of ideas. With so much downtime on the road, Charley helped inspire
many hours of stimulating conversation. Charley was a cynic, and a
romantic as well. He enjoyed almost everything he did, despite his
increasing bitterness in his unworkable marriage with Susan.

Eating was another enjoyable pastime while traveling, and we
both liked Chinese food. We also shared a common interest in bluegrass music. We listened to Bill Monroe, Doc and Merle Watson,
and Jerry Garcia's group, Old and In the Way. Much like the basketball that Charley and I valued, good bluegrass results from a team
effort in which the individual players are careful not to overwhelm
the musical understanding of the band as a whole.

Teamwork was not a normal part of CBA players' game plan.
They knew that only numbers attracted the attention of NBA scouts,
so, win or lose, they were unhappy if they didn't get their personal

quotas of points or rebounds. My idea was to employ two platoons of players working in eight-minute rotations. That meant the starters could only expect to play thirty-two minutes per game, and the bench players only sixteen—so everybody was unhappy. Another problem I had with my team was that I'd arranged for all of them to receive the same paycheck—$350 per week. The minimum mandated salary was $325, and the maximum was $400, so I felt that since nobody in the CBA was making any real money anyway, there was no reason to create the kind of salary hierarchy that's caused so much trouble among NBA players. As far as I was concerned, it was the journey that really mattered.

After every Patroons' game-day shootaround, Charley and I would minister elbows and forearms to each other's back, hips, and ribs as we labored to play one-on-one on a fortuitously shortened full court. It is a dance that we've done hundreds of times over the years, and it sometimes still gave us tremendous pleasure—not merely to compete but just to do the dance. Charley and I have both suffered the pains of gout. As a result, his hands were stiff and arthritic, but then his hands were never Charley's strongest asset anyway. We had an unwritten understanding that I wouldn't apply too much pressure when he dribbled the ball. And as we huffed and puffed up and down the court, the fouler always called the fouls. We tried to play for thirty continuous minutes, and it was great fun for both of us.

After our game we sat in the steam room and continued our habit of talking about the aesthetics and values of the game. We discussed the coaches and the new ideas some of them have brought to basketball. We compared the various styles of play, always favoring team-oriented offenses as opposed to one-on-o e performances. We also traded our opinions of the players, looking for the ones who have the makings of champions. The ability of a player to pass the ball was always an important criterion for us. Is he only capable of making "bailout" desperation passes when he can't find a shot for himself? Or does a player understand (as hockey players do) that the most important pass is the pass before the assist-pass?

The Patroons finished second in our conference, and we had high hopes going into the play-offs. As extra inspiration, throughout the postseason play I wore the NBA championship ring that I'd won with the 1970 Knicks.

Each round was a best-of-five series, and we started off by coming from a two-to-nothing deficit to beat the Bay State Bombardiers. The Patroons seemed to bond after that series, and we went on to overcome the Puerto Rico Coquis and then square off against the Wyoming Wildcatters in the finals.

The Wildcatters were coached by Jack Schalow and featured Del Beshore, a guard with some NBA experience. I was very rigid in keeping the team's habitual rotation in effect, my philosophy being that I had an obligation to stay with the players who'd brought us this far. But Beshore had a tricky behind-the-back move that our own point guard, Lowes Moore, just couldn't handle. Just before the deciding game of the series Charley insisted that Moore's backup, Mark Jones, could contain Beshore. I resisted as long as I could, but Beshore continued to overwhelm Moore, so I finally relented and sent Jones after him. This matchup turned the game around and enabled the Patroons to win the championship. And I realized that stubborn coaches operate under a self-imposed handicap.

The entire season was a wonderfully satisfying experience for me, one that convinced me that I had a viable future as a coach.

FIVE

ONE ON ONE

CHARLEY

Like everyone else who follows the bouncing ball, Phil and I had our own pregame rituals when we played one on one. He'd shoot a few layup/baby hooks, then unloose a couple of jumpers from the free throw line. Perhaps ten shots in all and he'd be ready. As for me, what I really needed was half an hour on a massage table, then another half hour reconvincing myself that, yes, the orange ring was bigger than the ball.

I'd rebound his misses or fetch his makes, then toss him lollipop bounce passes more or less in rhythm for his next shot. His returns to me were always perfectly accurate chest passes with perhaps a little more snap than my gouty fingers could comfortably handle.

Nevertheless, the ball fits against my fingers just so, my fingers spread to fill the seams. *Swish! Clunk!* Both of us shooting until there's an ethereal link between each one of us as the ball rolls through the air, its soaring arc a fulfillment of man's wish to fly. *Clunk!* Until there's a conjunction between the corporeal body and the mystic hoop itself. Until the ball becomes a flashing synapse between our outstretched fingers and the roundness of the world, of our path around the sun, of beginnings and endings, of the congress of all things.

Our standard game was up-and-down on a smallish full-court, twenty-one wins (but the winner had to win by 2), switch sides when one of us (usually Phil) reached 11. Sometimes we played straight-up. Sometimes he spotted me as much as seven baskets. Years later our games would be regulated by the clock—thirty minutes, switch ends at fifteen—although Phil always kept track of the score.

He was younger, quicker, and more skilled than me. My "advantage" was size (about half an inch) and strength.

"Make it, take it," one of us would say, and the other would shoot from the top of the key to determine first possession. Usually his.

He'd invariably start with a pull-up jumper that I could never quite block. *Swish!* After he retired and the spring went out of his legs, his base was more stable (being closer to the floor), his wrist much looser, and his jumper far more accurate. *Swish!*

When Phil was with the Knicks, Red Holzman would never let him dribble the ball. But Phil routinely froze me with nifty crossovers and behind-the-back maneuvers.

Swish!

Sometimes when the score got tight, he'd turn his back to me and roll me into the pivot. My body memory is indelibly imprinted with his right elbow flexing thisclose to the bridge of my nose as he launches his left hook.

Swish!

As the years wore on, Phil would develop his right-handed hook shot. Certainly not because he needed another weapon to beat me. For Phil, to live was to grow. The path was the goal.

Swish!

And me? I tried to bang him around on defense, especially when he took me inside. I tried to pin his left arm and keep him from rotating his right hip. Yet I was always mindful of the acrostic scars that marked his spinal fusion, so I was careful not to Bogart his back. The best I could do was force him into shooting a turnaround jumper, which I could occasionally block.

"Take it, Phil. I fouled you."

"Nah. I should've made the shot anyway."

Clunk!

Ballhandling was never my specialty, so Phil normally waited until I reached the three-point line before confronting me on defense. Even then, he'd let me dribble leftward. In a close game, though, he'd attack me in the backcourt, and with his cobra arms and quick feet, he could steal my dribble at his pleasure.

So how did I score against one of the finest defensive players of his generation? I took long jumpers (and even old-timey one-handers), mostly from well beyond my range. I shot running baseline hooks with my right hand. And I tried to overpower him in the pivot and then either utilize some kind of duck-under or reverse move to the far side of the basket.

Clunk! Clunk! Swish!!!

And I did beat him once, during our partnership in Albany. We were playing upstairs on the sixty-foot court in the Steuben Athletic Club. My shot was falling that bright afternoon, Phil's wasn't, and I was a blink or two quicker than usual. We played as fiercely as though we were brothers—pronging each other with elbows, smashing shoulder to shoulder and hip to hip. I was ahead 20–19 (with no spot!) and he had the ball, dribbling and spinning into the attack zone. We both understood that if he scored now, the game would eventually be his. This was the play.

At the foul line extended, he pivoted leftward to the sideline and began his swift approach toward the basket. Realizing that he'd gained an irrecoverable half-step, I tried to swipe the ball from behind him. And, yes! He'd been a little lazy with his crossover and I managed to tip the ball away (in the process, however, I'd also bumped his hip and sent him sprawling to the floor).

"Yes!" I shouted, as I dribbled unimpeded downcourt and scored the winning basket.

"Foul," said Phil, still lying on the floor.

"Bullshit. It was incidental contact."

"Bullshit yourself, Charley. You knocked me down. It's a foul."

We jabbered back and forth for a while, our arguments getting more heated with every exchange. Then I said, "You mean you've never lost a game when a referee made a bad call?"

Disgusted, he stormed off the court and spent thirty minutes doing solitary yoga exercises in a side gym. It wasn't until we'd showered, dressed, and agreed that both of us were assholes that we were able to joke about the game.

Swish!

BUZZZZZZZZTTT!

I'd guess that my lifetime record against Phil is something like 1–250.

Years later, after one particularly combative on-court session, we showered, dressed, and went for a walk in the woods near Woodstock. This was late in the summer of 1989, a few days before Phil was to leave for Chicago and begin his first season as the Bulls' head coach. As we ambled about, he expressed some doubts about his future. Was he ready to take over the team? Could he deal with the players' massive egos? Would the Triangle work at this level? Were his Xs and Os up to par? Did he have the stuff to be a successful head coach in the NBA?

Yes, I said. Of course. He'd paid his dues in full. He had the mind, the heart, and the spirit to excel.

But were these qualifications sufficient unto the day?

Yes. Of course. Because he also had the wisdom of experience. Because he also had a vision. And above all, because he had personal and professional integrity.

That's when I predicted that he'd win five championships in Chicago.

And last year I predicted he'd win three in L.A. *Swish!*

SIX

PUERTO RICAN SUMMER AND THE BULLS

PHIL

Before the Patroons faced off against Wyoming in the 1984 CBA finals, our opponent in the finals of the Eastern Division was the Puerto Rico Couquis. While we were in San Juan to open the series, I was approached by some local businessmen from Quebradillas and offered a summer job coaching in what was called the Superior League. I'd be able to bring my family down there, and it was a perfect opportunity to augment my inadequate CBA salary.

I'd never lived in an equatorial climate before, nor had I lived with people of color. I'd taken Spanish in college, but I didn't have much of a working vocabulary, so I approached my Puerto Rican adventure with a great deal of trepidation. Quebradillas was about sixty miles west of San Juan in a very rural community, but it turned out to be a lovely place to live and work.

The Superior League comprised sixteen teams representing towns all over the island. Even though the players got paid anywhere from $10,000 to about $20,000 for the summer season, the league was officially sanctioned by the NCAA, so most of the players were veterans of some form of college basketball. Players on the Puerto Rican national team who participated in the Pan-Am Games and the Olympics were also eligible to play. Every team was allowed to hire two "imports," who usually came from some other Caribbean country. Otherwise, the only qualification was that one of the players' parents had to be a native of Puerto Rico. That meant there were kids from Connecticut, Los Angeles, Miami, Orlando, and New York (called NewYoricans), which just about defined the geographical areas where Puerto Ricans lived on the mainland. There were fifteen players on each team, and they ranged in age from fifteen to thirty-eight. I had an interpreter constantly by my side, and the kids were just great to work with.

There was always a trade wind blowing, so the temperature usually hovered somewhere between 85 and 88 degrees. Occasionally we'd see a 90-degree day with high humidity that was tough for me to take. But the ocean was all around us, so it was easy to cool off.

Sunrise was six a.m. every day and the sun would set precisely twelve hours later. The games were scheduled for eight p.m. when the island was pretty much cooled down. Most of the games were played in arenas called *conches* ("shells") that featured open-air sides. Basketball was by far the most popular spectator sport in Puerto Rico, with at least four games televised every week.

The teams were owned by the league and franchised out to local businessmen. There was a definite feeling of community involvement everywhere, so the rivalry between teams that represented neighboring towns was ferocious.

The Puerto Rican coaches were very astute, and the Superior League also had a long history of mainland coaches. Tex Winter won a league championship coaching Ponce in the early-1950s. When I first joined the Knicks, Red Holzman was spending his summers coaching in Ponce. Johnny Bach, who'd later become my assistant in Chicago, coached in Mayaguez. Other notable coaches include Larry Brown and his brother Herb, P. J. Carlesimo, Jim Boeheim, Lou Rossini, Del Harris, Doug Moe, Paul Westhead, and Sam Jones.

I soon found out that home teams rarely lost: There was one game in San Germain when the hometown timekeeper let the clock run out after the referee had called a time-out with several seconds remaining. We were behind by a point and we had the ball, so I ran over and protested to the refs. But in Puerto Rico, all the refs were homers (which was a sensible life-preserving attitude), so the refs simply said, "Game over," and tried to get off the court as quickly as possible. At that point, I took my argument over to the timekeeper. "What the hell're you doing?" I shouted. "There should be five seconds left in the game!" Then my assistant coach/interpreter/bodyguard pulled me away. I thought that I had a good case, but I was told that the timekeeper had just pulled a knife from his pocket and was about to attack me.

The first time I coached a home game at Quebradillas I noticed a large wooden box situated against the wall behind the last row of seats. What was that all about? It seemed that the mayor of Quebradillas was a rabid basketball fan. During a ball game a few years back he had been so infuriated by a referee's call that he pulled out a pistol and tried to shoot him. When someone grabbed at his arm, the mayor ended up wounding an usher. For this the mayor was fined, spent a few days in jail, and was not allowed to carry a firearm. But the punishment didn't deter him. The following season, the mayor came out of the stands to dispute another referee's decision, hitting the offending ref in back of the head and knocking him to the floor. Since then, whenever the mayor attended a home game, he had to be locked inside the box.

One of my players was Raymond Dalmau, who at age thirty-six was the most prolific scorer in the history of Puerto Rican basketball. But Raymond did not like the flex offense I was using. Nor did he like playing less than the entire ball game. Raymond had enough juice to have me fired after seven games. "Don't worry," the owner of the team said to me, "I've fired bigger names than you."

Fortunately the owner also had a ready-made parachute for me. He knew that the coach in the nearby town of Isabella was on the verge of being fired. The coach there was an American, Tom Sullivan, who'd run afoul of Alex Vega, his team's best player. As a result of their dispute, Sullivan refused to play Vega during a crucial home game, and all hell broke loose. While the fans rioted outside the arena and were tearing up the coach's car, the police had to take him down to the station house to save his life. (Coaches' cars were provided by the teams and were considered to be extremely valuable assets. The rule was that a coach never returned the keys to his car until he'd been paid his wages in full.) Three days later I was on the bench and coaching in Isabella.

I found out later that Quebradillas had been founded four hundred years ago, but there had been many big disagreements within the founding family over water rights at a nearby river. The result was that one side of the family remained in Quebradillas while another side moved across the river and founded Isabella—and the two towns had been battling ever since. There were similar stories of feuding towns all over the island. No wonder the fans were extremely emotional and the kids played all-out.

The nickname of the Isabella team was the Gallitos, "the fighting cocks," and from time to time when they played in Quebradillas a local fanatico would toss a plucked chicken out onto the court. This symbol of humiliating emasculation would invariably start a fight in the stands (which was why the courts were always surrounded by wire fences—although a player in Fajardo once climbed the fence to go after a fan). Perhaps that's why my new interpreter/assistant coach made road trips with a gun strapped to his leg.

The one town that had the most significant home-court advantage was San Germain, the site of a large convent. The story was that the nuns were using candles and exhortations to throw hexes on opposing teams. Once before a play-off game, it was said that the nuns had killed a chicken at midnight in a graveyard and then sprinkled the chicken's blood on the visitors' bench. At one time the owner of the Ponce team also owned a huge sugarcane plantation. To counter the nun's hexes and the intimidating San Germain fans, he packed the stands with about fifty of his sugarcane workers armed with machetes.

The only way into and out of Quebradillas was through a narrow mountain pass, where desperado fans would wait in ambush to stone the cars of any visiting team that had dared to win a game there. After games anywhere on the road, visiting teams would forgo showers and sprint from the court to their cars, hoping to get there before the locals punctured all their tires.

Above all else, my stint in Puerto Rico forced me to learn nonverbal methods of communicating. Smiles, frowns, raised eyebrows, and body language in general were just as important for setting a mood as was language. I also learned how to deal with zone defenses, and how to implement and counter various traps. The international rules were interesting, especially those governing technical fouls and time-outs. Every technical foul called on a player also counted as a personal foul, so the players had to be very mindful of how they spoke to referees. Each team was only entitled to two time-outs in each of the twenty-minute halves. The procedure was that a coach had to notify the official scorer that he wanted a time-out (some arenas actually had buzzers on the bench), which would then be called only when there was a stoppage in play. It's a great idea that kept the games moving along. Forty-minute games were completed in an hour and a half.

While the reduction of time-outs would not work in the NBA because of the need to create space for TV commercials, two of the international rules would certainly benefit the pro game. The international three-second lane measures twenty feet at the baseline, tapering to twelve feet at the foul line, and is trapezoidal in shape. In the NBA, the low post has become the scene of many brutal battles. But if the international lane were adopted, then the mid-lane and the low-post jockeying for position would take place the same distance from the basket, and the goal area would be decongested.

In international basketball, once a shot hits the rim, it's up for grabs, and there's no offensive or defensive interference. (Shots blocked on their downward trajectory are the only instances where goal tending can be called.) The advantage of this situation is that the rebounders don't have to wait for the ball to leave the cylinder to grab it, which means they don't have time to be fighting and throwing one another to the floor. Instituting the international no-goal-tending rule would de-emphasize power and physical strength under the basket, while helping those rebounders who are great leapers. Speed and quickness would be just as valuable as muscle power.

Back on the mainland, Charley's role was expanded in the 1984–85 CBA season when the league saw the importance of a team's carrying a full-time assistant coach. Our van now contained nine players, myself, Charley, and also a radio man, Joe "Mr. Metameucil" Hennessy. It was jacket and tie at home and away for Charley, and the Patroons proved to be the best team in the league. Our only two-game losing streak occurred during a stretch of four games in four nights in four different cities.

Life on the road wasn't always pleasant, but Charley and I were focused on trying to get the guys to play for the sheer joy of the game, so we gave them as much of ourselves as we could. And with Charley's sense of humor and my increasing focus on the team as community, these men found a way to enjoy the life and enjoy each other's company.

We had another successful season, losing to Bill Musselman's Tampa Bay Thrillers in the conference finals. The following year, Charley's last as my assistant, Musselman beat us in the play-offs again, this time in the first round.

During these developmental seasons, Charley and I would always keep track of how basketball was evolving elsewhere. College hoops was being dominated by North Carolina and Georgetown, with surprises along the way from Villanova and North Carolina State. And the NBA was ruled by two teams, the Los Angeles Lakers and the Boston Celtics. As we'd watch an NBA contest, Charley would tell me, "Phil, you'll be there. Just be ready for the opportunity when it comes."

I also continued to develop the flex offense and see if it could work in pro ball. The constant motion appealed to me, as did the unselfishness demanded by the format. But by my third year in the league, when I couldn't seem to recruit mobile, outside-shooting, good-passing big men, I went to the Hawk series. In retrospect, I didn't pay enough attention to team defense. The only deviations from our straight man-to-man were full-court and half-court zone defenses.

In 1987, after four years of coaching year-round in both the CBA and Puerto Rico, I decided that I'd gone as far as that road could take me, so I resigned from the Patroons and also severed my ties with the Superior League. My future was decidedly unsettled. I took an aptitude test that accurately reflected my interests in cooking and in outdoor activities, and suggested a career in either the ministry or law. Perhaps I'd go back to school and get a law degree. Maybe I'd get involved in the health club again. More than anything, I had faith that something would turn up.

In June I attended the NBA's predraft camp in Chicago. That's where sixty or seventy college players are invited to take part in various drills and scrimmages in the hope of improving their draft position. It's also a great time for unemployed coaches and scouts to schmooze with general managers and NBA brass. At the time the Knicks' coaching job was open, and they interviewed me while I was there. I spent the rest of the spring and summer in Montana waiting for the Knicks to call, but they eventually hired Rick Pitino. When nothing else turned up, I returned to Woodstock so that my kids could go through another school year there.

Strictly on a hunch, I called Jerry Krause and asked if the Bulls needed a territorial scout to cover the NBA teams on the eastern seaboard. "No," Jerry said. "Our coaching staff does all of our NBA scouting." Then a week before the Bulls' training camp opened, Krause called and asked if I was interested in interviewing for a position as an assistant to Doug Collins.

This was a total surprise for several reasons: It was back in the summer of 1985 that Krause had first expressed an interest in having me join the Bulls organization. Stan Albeck was the new coach, and Krause was looking to fill out the coaching staff. I was coaching in Puerto Rico when the summons came, and I arrived in Chicago for the interview wearing a full beard and dressed in tropical attire—khaki chinos, sport shirt, sandals, and a beautiful Ecuadorian straw hat replete with a blue parrot feather. Albeck balked, and I was never offered the job. The media has repeatedly opined that I was turned down because of my outfit, but the real reason Albeck nixed me was that Krause had vetoed his first choice, John Killilea, and they were playing tit-for-tat.

When Krause called again three years later, I really didn't have many viable alternatives if I wanted to stay in basketball. Besides, I felt that my full dose of the CBA had totally prepared me for the next level. This time I was clean-shaven and wore a tie and jacket.

My annual income during my four CBA years had never reached $50,000. June and I had been forced to dip into my NBA nest egg (our savings and various investments), but with four children all within six to ten years of going to college, I knew that I'd have to get back into the NBA or move on to some other lucrative job. June and I discussed the trials and tribulations of the NBA lifestyle—how consuming it was, how exciting and how financially rewarding, balanced against the loss of family time. I knew how much more demanding coaching was than playing. Nevertheless, I felt I'd already had a positive influence on the most important part of my children's lives, their preteen years. I also believed that our family would be able to retain our core values even if I found employment in the NBA. So I agreed to travel to Chicago for an interview.

Four days after I returned from Chicago, Krause called and offered me the job, pointing out that I had to leave immediately. The kids were already in school, and June had a position setting up a hospice organization in Ulster County, so I accepted Krause's offer and was off to Chicago on my own. But I left with a sense of relief, knowing that my family would be provided for. Above all, I also felt blessed and thankful that I'd been given a second chance.

At the same time, even though I had no ambition to ever become a head coach, I believed that I belonged in the NBA. My only intention was to immerse myself in my job and relearn the league. Unlike my previous stint in New Jersey, the Bulls' assistants were treated handsomely. We each had our own office, our own videotape machine, and we were responsible for scouting upcoming opponents. Clearly, the Chicago Bulls was an organization that took their business seriously.

It was in Chicago that I served my final apprenticeship and, notwithstanding what I came to learn from Doug, my mentors were the other two assistant coaches, Johnny Bach and Tex Winter.

Johnny had grown up in Brooklyn, and had played baseball and basketball at Fordham University in the Bronx. When World War II broke out, he moved on to Brown University, where he attended Officers' Candidate School. From there, Johnny saw action in the Pacific theater and was part of the naval fleet that bombarded the beach at Okinawa for forty-eight consecutive hours prior to the infantry assault. After his discharge, he played one season with the Boston Celtics (1948–49) and also served as a bullpen catcher for the New York Yankees. Eventually he wound up coaching basketball, first at Fordham University (1950–68), and then at Penn State (1968–75). Johnny's next step was the NBA, serving as an assistant (and later a head) coach with Golden State. In the infamous 1972 Olympic Games (when the Russians were given three last-second chances to win the gold-medal basketball game against the United States), Johnny also assisted Hank Iba, and that's where he met Doug Collins.

Johnny had a brilliant basketball mind, yet instead of being associated with a particular system, he was essentially a pragmatist. His expertise was defense, and his scouting reports were incredibly meticulous. Blessed with a photographic memory, Johnny knew a million ways to win a ball game.

One day, early in my first season with the Bulls, I was watching a Milwaukee Bucks' game tape, just trying to get a feel for what the other teams in our division were doing. "Johnny," I said, "Milwaukee's running some kind of offense that I can't identify. Come on over and take a look." So he slid his chair up in front of my VCR, watched for about ten seconds, and then said, "Oh, that's Horst Pinholster's pinwheel offense?"

"Who?"

"Horst Pinholster. He was an innovative coach back in the fifties."

A few days later, Johnny presented me with a book that detailed Pinholster's pinwheel offense.

After having been away from the NBA for five years, I had a lot of catching up to do. What I discovered was that everybody pretty much ran the same offensive sets, and there wasn't any kind of flow from a full-court to a half-court situation. Teams would look for a fast break, then if it wasn't there, they'd pull the ball back out and the coach would call a number. Motion offenses were popular, plus the old standbys—single-doubles, various box sets, and different forms of Hubie Brown's Hawk series.

Doug preferred single-doubles, Hawks, and anything that could create isolation opportunities for Michael Jordan. Every so often, Doug would come into practice and add another set that would be effective for a week until the other teams got wise to it. Rather than having his own definitive system, Doug had a playbook offense. With Michael the focus of every play anyway, Doug's main concern was how to keep the defensive help away from him.

During practice, only Johnny and I were allowed to join Doug on the floor. That's because Tex never really got along with Doug and was banished to the sidelines, where he would sit on a chair and take notes.

The biggest problem between Tex and Doug was Tex's feistiness during ball games. "Damn guy isn't doing any work," Tex would grumble whenever a player was loafing. Then he'd get into the player's face during a time-out. "You'd better start working hard out there, or else…" Most head coaches would find Tex's comments to be distracting, and Doug was no exception. The two of them were very much alike—impatient and impulsive. Tex was forbidden to sit on the Bulls' bench during games.

Later, I would find that Tex had a God's-eye view of basketball, and that his caustic commentaries were extremely valuable. If Michael was screwing up, Tex would say, "You've got to get him out of the game, Phil, he's trying to score every time he touches the ball. He's not allowing us to run our offense." And I'd say, "Just wait, Coach. Michael just needs to get a feel for the game, then he'll get back to the Triangle. We've got to be patient with him." Tex's tendency to become easily exasperated and my penchant for long-suffering worked well together.

Even though I was the junior member of the coaching staff, Doug wanted me to step up and contribute what I knew. Before too long, I was able to develop a distinctive voice, which led Doug to give me more and more authority. When Doug got tossed from a game during my second year, he actually handed me the play sheets and told me to take over. This was a significant move because it showed the team that I was no longer just part of the chorus, and that Doug trusted me to make on-the-spot decisions with a ball game in the balance. I'm forever grateful to Doug for allowing me to establish credibility with the players.

Doug was a very intelligent man with a wonderful grasp of the game. As a player, he had been a terrific scorer who was selected to four All-Star games. The only two NBA coaches he ever played for, Gene Shue and Billy Cunningham, were also accomplished scorers. Accordingly, Doug favored players who could shoot, and whose ball-handling capabilities could break down a defense and get them to the free-throw line at the end of the game. Doug's special passion was ball control, and he placed a high value on each possession. Turnovers were anathema.

Doug's defensive philosophy came straight from Hank Iba: always rotate both guards back whenever a shot goes up to absolutely prevent any fast-break scores. At one time Doug did explore the Triangle, but he soon scrapped it because the Triangle is often run with a guard in the corner, which makes it difficult for him to retreat to midcourt when a shot is taken. In the Triangle the responsibility for rotating back is often placed on a guard and the small forward. This was too much of a deviation from Iba's principles for Doug to embrace.

Doug did most of his defensive teaching in preseason and in the shootarounds that preceded ball games when he emphasized a variety of defensive rotations and situational defenses. He preached team defense, but he also taught individual defensive skills: Time-delay the cutters. Arm-bar the cross-pick. All of his defensive techniques were right on. Like Kevin Loughery, Doug aimed to take an opponent out of its favorite offensive sets by employing a wide range of doubleteams.

It's interesting to note that 90 percent of the ex-players who've become coaches have been guards. I guess that's because guards do a lot of thinking with the ball in their hands, and everybody sees them as leaders. How many big men have been good coaches? Alex Hannum, for sure. Joe Lapchick with the old New York Knickerbockers. Bill Russell? He did win a couple of championships—not because of his coaching ability but because he was still playing. Rudy Tomjanovich is a good coach. He's six-eight, but his credentials as a big man are suspect because he was more of a shooter than a rebounder or picker. I considered the six-foot-five Jerry Sloan to be a big man because of the way he played—rebounding, setting picks, and tough enough to defend power forwards. Larry Bird was well on his way to becoming a good coach when he quit after only three seasons. I've always thought that Dave Cowens was a good coach. Paul Silas, too.

Anyway, it was Doug who introduced me to the benefits of making assistant coaches responsible for advance scouting. I also admired his sense of organization and his game preparation. In addition, Doug was an advocate of the extensive use of videotapes and editing machines.

As much as I appreciated his basketball know-how, Doug and I didn't always operate on the same wavelength. Doug's personal style of dealing with people was confrontational. If something irritated him, he'd be visibly upset until the situation was resolved. Charles Oakley used to constantly complain about not getting enough shots. "Michael got forty shots," he'd say after a game, "and even though I did all the dirty work, I only got five." Doug would have a hard time swallowing this kind of stuff, so those kind of comments from Oakley would always upset him.

But the team was successful. My first year in Chicago, we won fifty-two games, and the next season we won forty-seven.

Through it all, Tex and Doug continued to have forceful disagreements. Tex didn't necessarily want Doug to run the Triangle, but he did think that the team needed some kind of definable system. Tex felt that when Doug called every play from the sidelines, he prevented the team from developing a rhythm. Tex and Doug didn't go so far as to berate one another, but their antagonistic relationship made everybody uncomfortable. Tex was so distraught that he was looking forward to retirement.

I'm sure that if I hadn't been named the Bulls' head coach in 1989, Tex would indeed have left the game. That would have been a great loss for the game of basketball.

While I was with the Bulls, Charley was the head coach of the Rockford Lightning, just seventy miles west of Chicago, and I was able to watch his team play several times. Charley expanded the flex offense so that it had over fifty options. He had a really good feel for coaching, and his teams responded well to him. He had great success at Rockford and later in Oklahoma City. Always a passionate coach, Charley sometimes got into trouble with his desire to find a perfect offense and have the game judged by perfect referees. After one of his games, Charley had the dubious distinction of having to be bailed out of jail by his players, after he was arrested for assaulting the opposing coach.

In the mid-1990s, Charley and the CBA parted ways after a tough coaching experience back at the place where he started, Albany. After that, Charley found himself at home in Woodstock in front of his typewriter.

Even in the few years since I'd coached the Patroons, the CBA had dramatically changed. More and more of a team's best players were either being called up to the NBA—Charley once lost both his starting center, Ken Bannister, and his starting point guard, Dominick Presley, to NBA teams during Rockford's playoffs—or jumping ship and signing on with European ball clubs. In Charley's last few years in the CBA, his (and every) team's roster was so unstable that it was virtually impossible for any coach to get beyond Ws and Ls. As much as Charley wanted, and even tried, to implement the Triangle, he never really had a chance.

We had coached together for three years, against each other for one season (my Patroons beat his Spirits six out of eight games), and for five years we'd been coaching at different levels of professional basketball. But now our paths diverged—I was still sitting on the bench, while Charley was sitting in front of his keyboard. If Charley could never fully participate in the Triangle, at least he'd become a true believer and an eloquent advocate.

When I succeeded Doug, there was the glimmer of a chance for Charley to join my staff after assistant coach Johnny Bach left. I respected Charley's eye for the game almost more than anybody else's, and I wanted him there with me. But I also knew that bringing such a close friend on board the Bulls' coaching staff might be seen as compromising my integrity. It was a hard decision for me, and Charley had a tough time accepting it. I could certainly understand his anguish and extreme disappointment; our friendship became strained and we didn't talk to each other for several months. In fact, it wasn't until a couple of years later, when we were both pallbearers at Eddie Mast's funeral, that we became totally reconciled.

Years later, I told Charley that I'd probably made a mistake by ever encouraging him to abandon his primary calling in order to become a basketball coach. Although I can't say exactly when I realized this, I knew by this time that Charley had more to offer our society through his talents as a writer. Since then, being outside the whirlwind of professional basketball, Charley has had the opportunity to discover himself spiritually, and I can see that what happened was the right and inevitable decision for us both, but at the time it was not an easy thing for our friendship.

Charley went on to write three more books during that time (*The Cockroach Basketball League*, *The House of Moses All-Stars*, and *Barney Polan's Game*), each one receiving more attention than the last, and I think he is truly at the top of his game. It's generally acknowledged that he's the sport's greatest champion when it comes to translating the game of basketball into words that capture its spirit.

For the past fourteen years we've been jointly teaching a class at the Omega Institute in Rhinebeck, New York, on the joys of basketball. The class started out to be about competition and the addiction of basketball junkies, but after the death of our mutual friend Eddie Mast, Charley and I started talking about age, and the waning of our abilities to play basketball. The class is called "Beyond Basketball," and teaching it has been enriching for both Charley and me, maybe even more so than for our students.

SEVEN

THE COCKROACH BB ASS.

CHARLEY

After three seasons with Phil and the Albany Patroons, I was named head coach of the Savannah Spirits. This promotion had less to do with my mostly irrelevant résumé (which features a master of arts degree in medieval literature) than it did with the impressive roster of benefactors who called the Spirits' general manager, Robb Larsen, on my behalf. This list included Phil, Jerry West (whom I barely knew and who called only because I asked him to), Bill Fitch (whom I had interviewed once for a magazine article and who called Larsen at Phil's behest), and Red Auerbach (who owed me a favor). Larsen, of course, was thrilled to schmooze with all of the above and therefore considercd me to be a qualified coach by association. (My most significant competition was an ex-waiter who ran errands for the Lakers and was being promoted by Pat Riley.)

During my nine years in the CBA, the league included as many as sixteen teams, but most often fourteen, circulating among a total of forty-three different cities. When I joined the Spirits in 1986, the franchise had just relocated from Detroit and included only three holdover players from a talented yet undisciplined squad that had struggled to underachieve a record of 24–24: Steve Rambadt (with his 2.0 ppg and his perpetually aching back), Alvin "Bo" Dukes (a squat five-foot-six guard who could do everything except shoot and defend), and Tico Brown (the league's leading scorer).

Going about my business in Savannah always brought a tear to my eye and a tickle to my throat. That's because there was a paper bag factory near the airport, and whenever the wind was wrong, the stench was reminiscent of cockroach spray with musky overtones of boiled cabbage. The aroma was particularly overpowering when the factory cranked up on Monday mornings, strong enough to cause birds to drop dead from the sky. Strong enough to force the airport to reroute approach-and-departure patterns.

When questioned, the locals took deep, defiant breaths and claimed that everything smelled just fine. When pressed further, native Savannians declared that the factory employed four thousand workers and lowered real estate taxes all over town. Sure, but I spent my first two months there clearing my throat and coughing, constantly on the verge of bronchitis.

On the upside, the seafood was always fresh, and wonderful restaurants abounded. The recently renovated waterfront area was quaint and thronged with tourists who marveled at the charms of the Southland, studiously ignoring the smell, not to mention the oil slicks and dead fish floating on the Savannah River.

The downtown area was dotted with restored colonial houses and lush pocket gardens, bracketed with wrought-iron fencing and gold-lettered historical markers. The oldest synagogue in America was over on Elm Street. A Revolutionary War cannon sat on Bay Street, aimed inland at the Stars and Bars Bar. There was even an oldies station on the radio, WREB. The city's main traffic artery was entirely shaded by gracefully drooping cypress trees and was called Victory Drive, presumably named to celebrate Sherman's decision not to torch Savannah. The air was always wet, and even the trees seemed mildewed.

The metro population of 150,000 was 52 percent black, yet people of color out on the streets still felt compelled to cast their eyes to their shoes whenever they passed a white. The crime rate was high—assaults, rape, burglaries—but the average cracker on the street was thrilled that most crimes were black-on-black. Nor did the yokels think twice about casually referring to ballplayers as "niggers" to their faces.

The owner of the team was a black man, Reggie Henderson, who owned a chemical laboratory back in Detroit and would eventually be indicted by the federal government for fraud. Henderson visited Savannah only once and showed more of an interest in bedding cheerleaders than in letting me trade for the players I needed.

My wife, Susan, and my two children, Darrell and Alexandra, stayed behind in Woodstock, New York, while I enjoyed the freedom to choose between Chinese food and pizza, use the bathroom without having to wait on line, leave yesterday's newspapers scattered about the living room floor, and obsess about my team.

I was also free to institute an expanded version of the flex offense and box set that Phil had taught in Albany, but I was somewhat surprised when both strategies proved effective. Even more rewarding than my early experimentations with Xs and Os was the camaraderie I enjoyed with the guys. Tico, Bo, and I came to respect each other's passion for the game. After road contests we'd often convene in my hotel room for postmortems over beer and pizza. Under the pressures of long seasons, endless waits in airports, and intense ball games in hostile arenas, it's only natural that close friendships are forged. But when the buzzer sounds in the last game of the season, everybody goes home, and basketball friendships rarely survive.

To save costs, we were always booked on the first flight out of town—usually around six a.m., which necessitated a four o'clock wake-up call. Traveling from Florida to Washington, from Maine to New Mexico, a CBA team moved through the airports like a wolf pack. It was a mucho-macho male reality where the only purpose of young women was to be whammed, bammed, and thank-you-ma'ammed. There was one player who, for example, while being treated for a virulent case of gonorrhea, went out of his way to bed down as many Georgia peaches as he could pluck. When I discovered the situation, I attacked him: "Cedric, you selfish son of a bitch! Why don't you put your dick in jail, at least until you can't infect anybody?"

He just shrugged and said, "A man's gotta do what a man's gotta do."

It was an attitude I detested, and I made my feelings well known. But the players (white and black) just laughed behind my back and persisted in proselytizing their jockhead mentality.

If I couldn't reform the sexist mindset, I did feel good about the hoop-time job I was doing, maximizing our strengths and hiding our weaknesses. I eagerly looked forward to every ball game and every practice session.

The referees were a constant problem for me—maybe because I always demanded justice and fair play. They seemed to have no appreciation of the beauty of the game—and how could they, when they were trained to focus on mistakes and blunders? Being a mere rookie coach, all I could do was stomp my way up and down the sidelines, yowling over every perceived miscall. One result of this misguided strategy was that I led the league in technical fouls.

Too bad the Spirits didn't lead the league in anything but steals. Except for losing all eight games we played against Bill Musselman's championship-bound Tampa Bay Sizzlers, we split our remaining forty games. We were in a battle for the last play-off slot until the final week of the season, then Tico twisted his back in a home game against the Pensacola Tornadoes. In those days, the players' physical welfare was certainly not among the league's top priorities. (Remember, during my tenure with the Patroons, even I, with my blatantly bogus credentials, had been officially certified as a trainer.) So when Tico went down, there were no medical personnel on hand, no emergency equipment whatsoever, and Tico had to be carted off the court lying atop a door that had to be hurriedly detached from a storage room—like the mortally wounded Achilles being carried off the battlefield on his shield.

With Tico out, we quickly fell to the bottom of the league.

Ah, the indignities of life in the CBA! Where a player was actually traded for a blow job executed by one team's secretary upon the other team's general manager. Where a certain coach's fate during a locker room disagreement with a bench warmer was to be lifted off the floor by the player and stuffed headfirst into a toilet bowl, which the player flushed and reflushed until a security cop interrupted the attempted coachicide.

The Spirits' play-by-play announcer was none other than Craig "Bibs" Kilborn, future TV star, who was then malnourished and chronically broke. At the time, Craig was easy to like, always personable and of good cheer, but arrogant and opinionated. We spent a lot of time together, most of it arguing. Credit me for buying him savory meals at least four times a week to augment his $25 per game salary.

Here's an incident that reveals exactly where each of us was at the time: At a rangy six-foot-five, Bibs fancied himself quite the ballplayer and, truth to tell, he wasn't nearly as bad as I wanted him to be. One day after practice, he challenged me to a game of one-on-one, make-it-take-it, eleven wins. Sure. No problem. But I couldn't cope with his quick moves, young legs, and general exuberance. Then, with the score 10–6 in his favor, Bibs made a mistake. "Charley," he said, "do you want me to end the game with a graceful shot from the outskirts, or a scintillating drive to the hoop?" I chose the latter, and as Bibs approached the shadow of the basket, while ostensibly trying to block his shot, I knocked him on his ass and slightly bloodied his lip. After he badly missed his subsequent outside shot, I took over the game—backing him slowly and relentlessly toward the hoop, and using my face-seeking elbow to keep him away from the ball. The victory was mine, 11–10, but Bibs complained, "That's not basketball."

"It is in the Bronx," I said.

I wasn't at all surprised when Larsen sandbagged me at season's end, but a new round of celebrity endorsements gained me the coaching position at Rockford, Illinois. Tightly wedged into the very buckle of the Rust Belt, Rockford was once rated the worst city in the country by *Money* magazine. Rockford featured the emptiest libraries in the Western Hemisphere, only two decent restaurants, a highly advanced mall culture, and scores of rabid basketball fans.

The Lightning's owner was Jay Polan, a kindly man who owned a charter bus service in Chicago and allowed me to face the consequences of my own decisions. Because Polan passed the players illegal bonus bucks under the table, at various times during that first season the Lightning fielded several once and future NBA players— Fred Cofield, David Wood, Carl Henry, Jim Lampley, Pace Mannion, Pete Myers, Brad Wright, Elston Turner, Kannard Johnson, John Schweitz, Scooter McCray, Richard Rellford, and Alfrederick Hughes (who, when he first joined the team, introduced himself to me as "Al," to the general manager as "Fred," and to Jay Polan as "Rick"). Polan likewise illicitly arranged to personally pay for any and all technical fouls I accrued—a total that came to over $1,400. Once again I led the league.

As part of the NBA-CBA contract, the NBA was responsible for paying, scheduling, and supervising all the CBA's refs, but the difference between the officiating done in the two leagues was profound. In the NBA the refs determine the outcome of approximately one ball game in ten, while in the CBA the results of two-thirds of the contests were determined by the refs. In the CBA, every close call was unduly influenced by two factors: which team was wearing the white uniforms? and was one of the teams coached by either a former NBA player or a former NBA coach? Home teams and NBA veterans got the breaks. Imagine how difficult it was for civilian-coached teams to win on the road. Yet no matter how blatantly biased or erroneous the refs' calls might be (like the game I lost to Tom Nissalke in Jacksonville when Hank Armstrong called two fourth-quarter fouls against the home team and twenty-four against Rockford), there was no redress for the losers.

Why was all of this possible? Because nobody in the NBA really cared about us. And, more specifically, because Darell Garretson, the NBA's supervisor of officials, believed that the CBA had only one function—to develop refs for the league.

Refs, lawyers, and cops. Whistles, writs, and guns. Even in the best of circumstances I consider basketball officials of any ilk to be a necessary evil.

For sure, I deserved many (if not most) of my T's. And just as certainly I was unjustly "whacked" and even "tossed" by shortsighted referees. Like the time in Wichita Falls when a drunk sat directly behind me, loudly excoriating the refs in a thick southern drawl whenever a call went against the hometown Texans. Yet it was I who was booted midway through the second quarter by Duke Callahan. "I've heard enough from you, Charley," Callahan shouted as he pointed offstage right. Or the time I was standing in a perfectly legal out-of-bounds spot in front of my bench in Rochester, Minnesota, silently observing the action, when a wayward ref blindsided me. Since I was about ten inches taller and fifty pounds heavier than he, the ref crashed to the floor. My bench players laughed to beat the band, and I quipped to the still-sprawled ref, "Was that a charge or a block?" I thought it was a good line, but it got me booted from the premises. Or the time a particularly myopic ref failed to see one of my players dribble twice on his way hoopward and tooted him for walking (thereby negating the dunk shot that would have tied the score late in the fourth quarter). Yet he banished me just for asking a pair of purely rhetorical questions: "What are you? Fucking blind?"

Etcetera.

The Lightning finished with a record of 37–17 and lost in the conference semifinals to Cazzie Russell's Wyoming Wildcatters (the deciding game being a quadruple-overtime heartbreaker).

Phil used to say that a CBA coach learns more about his profession during a single season than a college coach does in five years. So, after one season in Savannah and one in Rockford, I'd quickly established myself as a more than capable veteran coach.

At the same time, I'd also developed a narrow vision of the game: all my perceptions depended on whether we won or lost, and this retroactively colored my entire experience of the game. Winning made it enjoyable, losing was always irredeemably painful. My self-definition depended upon the scoreboard. A win made me feel righteous and benevolent. A loss, and I was a despicable human being.

Fortunately the Lightning won enough to boost my self-esteem and to secure a new contract for the 1988–89 season. Susan and I decided to move the family to Rockford for the school year.

My second year with the Lightning was even more successful than the first. Our regular season record was 34–20, and paced by Mannion and Dwayne McClain, we gained the championship series (only to be swept by a team of druggies and thugs from Tulsa assembled by Henry Bibby). A providential season overall, except that my relations with the CBA's officiating staff grew even more contentious.

In retrospect, I can see how much resentment and outright anger was boiling inside me, never far from the surface. In addition to all of the unresolved issues surrounding my father's illness and the physical and psychological abuse I'd suffered at his hands, my barely suppressed rage was also fueled by my failing marriage.

Susan and I were hopelessly caught in what I call the Jewish Death Grip. Each of us had been conditioned to secretly condemn ourselves as being weak and selfish individuals who were absolutely undeserving of any genuine happiness. Neither of us had ever been able to measure up to the expectations of our respective parents, nor to the idealized images we saw on television. It was much easier for us to blame all of our own real and imagined inadequacies on each other than to take responsibility for our own lives. There was something safe (if agonizing) about this relationship, which is probably why our marriage lasted twenty-six years. It has also been said that the main reason why "basketball marriages" last so long is road trips!

Writing served many purposes for me; it was a safe retreat from the many painful realities of my days and ways. Writing fiction allowed me to impose some kind of order and meaning upon the otherwise ruthless and chaotic circumstances of the waning century.

I created my own guiding principle—"Life is a metaphor for basketball"—because for me the game was the world. At the time, I believed that all of life could be experienced within the white lines— from the birth of consciousness to physical death. And like life, the only constant aspect of hoops is that it continually changes. The essence of basketball, like the essence of life, is forever elusive—neither one can be frozen in time and thereby defined. To somehow discover the truth in one form of human endeavor is to discover the truth in everything we do, have done, and dream of doing. That's why writing, for me, is not a choice; it's an imperative.

Ironically, coaching actually took me away from the game I loved.

The distractions were overwhelming: knuckleheaded players who controlled my destiny, misguided owners, media Muppets greedy for controversy and scandal, arrogant refs, four a.m. wake-up calls. The game at hand was moving beyond my reach. Writing about how I saw the game, how I felt it, was the only way to hold on to a beautiful memory.

Dorothy Parker once said, "I hate writing, but I love having written." For me, the reverse is true. The mindful act of doing is what counts—just like a ball game where the playing is the thing itself. I love the process of writing, playing alphabetical jazz on my keyboard, being baffled and amazed at the words that leap from my fingertips, at the connections that form almost organically, cobbling words and sentences, getting closer and closer to the core of reality. Then, when a book is completed, I'm happy to release it into the world, where it will thrive or vanish according to its own merits—while I make another attempt to say the unsayable.

Phil was named the Bulls' head coach in the off-season, and for a while I sparkled with hope that he might be able to bring me in as an assistant. But, no. Jerry Krause still had a veto in the hiring of the scouts and the coaching staff, and I was the spirit of Woodstock Past, an embarrassing reminder of Phil's heyday as a hoop-o-hippie. Krause even called me to say that he thought I was well qualified but that Phil's assistants had to be former NBA players. "Those are the only guys today's players have any respect for," Krause told me. "I give you my word, Charley. I'm forced to hire an ex-player." Shortly thereafter, Jimmy Rodgers was hired, an outstanding assistant who had never played pro ball at any level. And I was left to wonder exactly what the "word" was that Krause had given me. "Bullshit"?

My father used to tell me this: "Always expect the worst and you'll never be disappointed." And I believed him. So I'd harbored no abiding fantasy that Phil would someday be able to bring me into the NBA. I was pained, however, by the fact that although Phil knew I had little respect for Krause, it was Krause who called to tell me the bad news. I had a tough time forgiving Phil for allowing that to happen.

My third season at Rockford was catastrophic. Even before the season began, Jay Polan was convicted of attempting to bribe certain members of the Chicago City Council in order to obtain lucrative contracts for his bus company, and was sentenced to eighteen months in a minimum-security prison near Santa Barbara, California.

In Jay's absence, the Lightning's affairs were governed by Jerry Frank, a minority partner.

Jerry was obsessive about cutting costs and turning a profit, something that Jay had never accomplished. When I told Jerry that I needed to either trade for or buy an experienced (and therefore expensive) backup center, his response was, "There's a million *schvartzas* hanging around playgrounds in Chicago that would play for peanuts."

Add Jerry's unreasonable frugality to my unrelieved and mounting angst, and I was an accident looking for a place to happen. That place turned out to be Cedar Rapids, Iowa.

Christmas 1989. Whereas Jay Polan had always presented me with a holiday bonus of $700, Jerry Frank gave me a small jar of strawberry preserves. A very small jar.

Also, since the bus ride from Rockford to Cedar Rapids took four hours, Jay had always allowed the team to travel there the day before the game. Jerry, however, insisted that we leave at eight a.m. the day of the game. "You'll get there in time for a noon shootaround," he reasoned, "and I'll save a day's per diem and a big hotel bill."

I begged Jerry to reconsider. "This is what'll happen if we do what you want: the game will be close for three quarters, then our players' legs will turn to rubber, and we'll get blown out in the fourth quarter."

"You're the coach," Jerry said. "It's your job to make sure that doesn't happen."

The night before we left for Cedar Rapids, I received a disquieting phone call from the coach of the Rapid City Thrillers, Eric Musselman (Bill's son). It seems that the Thrillers had just played a game at Cedar Rapids against the homestanding Silver Bullets, coached by a notorious jackass named George Whittaker (and owned by Kevin Krause, whose only other claim to fame was to have proudly served as the "Herky the Hawk" mascot for four years while a student at the University of Iowa). Anyway, Eric's complaint was that late in the fourth quarter, with the Silver Bullets ahead by twenty-four points, Whittaker had ordered his team into a full-court press.

"It was like he was kicking us when we were already down and out," Eric told me. "Like he wanted to beat us by a hundred points if he could. It was humiliating, and my guys were totally pissed. I had to stop a couple of them from busting Whittaker's ass."

In my fourth continuous season of employment, I was the CBA's senior coach, and as such Eric asked me to speak to Whittaker and explain the error of his ways.

No problem.

We did indeed arrive just in time for our appointed shootaround, and just in time, too, for me to catch up with Whittaker as his team was leaving the court. He was a round-faced young man with Shirley Temple curls. When I repeated Eric's accusations, Whittaker appeared insulted. Yes, such a tactic was deplorable, said Whittaker, but he pleaded his innocence. "I don't even have a full-court press," he insisted. "And even if I did, Charley, I would never do anything as disrespectful as that."

Okay. Fine. Terrific. Thanks, George. You're a helluva guy.

Come game time my prophecy came to pass: we lost each of the first three quarters by one point and got our doors blown off in the last quarter. Then, lo and behold, the score was 112–79, with 1:17 on the game clock, when I heard Whittaker shout out, "Red! Red!" thereby ordering his team into a full-court press.

Jumping up from my seat, I glowered downcourt to where Whittaker likewise stood in front of his bench. "That's bullshit!" I yelled at him.

"Fuck you, chickenshit!" was Whittaker's response. Then he waved his hands, challenging me, beckoning me to approach him. "Come over here and do something about it!"

And I couldn't take it anymore. The game. The CBA. My life. "YOU MOTHAFUCKER!" Some last vestige of self-control snapped, leaving me wild and bellowing, a wounded beast suddenly turning on the hunter, charging downcourt, out of my mind with rage, intent on obliterating Whittaker, who moved to hide behind his bench players. I think I could have actually killed him.

But thankfully one of the referees, Jim Kinney, grabbed me in a bear hug from behind, pinning my arms and swooping me off my feet. "It ain't wuth it, Charley," he said in my ear. "Carm down. It ain't wuth it."

"It is! I'm gonna kill the bastard!"

Slowly Jim increased the pressure on my chest so that I had to gasp for breath. "It ain't wuth it." He carried me toward the baseline, where the desperate need to breathe, to inhale, to live, suddenly overrode my anger.

"I'm okay," I said. "Thanks, Jim. I'm okay. Let me down."

He released me gently. "I have to cawl a couple a T's," he said, almost apologizing. "You're ejected."

"I understand. I'm okay."

So I walked slowly off the court, the fans in an uproar behind me, hurling abuse, paper cups, and crumpled newspapers as I entered the tunnel that led to the basement staircase, thinking, hoping, that this fiasco would motivate my players for our next game. Then, just as I reached the top of the stairs, gathering my body for the rhythmic descent into the basement, a hand seized my right forearm.

"What?"

It was a cop. About five-eight, a solid 170 pounds, wearing his play-hat with its shiny black brim, a badge on his hat, a badge on his chest. The nameplate above his right breast pocket said, "G. Murray." His eyes were gray, almost colorless. There was an oversized six-shooter strapped to his waist.

Now his other hand locked onto my left forearm. "Let's go," he said. The force of his grip nearly tilted me headlong down the steps, and he had to yank me back to right my balance.

"I'm going," I said, then shook him loose. "Get the fuck *off* me. This has nothing to do with you."

He clutched at me again, and I repeated, "Get the fuck *off.*"

When we arrived at the bottom of the stairs, he pushed the small of my back, propelling me toward the locker room. "Get away, leave me alone." Then he shoved me into the locker room and slammed the door behind me.

"Fuck you!" I shouted at him through the closed door. I kicked every dented, rusty locker from one end of the room to the other.

Right then, at that very moment, everything that had happened was someone else's fault. Jerry Frank's. Whittaker's. Murray the mini-cop. I was the outraged innocent, and the role felt highly gratifying.

But then I realized that I was thirsty, so I ventured into the hall-way to find a water fountain, and all hell broke loose.

Evidently the game was over, because here came Whittaker, bop-ping down the stairs and happy to be a winner, feeling invincible, knowing that he was a genius.

I rushed toward him, and suddenly we were face-to-face. I clenched my right hand. Instead of moving to defend himself, he stared at me, speechless, apparently shocked at my riotous fury, his mouth twisted into a vacant grin. I no longer wanted to hurt him, yet some red-eyed, swaggering compulsion moved my fist in a threaten-ing arc. Whittaker never retreated as I swung weakly and missed his face by at least a foot.

All at once something grabbed at my neck from behind. My legs were shoved forward, and I tumbled to the floor. I found myself on my back, with the minicop jamming a forearm against my throat and a knee into my chest.

By then, my players had arrived. "Get off him," one of them shouted, and another said, "Let him up."

The cop backed away, and I was helped to my feet, but suddenly the cop was at me again, his left hand poking my chest, his right hand balled into a fist.

"It's over," one of my players said. "Let him alone. We'll take him into the locker room."

The players slowly formed a circle around me and Officer Murray. Large black men closing in behind him, cutting off his only avenue of escape. The cop's right hand moved slowly toward his gun, carefully unsnapping the strap on his holster.

"How many of us can you shoot?" I asked him. "How many bul-lets do you have?"

Now the cop stepped back, holding his hands open in front of his chest, allowing the players to hustle me back into the locker room.

Inside, nobody quite knew what to do. So we moved in an aimless circle, waiting for the music to stop. We had the feeling that we were all under siege, and none of us was eager to leave our sanctuary.

"I'm proud of you," one of the players said. "You stood up for us. You did what you had to do."

But then the door burst open and a dozen cops poured into the room. The biggest one—six-five, 240 pounds—the one with the angriest face—said to me, "Come outside, we want to ask you some questions."

"Ask them in here," I said.

"Come outside," he insisted. Officer F. Jablonski.

"They're gonna bust you," a player said, and the entire team surged forward to shield me. But the cops waved their nightsticks, and the players retreated. Then Jablonski grabbed my necktie, yanked me through the doorway, and slammed me face-first against the wall. My arms were pulled behind my back, and my wrists were cuffed. And the peace officers swarmed around me as Murray stepped up close in order to bang his nightstick against my legs and thighs. "You fucking cowards!" I shouted. I would have said more, but the handcuffs were immediately ratcheted a notch tighter.

I was pushed up the stairs, outside the arena, and into the backseat of a squad car. A photographer flashed his gizmo as the car door slammed shut.

Officer Half-Pint drove while Jablonski rode shotgun. In the cramped backseat with my wrists tightly manacled, I couldn't twist or angle my legs without some part of my body suffering. Jablonski recited my rights in rapid-fire delivery. I couldn't understand most of what he said, but I didn't dare ask for any clarification. I was a prisoner.

"What happens now?"

"You'll get booked," Murray said without a trace of hostility. Just doing his job. The law-abiding citizens of Cedar Rapids could rest easy tonight.

"What's the charge? Did Whittaker file charges?"

"No," said Murray. "We'll file charges. Resisting arrest. Just cooperate and behave yourself."

"You know something?" I said to G. Murray. "You'd make a terrific referee."

Later, after I'd been booked, fingerprinted, mug-shot, and sequestered in a small cell, my players chipped in for my $400 bail and were waiting for me in the bus. When I joined them, they applauded and hooted and treated me like a hero. One player handed me two McBuggers and a Coke, saying, "You're always hungry when you're let out of jail."

"Ain't no big thing," another said. "Most brothers, if they live in a big city, have been in the joint some time or other. Me? Yep. I had a fight with some white dude in a bar. I stayed in jail overnight, and the school got the charges dropped. Actually I didn't mind it 'cause I scored some pretty good weed."

And their testimonials continued:

"I got caught drunk driving when I was in school, and they also got them to drop the charges."

"I beat up some girl the year after I got out of school. She let me stay in jail for two days, then she dropped the charges. She was a good piece of ass, man. The day I got sprung, I moved in with her."

"Not me, man. I've never been busted. My momma would kill me if I even got a parking ticket."

The Lightning finished out the season at 22–34, and Jerry Frank canned me. Oh, well. Another round of celebrity references, and another job was in the offing—this time with the Oklahoma City Cavalry, an expansion team.

OK City… The wildest West, where even the shortest drink of water proudly wore a ten-gallon hat. Where barbequed anything (including bologna) was treasured as being top-of-the-line eats. Where the airport was named after Will Rogers, who perished in an airplane crash. I was officially welcomed to town by Abe Leamons, the legendary cornpone coach of Oklahoma City University, who said, "So you're the Jew coach from New York that's going to set this town on fire?" And it went downhill from there.

Simply put, by now I was burned out, depleted, exhausted, bored, and in it only for the money. The game held no charm for me anymore, and my only goal was to survive the season without getting fired. Which I did. Barely.

We were 5–3 and hopeful until our high scorer, Luther Burks, sprained an ankle. Our final mark was a dismal 18–38, and guess what? Two days after the season was over, I was presented with still another pink slip.

But, hey. Not to worry. A few more calls from the right people, and I wound up back in Albany, as head coach this time.

Albany is the capital of New York, and as such has the largest per capita population of lawyers in the country. The city also had delusions of grandeur, nary a decent eatery, and an alarming number of ambulatory alcoholics.

Even worse was the fact that I would be succeeding George Karl, who was currently back in the NBA coaching the Seattle SuperSonics after leading last season's Patroons to an all-time best CBA regular season record of 50–6 (before losing in the second round to Wichita Falls, the eventual league champs). It was a tough act to follow—especially since the only returning player was Jeff Sanders, a selfish onetime NBAer who played dead more often than he played hard. My contract called for $50,000, but only 30K of it was guaranteed. My goal was to last long enough to collect the other $20,000. With such a defensive mindset, it's a wonder I lasted as long as I did.

So that I wouldn't be bored, I decided to forgo the flex, discard the box, and employ the Triangle offense. I studied Tex's book, carefully questioned Phil, and perused with as much diligence as I could muster a Bulls training film that Phil had given me. It was all I could do to learn the basic formation, the key passes, and a few specialty plays. But if I knew the parts, collating them into a cohesive overview was beyond my capabilities. My biggest problem was feeling exhausted even before training camp began by the inevitability of having to teach and reteach the Triangle to the long procession of players (twenty-one, as it turned out) who would be wearing Patroons' uniforms sometime or other throughout the season. So, in my version, the Triangle was a series of plays in which I signaled the key pass. It was an execution offense played station-to-station with no continuity.

Even worse, Jeff Sanders had played for Phil in Chicago and certainly knew more about what was really what than I did. But I felt too insecure to ask for his help, and he certainly didn't volunteer. (It was Sanders, by the way, who, even though he was averaging forty-seven minutes of playing time per game, complained to the media that I was "messing with his minutes.")

After limping out of the gate with a record of 2–6, I trashed the Triangle and reinstated the sturdy flex. Might as well go to hell with what I knew.

The Patroons' biggest wig, Joe O'Hara, fired me just before my guarantee ran out. Once or twice the Patroons had come within a game of .500, but that was as good as it ever got. My last CBA season concluded with a record of 19–22.

And I was compelled to realize that coaching was not my path. For me, coaching was too public and too competitive, too ruthless and too life-consuming.

I finally had to face it—I was a writer. I needed to edit reality, over and over again, until I got it right.

Phil may blame himself for encouraging me to become a coach, but in truth my several seasons on the bench were invaluable in deepening my understanding of myself, of the game, and of what winning demands of coaches and players. Now that I've been divorced from the CBA, and from Susan, and have retired from my elbow-brandishing on-court follies, my love for basketball is unadulterated and sincere again. I am free to worship the truth of the game, and I have all of my hard-won understandings to share.

Instead of striving to achieve the "perfect" play, the "perfect" game, and the "perfect" season, my ambition now is to write the perfectly imperfect book.

EIGHT

TRIANGULATION

PHIL

When I was an assistant with the Bulls, I applied myself diligently to learning the current state of NBA basketball—which teams were doing what on offense and defense. And my primary concern was how I could help the Bulls win a championship. During my tenure as one of Doug's assistants, we'd made a major trade (Charles Oakley to the Knicks for Bill Cartwright), and had limited success. Our regular season win total had slipped from 50 in 1987–88 to 47 the following season—but we did reach the Eastern Conference finals in 1988–89, losing in six games to Detroit.

After the season, there were several rumors about other teams being interested in hiring me to run their programs. Supposedly, the Timberwolves had asked Krause about my availability and so had the Knicks, but since I was under contract with the Bulls, Krause wouldn't let any other team talk to me. I'd discovered that the Knicks' interest in me was serious during an informal discussion I'd had with Dickie McGuire, my former coach. Of course, I'd relayed this news to Krause, and I think that this information created a sense of urgency in the Bulls front office.

Prompted by the rumors, Krause asked me if I'd rather coach the Knicks or the Bulls. The Knicks hadn't yet offered me a job, but I said, "I think New York can win one championship, and I also think the Bulls can win multiple championships. If the decision was up to me, I'd rather be with the team that has the brightest future in the league. The Chicago Bulls."

About two weeks later, right after the college draft of 1989, the Bulls released Doug. Within a few days Jerry Krause called me in Montana and, knowing that I was on a party line, told me to call him back from a "secure phone." I rode my motorcycle to the nearest town and called Krause from a pay phone, and that's when he offered me the head coaching job. Besides the outright elation, I also felt the need to start living my life more cautiously, so I rode my motorcyle back home at a reduced speed.

When the owner of the team, Jerry Reinsdorf, was questioned about the decision to replace Doug with me, he said, "I thought that Doug did a good job getting the Bulls from A to B. But we think that Phil can get us a championship."

Krause and I conferred about what my specific responsibilities would be. I would control the travel schedules, and the procedures for scouting our opponents. We would discuss all player personnel decisions, and although Krause encouraged me to retain the existing assistant coaches, we each had veto power over who would fill the vacancy on the coaching staff. When I proposed Jimmy Cleamons, Krause readily concurred. It was also made clear that I could use whatever system or style of play suited me. At this point there was no question in my mind that the Triangle was, in fact, the very system I'd been seeking for so long.

My official introduction to the Triangle occurred during the summer of 1988 when Tex and I coached the Lakers' entry in the L.A. Summer League. Even though there was no chance that Doug would incorporate the Triangle during the upcoming regular season, Krause thought it would be beneficial for me to learn the offense from Tex. By our second summer semester together, Tex was allowing me to teach the offense in our practice sessions and also to coach every other game.

The Triangle was a more evolved version of the offense the Knicks had run under Red Holzman, and it programmed all of the instinctive movements that both Red and Bill Fitch had encouraged. Essentially, the Triangle was a vehicle for integrating mind and body, sport and spirit, in a practical, down-to-earth form. It was awareness in action.

I also like to think of the Triangle offense as five-man *tai chi*. The basic idea is to orchestrate the flow of movement in order to lure the defense off balance and thereby create undefended spaces on the court. The system gets its name from one of its most common patterns of movement: the sideline triangle.

This is how it works: as Scottie Pippen, for example, dribbles the ball across the midcourt line, he has a companion guard (John Paxson) stationed fifteen to twenty feet away on the same lateral plane. Pippen then makes a wing entry pass to forward Michael Jordan, who's above the free-throw line extended. On the pass, either Pippen or Paxson fills the corner on the ball side, and either the center (Bill Cartwright) or the weak-side forward (Horace Grant) moves to occupy the strong-side low post. The Triangle is now formed—Jordan with the ball, Grant or Cartwright in the post, Pippen (or Paxson) in the corner. In addition, you'd have Paxson (or Pippen) at the top of the key. With only one pass having been made (to MJ), the four players without the ball can potentially fill any of the other four spots (the exception being the center, who can only occupy the low post, the weak-side forward spot, or execute a corner fill), and any two of them, plus the ball carrier, can complete the triangle. The rhythm of the offense requires MJ (with the ball) to take his time (a two-count is long enough), be a threat to shoot or penetrate, and thereby allow time for his teammates to move appropriately. Now MJ can read how the defense reacts to the movements of his teammates and make an expedient pass. This preliminary process of forming a triangle is called "lining up the defense." MJ is now capable of passing the ball to any of his four teammates, but the optimum pass is the one that creates the deepest penetration, which would be to Cartwright, since he's the closest to the basket. If this pass is available (called the "number one key pass" in Tex's terminology), and Cartwright catches the ball, then the defense is forced to make dramatic adjustments, since Bill is only one dribble away from a good shot. Depending on how the defense does respond, a series of simple offensive movements is initiated. If MJ's "key" pass goes to Pippen at the top of the key (which swings the ball to the opposite side of the court) instead of into Cartwright, then a different series of movements ensues. And so on.

The idea is not to go head-to-head with the defense. In fact, the offensive players will always take the path of least resistance and move into open areas. Since all four possible passes cannot be denied without making the defense vulnerable to reverses, backdoor cuts, or alley-oop plays, MJ must read the defense and simply take what they give. This kind of movement requires complete coordination, with all the players thinking and moving in unison. Instead of following dotted lines, they're reacting to the defense, so each player must be totally aware of what's happening on the floor. Executed properly, the system is virtually unstoppable because there are no set plays (only a series of possible options), so the defense can't predict what's going to happen next. If the defense tries to prevent one particular move or pass, there are always alternative moves and passes.

Tex's way of teaching the formating of the offense (which is the most critical consideration) is to break every possibility down into its constituent parts. For example, when Pippen makes the wing-entry pass to MJ, the way in which the defense chooses to pressure Pippen and Paxson will determine which one of them moves to the corner. The timing and rhythm between Pippen and Paxson must be established before the entire five-man offense can operate smoothly. So Tex will drill this particular two-man sequence until it becomes instinctive. After Pippen makes the wing-entry pass to MJ, Pippen and Paxson have five distinct options—the corner fill, the basket cut, the diagonal cut, the outside cut, or the inside cut. Drill, drill, and redrill—then put all the parts together.

Behind every cut, every pass, every screen, every single possibility, stood Tex's Seven Principles of Sound Offense.

A sound offense…

1. Must penetrate the defense
    A. Create good % shots. Define what is a good shot for each player.
    B. Stress inside power game. Play for the 3-pt power play.
    C. Break down all defenses from full court presses to double teams.

2. Basketball is a full court game, end to end play. Skills must be learned at fast-break pace. *Know* the optimum speed and work to increase it. Transition basketball starts on defense. Look to run!

3. Provides proper floor spacing 15'–18', creating an operating room and clearing area on the court. It keeps the defense *occupied* on and off the ball.

4. Provides player and ball movement *with a purpose*. There is only one ball and five players. All things being equal, a player is without the ball 80% of the time.

5. Provides strong rebound position and good defensive balance on all shots.

6. Provides the player with the ball an opportunity to pass to any of his teammates. (The offense should also provide a counter to whatever action the defense may take.)

7. Utilizes the abilities of the individual players. Must create high % shots for a team's best shooters, rebound opportunities for bounders, driving opportunities for best drivers, etc. affords the opportunity to play out of a flexible format rather than be restricted to a definite set play.

Of all the systems I've ever seen, the Triangle is the only offense that fully satisfies these almost biblical requirements.

I'd say that about fifteen times every season, I've used a Magic Marker to write the Seven Principles on the ceramic board in the team's council room. This has been one of my routine corrective procedures whenever my teams play sloppy basketball. "Of course," I'd tell the players, "you guys all love the Seventh Principle because you're looking to see what the Triangle can do for you. In reality, what counts is what you can do for the Triangle."

Besides the offensive efficiency that the Triangle brings, it also relaxes the often tense relationship between a coach and his players. Having a clearly defined set of principles to work with reduces conflict because it depersonalizes criticism. The players understand that the coach isn't attacking them personally when he corrects a mistake, but simply trying to improve their understanding of the system.

During my rookie season as the Bulls' field commander, I thought that using certain aspects of Doug's offenses might help the players ease into the Triangle by providing a sense of continuity. Doug wanted MJ on the wing in fast-break situations so that when he received the ball he could quickly attack the basket. Like Doug, I also felt that Michael was somewhat uncomfortable handling the ball in the backcourt. Also, since Michael was already responsible for so much scoring, posting up, defending, and rebounding, I was afraid that the extra burden of hauling the ball up and down the floor might wear him out. So after conferring with Tex, I decided to make a format change from the traditional two-guard front and introduce the Triangle as an offense that featured a one-guard front.

Michael, of course, had played collegiately for Dean Smith at North Carolina, where he'd been trained to operate within a structured system. He was a gifted athlete with enormous confidence in his own abilities who had to be influenced into sacrificing for the team. I had to match his stubbornness with my own and constantly reassure him that the Bulls were on the right track. "Stay with it," I told him. "You don't have to worry about the fact that Cartwright isn't a good passer, or that the ball might wind up in Grant's hands with the shot clock running down. Because we'll teach the players to read the defense, so you'll always wind up with the ball in critical situations. Trust us, Michael, and everything will work itself out."

Michael continued to be dubious. He joked that the Triangle was "an equal-opportunity offense." In addition, because Cartwright needed so much time and space for his post-up moves, our version of the Triangle generally emphasized outside shooting and not one-on-one penetration—leading Michael to call it "a white man's offense."

The one factor that eventually made Michael yield was his competitive nature. He'd rather score thirty points and win than score forty and lose—which can't be said for all NBA players. What the Triangle did for Michael was put him in so many possible spaces that the defense couldn't anticipate where he'd be when he received the ball, and was unable to quickly double-team him.

It actually took the Bulls about one and a half seasons to become fluent with the Triangle. And it wasn't until Michael returned to basketball from his fling with baseball in 1995 that he became a true believer.

Scottie was a much easier sell, partially because we both joined the Bulls at the same time, and we developed a close relationship. When I was an assistant coach, I would lace up my sneakers and work with Scottie one-on-one. My point of emphasis was teaching him how to make a dribble move, then pull up and shoot. Whatever the reason, Scottie eagerly immersed himself in the intricacies of the Triangle—so much so that he became the organizer of the offense. It was Scottie who made sure that everybody was in the proper position so that we'd be ready to spin the wheel. And it was Scottie who was also our defensive overseer on the court. Sometimes I'd gasp when an otherwise intelligent player would either double-team the ball when he wasn't supposed to, or confound our game plan by rotating into a *verboten* area. When I'd challenge the player about his transgressions, he'd more than likely say, "Scottie sent me." Then I'd question Scottie, only to find that his on-the-spot reasoning made sense.

Michael really didn't want to be a team leader, but his inspirational play thrust him into that capacity. Scottie (and Bill Cartwright) were the unsung team leaders—talking privately to the players, helping them accept their roles. If Michael Jordan's genius amazed me, I had almost a parental sense of pride in Scottie Pippen's achievements. It was Scottie who helped his teammates find their comfort zones within the team's framework by constantly acknowledging their contributions.

Our one-guard alteration of Tex's grand scheme had John Paxson carrying the ball upcourt, Michael and Scottie running the wings, Horace Grant as the post sprinter (the first big man to storm his way to the basket in a fast-break situation), and Bill Cartwright trailing the action as the bounder. With this alignment we were able to easily flow from our full-court to our half-court offense.

We won fifty-five games in my first year as Chicago's head coach, and in the play-offs we cruised past Milwaukee and Philadelphia to reach the Eastern Conference finals. Then the Detroit Pistons put heavy-duty pressure on Paxson when he had the ball, double-teamed MJ anyway, and beat us in seven games.

The following season (1990–91), I let Tex convince me to institute his two-guard front. This double-barreled formation allowed us to reverse the ball more easily, and also to build our triangles in several different ways. In addition, with Scottie Pippen available to carry the ball across the midcourt line, his ability to get to the basket with either his right or his left hand and to pull up and shoot made us more versatile in fast-break situations. From there the Bulls took off on a good roll that lasted for the next eight years.

Over the next several seasons, I tinkered with the Triangle. I put in a wing button hook that we used to spring-load the offense a little quicker than the standard entry passes. I put in an open set, as well as several of the UCLA functions. In truth, the Triangle can be used as a starting point to get into any of the basic pro offenses. According to Tex, that old standby, the single-double, originally came out of Sam Barry's center-opposite.

Tex also loved to mess around with the Triangle. He'd see some sort of action that we hadn't yet featured, and he'd find a way to fit it into our existing structure.

Judging by Tex's very demanding standards, the Bulls' most flaw-less execution of the Triangle took place during the 1993–94 season while Michael was off playing baseball. Without Michael's creative genius, we had to rely solely on the system to create our shots. That meant we had to be more precise than ever before, and our timing had to be impeccable.

All told, the Bulls' version of the Triangle featured approximately forty possible options. We didn't have any pop-up wing shooters, so we didn't need to add any single-doubles or motion actions. These two options would have added perhaps another ten possibilities. (By contrast, even with the single-double action that I put in for Glen

Rice, the Lakers finished the 1999–2000 season with about twenty options.) In theory, with sufficient time and sufficiently skilled players, the Triangle's possibilities seem almost infinite.

As the Bulls progressed and perfected the Triangle, it became clear that the referees had little understanding of what we were doing. In my discussions with them, the refs would claim that they didn't care about what kind of offense any team used, that their job was just to call fouls and violations. Even so, I've always felt that the NBA's officials were confused by the Triangle.

In the normal unfolding of a pro offense, two guys are in the parking lot, and there's an isolation situation setup either along the baseline or in the low post. Once the ball is dropped into the post, maybe two players execute some kind of minimal crossing action and that's it. The total spotlight is on the guy with the ball, and all of a sudden his solitary defender is entirely exposed—every hand check, every hip bump—so it's easy for referees to identify defensive fouls. In fact, too many coaches deliberately run isolation (and/or screen roll) offenses solely to expose the defense and enable the refs to call fouls. To me, playing to the referees in this way is an unfortunate distortion that diminishes the game.

On the other hand, whenever the ball is moved into the low post in the Triangle, the other four players are in constant motion—cutting, squeezing, running weak-side exchanges. Now the referees can't zero in on such a small area of the court. They have to look through and into an entire choreography of moving bodies to see the total action, something that they're reluctant to do. The result is that the Bulls frequently lost fouls. Even with Michael Jordan, Chicago always ranked in the bottom half of free throws attempted.

In addition, referees tend to ignore the illegal defenses that most teams use against the Triangle. When Dennis Rodman played for the Bulls, his defender would simply ignore him on the wing and sink back into the lap of our center. This was an obvious (and continuous) case of illegal defense, but the referees chose to let it pass.

I always tell my players to play above the refereeing, that is, not to waste any energy worrying about what has or hasn't been, will or won't be, called. If we play with energy, poise, and unselfishness, we'll be playing the game the right way, and the referees will call what they see.

The truth, however, is that NBA referees invariably make the defensive players the focus of their attention. So if an offensive player hits his defender with a forearm and then steps out to receive the ball, the whistle rarely sounds. Yet if the defender retaliates with a slight bump, that's the foul the refs will call. The offensive players are the actors, the defensive players are the reactors, and the referees usually see only the second foul. Consequently, I exhort my players to play defense with an anticipatory attitude rather than a reactive one. The idea is to make the offense react to the defense so that the second foul can be tagged on the offense.

Another annoying aspect of the way referees regulate the game is the atrocious footwork they permit. When I was growing up, learning the proper footwork was considered to be the most essential part of the game. During normal practice sessions my teams work on fundamental footwork for at least thirty minutes. But come game time I'm appalled at what guys get away with. Today's players don't know how to pivot properly, so they'll routinely pivot on one foot, pause, pivot on the other foot, and then make a move toward the basket. And the referees never watch a player's feet, so they just suck on their whistles.

There's no question that the referees willfully allow certain prominent players to get away with illegal footwork. Reggie Miller, for example, is notorious for stepping out of a down-screen, taking three small skip-steps to the far side of the three-point line, and then launching a shot. All this without ever dribbling the ball and without ever being called for walking.

Karl Malone is another one. When he has the ball on either baseline, Malone likes to make a step-out move and shoot a jump shot. The problem is that he shuffles both feet before he shoots. I finally convinced Mike Mathis to call Malone for walking during the Bulls' second championship series against Utah in 1997. Giving All-Star players an illegal advantage makes them all but unstoppable.

Then there's the Georgetown Gallop as practiced by Dikembe Motumbo, Alonzo Mourning, and Patrick Ewing. In theory, they're

entitled to pick up their dribble, then take two steps before shooting. The reality is that they take three steps. This maneuver is similar to the European one-two-three step that drivers use to avoid
defenders in the lane. Whatever term is applied to this patently illegal action, if the refs aren't going to call it, then coaches have to be
allowed to teach it—and this is where coaches and refs wind up in
philosophical arguments. Every player should have to play by the
same rules.

I'm also disturbed at the way the players are permitted to dribble
the basketball. It seems that all the young players carry the ball, even
when the defense isn't pressuring them. Even worse, whenever they
change direction or make an offensive move, legalized palming
makes them impossible to stop. Because one-on-one defense has
become such a hopeless situation, defenses are forced to either sag or
double-team, which then forces the offense to swing the ball until
someone can shoot a three-pointer. So, instead of opening up the
game, the license given to palming has flattened it out and created a
standardized NBA offense.

In their effort to inject more offense into the game, the NBA
Rules Committee has also legislated against the defense by disallow-
ing hand checking (stiff-arming a ballhandler's hip or back) and arm
checking (using a bent forearm to bang a cutter and knock him off
his path). It's interesting to realize that in many ways the college
game is more physical than the pro game. Of course, the players are
bigger, stronger, and faster in the NBA, so there's more physical
intimidation and more hard fouls committed. But the college game
still endorses hand and arm checking as a legitimate means of playing defense. When it comes to guarding dribble-penetrators and cutters, NBA rookies have to learn to move their feet and play with
much more finesse than they needed in college.

Once an NBA player leaves the floor to shoot the ball, however,
the defense has a distinct advantage. NBA players get fouled virtually every time they shoot the ball in traffic. The type of contact
may vary—knee to knee, hip to hip, hand to elbow—but the
defender is allowed to interfere with a shooter's balance. That's one
reason why shooting percentages are not as high as they should be.

Whenever players do get free shots, their field goal percentages just skyrocket.

This particular situation occurred after the NBA went to three referees: I'm convinced that two referees could see the game much better than three can. The two-referee tandem required a much higher degree of athleticism, and both referees had to be in really good physical condition. The referee at the top of the floor had to anticipate a fast break and beat the fast-breaking team to the baseline. In a half-court set one ref was positioned on the baseline just outside of the pro lane, but nowadays, the baseline ref sets up about two steps from the corner, where he can't really see what's happening in the lane. This means that savvy teams can simply sink their defense into the lane and are free to maim any ballhandler who approaches the basket.

Generally, the three-referee format requires the refs to be stationed in predefined zones somewhere at the edge of the court, which results in their being too far away from the action. Referees will then use the fact of being in their assigned zones as excuses not to make calls on the margins of these areas. "That wasn't my call," they'll say when a noncall is challenged. "That space is Joe's responsibility." Older basketball fans will notice that today's referees are never in front of fast-break situations. In an up-tempo game, the refs will make calls from behind the action or from the side, and they'll also make guess calls (or no calls at all) because of their poor sightlines. At the same time, there are some limited advantages to having three referees—mainly their ability to see three-second violations, and to identify illegal defenses.

It's understandable that the vast majority of NBA coaches are simply afraid to talk about how the game is officiated. We're intimidated by the absolute power of the referees to control a ball game. I also feel that most referees want to be coached in some fashion and encouraged to become better at their jobs. I think they like what they're doing, that they have a sincere desire to improve both the game and their own performance, and that, in fact, today's NBA referees are better than ever.

When Darell Garretson was in charge of the officials, the referees were much more caustic and difficult to deal with. Garretson felt that the NBA was strictly a players' league, so the referees were encouraged to talk to them. But since Garretson felt that the coaches whined about every call that went the other way, they weren't permitted to voice their opinions at all. That's why, during the 1996–97 season, I decided to just sit down, shut up, and let the referees alone to do the best job they could. How can they make clearheaded judgment calls when both coaches are constantly barking in their ears?

I came up from the CBA, which was a developmental league for referees like Steve Javie, Ronnie Nunn, Bob Delany, and Darell's son, Ronnie Garretson, guys who have become the best referees in the NBA. Perhaps it's due to our familiarity, or the year I spent out of the league, or perhaps my style has changed, but I find these guys much easier to work with than the veteran holdovers from Garretson's regime.

After Garretson retired three years ago, the referees became much more friendly and talkative. Some coaches, however, have taken advantage of the more relaxed conditions. Guys like Gary St. Jean and Jeff Van Gundy habitually step over the sideline onto the court and wave their hands, trying to distract opponents as they shoot the ball. Or else you'll see coaches strategically positioned near a sideline trap, again waving their arms to effectively make a two-man trap into a three-man trap. I know that coaches have to get totally involved in the game, but there should be certain limitations.

I used to get very anxious when I was informed who the referees would be for any given ball game. Once the starting lineup is given to the official scorer about twenty minutes before game time, the coach is free to ask him who will be working the game. And I could always find something wrong with the referees: this guy is a homer, that one lets offensive rebounders get away with murder, the other one will T you if you look cross-eyed at him. Kevin Loughery always said that coaches would be better off if they scouted referees instead of scouting the opponents. But that kind of thinking winds up being too distracting, so a few years back I just stopped asking the official scorers to identify the refs.

When Dennis Rodman was with the Bulls, I was very much concerned with preventing him from confronting referees. Joey

Crawford always had a low tolerance for Dennis's bedevilments, and if Joey was working one of our games, I'd have to warn Dennis not to give him any lip because Joey would only get back at him with a critical call late in the game.

Otherwise, I've found that the best way to deal with referees is just to do your job and let them do theirs.

II. BEING THERE

NINE

T FOR TWO
(TEX AND THE
TRIANGLE)

CHARLEY

At age seventy-eight, Tex Winter prides himself on being fifty-four years in the business—"longer than anybody else," he says. He is a revered relic from the pre-Celtic twilight of the game, equally famous for evolving the Triangle (aka triple-post) offense, for being upbeat, forthright and honorable, and for never refusing a free meal. But today, as the Lakers cruise through a midseason practice, Tex is disgusted by the team's nonchalant attitude.

In Tex's hoopocentric view of the universe, laziness is a cardinal sin, an unforgivable dissing of the game's eternal verities. "Let's go!" he shouts at large as he stalks the sideline. His black Lakers sweat suit bulges at the waist, his jutting chin is rigid with frustration, and his blue eyes sweep the court to register even the smallest misdeed.

The players are casually involved in a routine ballhandling drill that posits an imaginary defender and requires each player to escape by executing a standard crossover dribble. "Be sharp!" Tex says, even as he pauses to push a small plastic comb through his dense gray hair.

When he realizes that his commands are being ignored, Tex finally steps across the sideline, stations himself in front of Shaquille O'Neal, and with surprisingly nimble feet assumes a classic defensive stance. Pawing at the ball, Tex forces O'Neal to make a swift and precise crossover. Robert Horry is next up, and under Tex's soft pressure he is likewise compelled to work a little harder than he really wants to. Rick Fox and Ron Harper follow and dance around Tex in high seriousness.

As Tex recrosses the sideline, he turns and says to me, "I always half expect one of these guys to stick an elbow in my face."

After practice, Tex agrees to chat about the whys and wherefores of his favorite offense, and because of various time restraints, PJ's beachfront house is the most convenient site.

"Is that okay with you, Phil?" Tex wants to know.

"Sure, as long as you don't ransack my refrigerator."

On February 25, 1922, in Wellington, Texas, Ernest and Theo Winter became the proud parents of Mona Frances Winter. Fifteen minutes later the doctor informed the Winters that another baby was on the way. "No, no," Theo said. She gave the second child, a boy, to the doctor, who offered to raise him as his own. By the next day, Theo had changed her mind. She said it was all a misunderstanding, and she wanted the boy back. The name she eventually chose for her son was Morice Fredrick Winter.

Ernest died in 1933, and a year later Theo moved the family to southern California and young Morice underwent a name change. "With all of the Texans running around down there in Wellington," he says, "it would be too confusing to call each other 'Tex.' I didn't become Tex until I moved to California, and I haven't been able to live it down since. The Texans, of course, believe that my nickname is something that I have to live up to."

Measuring a very un-Texan five-foot-six and 125 pounds, he first played organized basketball as a sophomore in Huntington Park High School and also competed as a high jumper on the track team.

Tex's leaping ability translated in a school record of six feet three inches in the high jump as a sophomore. "But after I started growing and gaining weight," he recalls, "the high jump became a struggle. That's when I started messing around with the pole vault. I liked the excitement of the increased height that the bamboo poles made possible. By my senior year I was vaulting just over thirteen feet, which was pretty good for a schoolboy in those days."

In time, Tex became a world-class pole vaulter with a personal best of fourteen feet four inches. These days he sneers at the new-fangled composition poles used in competition. "As old as I am," he says, "if you put one of those in my hands I guarantee I'd vault ten feet."

But basketball was his true love, and after graduating from high school in January 1940, Tex played college ball for Compton Junior College, Oregon State, and (after he was honorably discharged from his duties as a navy test pilot), at the University of Southern California.

The Trojans' coach, Sam Barry, had played for tiny Augustana College in Wisconsin and had learned his Xs and Os as a graduate assistant to Dr. Walter Meanwell at the University of Wisconsin, who taught a "criss-cross system of offense." (The English-born Meanwell was elected to the Hall of Fame in 1959, and Barry would join him there in 1978.) At USC, Barry's offensive philosophy emphasized half-court patterns that allowed for good spacing, cutting, and snappy passes. The mainstay of his offense was the "center opposite" with an option called "reverse action." This was the genesis of the Power Triangle.

Even though Tex was a senior and new to the program, he earned a starting spot in Barry's backcourt. "I'd always made A's in geometry," Tex says, "so it was easy for me to figure out all the different angles in the offense."

There were two future NBA players on that team—center Alex Hannum and backcourtsman Bill Sharman. "The offense created very good shots for us," Tex says. "As a team our field-goal percentage was in the high thirties, which was considered outstanding at the time. I wasn't a high scorer by any means, and I took only seven or eight shots a game. The two-hand set was my bread and butter. Some of my old buddies and old girlfriends who remember seeing me play say that I played like Steve Kerr does today. Of course I never had Steve's range, but I take the comparison as quite a compliment."

After Tex graduated in June 1947, he became an assistant coach at Kansas State under Jack Gardner. "Jack had played for USC in the early thirties," Tex says, "and he wanted a Sam Barry disciple to help run the same system. I took the K State job because Sam darn near insisted on it."

Besides Gardner, Phil Woolpert at San Francisco and Pete Newell at California had also played for Barry and perpetuated the center opposite. Both coaches would later win NCAA championships, Woolpert with Bill Russell and K. C. Jones, and Newell with Darrell Imhoff.

It was at KSU, however, that the center opposite offense began to evolve into the Triangle: "Jack and I decided to bring the center to the ball side to form a triangle. But Jack wanted more continuity, so instead of a guard moving to the top of the key and holding like we do now, the guard would automatically interchange with the wing on the weak side. We wound up winning the Big Six conference for the first time in over thirty years."

In 1951, KSU lost to Kentucky in the NCAA finals. "By then I had installed a lot of my own ideas into the system," says Tex, "and I developed many of the drills I still use today. I was interested in basketball as a team game. Unselfishness. Oneness. The kinds of things PJ talks about these days, getting all five players involved. Which was something that Michael Jordan had a great deal of trouble accepting. I was also interested in ball-and-player movement with a purpose. Good spacing so that the defense has too far to go to effectively trap and double-team. Overloads and quick reversals to beat zone defenses. In the final analysis, however, the aim was to get the ball into the hands of certain players in their own comfort zones. More than calling it a system, I prefer to identify it as a philosophy."

The following year, Tex moved on to become the head coach at Marquette University, a Jesuit school. "I was treated wonderfully well there," Tex says, "but I really didn't like the severe winter weather in Milwaukee. I was also very naive about the Catholic religion, and that was somewhat uncomfortable. One time a priest asked me, 'Are you going to mass?' And I said, 'No, I've already eaten.'"

Then, in 1953, Jack Gardner retired and Tex returned to KSU, where he remained for the next fifteen years. "We ran the Triangle Offense with great precision," Tex notes. "Good enough to reach the Final Four twice, losing to Elgin Baylor's Seattle team in 1958, and then to UCLA's runts in 1965." Tex was named NCAA Coach of the Year in 1958, and four years later published his seminal text *The Triple-Post Offense*.

The title notwithstanding, Tex's book covers far more ground than the 4,700 square feet enclosed by a regulation college/pro basketball court. In addition to delineating the theory and practice of the triple-post, Tex discusses every individual aspect of the game, from dribbling to passing, from body balance to shooting. His description of the attitude necessary for accurate jump-shooting is remarkably Zen-like:

> "[A good shooter] plays and shoots
> with aplomb, which frees his mind
> and body to perform the task at hand
> with relaxed abandon."

Tex also anticipates the modern-day development of sports psychology: offensive players must "realize things won't always go the way they would like and the defense is out purposely to see they don't." At both ends of the court, a player must become "so completely absorbed in playing the game that he is unaware of anything not directly concerned with it."

An entire section is devoted to "The Coaching Profession," and here Tex addresses such relevant issues as maturity, adjustability, humor, spirit, discipline, educational outlook, balancing "sentimentality" against "toughness," and coaches' burnout. "If a coach can spend a portion of the summer doing physical labor he is usually glad when the season rolls around again, and is more likely to appreciate the advantages of his job."

As advertised, *The Triple-Post Offense* also provides a blueprint for the offense in the form of thirty-six diagramed drills. The sequence begins with simple two-man exercises and inexorably builds up to the geometric offense that would eventually dominate the NBA. Once the basic triangle has been constructed, Tex offers forty-eight options divided into four series—the sideline triangle, guard dribble, guard inside cut, and the solo cut series. There are also strong-side and weak-side applications for each series.

In addition, each option is identified by a name, for example, "the dribble weave," "center rub," and "button hook." Tex stresses the importance of establishing a nomenclature. "Words mean more to the human mind than numbers. I can say to a former player 'guard quickie' and he'll know exactly what I mean."

After Tex had compiled a record of 262–117 at KSU, it was time to move on. "I was presented with the opportunity to coach at the University of Washington," says Tex, "and I accepted because I needed a change to revitalize myself. My wife, Nancy, was from Oregon, which made the Northwest especially attractive. In addition, Washington paid me more money to start there than Kansas State would pay me after fifteen years. Money wasn't the main factor, but it was important. I was also able to leave K State with a clear conscience because I knew I'd be replaced by Cotton Fitzsimmons, so the program was in very good hands."

As he recounts the unfolding of his remarkable career, Tex stares out at the panoramic view from Phil's living room. Tex appears to be communing with the smooth expanse of beach, and also the flashing sun that slowly plunges into the waiting sea. Somehow I feel like an intruder—me and the tiny whirring of my tape recorder.

Over the course of the next three years (1969–71), Tex coached the Washington Huskies to a laudable record of 45–25, but the times were a-changin' too quickly to suit him. "There was an increasing amount of turmoil in most of the colleges," Tex remembers, "and Washington was one of the target schools for racial protests. So we had ball games where our own black students were loudly rooting against the white players on the team. The whole scene was just awful. But the pro game was really coming to the fore at that time. Pete Newell was the general manager of the San Diego Rockets, and he eventually talked me into giving the pro game a try. But then, ten days after I moved my family to San Diego, the franchise was sold and relocated to Houston, which was not what I'd bargained for."

With the Rockets' relocation, Ray Patterson had replaced Pete Newell as general manager, and Patterson was itching to install his own man (Tom Nissalke) on the bench. Tex knew that his every mistake would be noted and that most of his achievements would be discounted.

Come what may, Tex was determined to utilize the triple-post offense in the NBA. "We had a lot of firepower on that team," says Tex. "Calvin Murphy and Stu Lantz were my starting guards, Rudy Tomjanovic and a rookie named Cliff Mealy were the forwards, and Elvin Hayes was our All-Star center. Mike Newlin was another rookie. Then we made a trade for Jimmy Walker, another high-powered scorer. One of our best plays was a backdoor cut we ran for Lantz. We also used a dribble weave with Murphy coming out of there shooting. But our defense was terrible, especially when Walker was in the game. He couldn't cover anybody. Didn't even want to. Still, it was Elvin who was my biggest problem. I certainly liked Elvin, he's a wonderful person, but he's always been difficult to coach, as many of these superstars are."

In 1969 "The Big E" had been the NBA's premier scorer (averaging 28.4 ppg), quite a feat for a rookie. His 17.1 rebounds per game also placed him fourth behind future Hall-of-Famers Wilt Chamberlain, Wes Unseld, and Bill Russell. Hayes's next two seasons were nearly as successful (27.5 ppg and a league-best 16.9 rebounds in 1970, followed by 28.7 points and 16.6 boards in 1971), even though the Rockets' record during his tenure was a paltry 104–142. Tex, of course, prized winning more than he did individual glory, and he was determined to teach Hayes how to be a team player.

"Everybody knew what Elvin was going to do whenever he caught the ball in the low post," Tex says. "He'd dribble once, then get off his turnaround jumper, but he was so strong and so quick that nobody could stop him. Whenever I asked Elvin to do something else, like pass the ball, he'd just say, 'I'm an All-Star. Why should I change my game? Asking me to pass the ball is like asking Babe Ruth to bunt.' But the truth was that Hayes had the worst fundamentals of any player I've ever coached. His footwork was terrible, and except for his one dribble-and-spin he just couldn't handle the ball. We had a lot of basic drills that he simply couldn't execute. He tried to avoid these drills by making believe he was hurt or by getting his ankles retaped. Finally he came up to me and said, 'Coach, it's too embarrassing for me to be out there.' So I excused him, and that's one of the reasons why I developed four-man drills. In fact I revised the triple-post into a four-man offense. Elvin just planted himself in the low post, and we ran our offense all around him. It would piss him off, but if he had really good position, we'd give him the ball and let him shoot."

(Tex would also piss off Hayes by inadvertently referring to him as "Alvin.")

With so many young players, Tex was pleased with the Rockets' season—winning thirty-four and losing forty-eight. Hayes, however, was demonstrably unhappy, mainly because his scoring dipped to 25.2 ppg.

During Hayes's initial four seasons as a pro, he'd worked under three different coaches—the others were Jack McMahon and Alex Hannum, who both subsequently blamed Elvin's stubbornness as the primary reason for their leaving San Diego. During an interview for an article I wrote for *Sport* magazine (February 1974), Hayes's voice rose an octave or two and his face twisted into a question mark when he talked about his former coaches: "How could Jack say I had him fired? Did I fire him at Cincinnati? At Chicago? At Pittsburgh in the ABA? The man was a loser wherever he went."

Of Hannum, Hayes said, "He was one of the lowest, most conceited people I've ever seen. He tried to control me like he was the Lord himself. But I know these people now—McMahon, Hannum, those sportswriters, those officials who make bad calls against me—they are the enemies of the Lord."

Hayes was not quite as damning in his appraisal of Tex Winter.

"Tex just didn't know what he wanted me to do," Hayes complained. "He told me to stop shooting completely. I was supposed to become a passer. I could have done more for the team selling peanuts."

Despite Hayes's skewed vision of the game, Tex enjoyed his initial foray into professional basketball: "I liked the idea that I didn't have to recruit players, or to worry about whether they were going to class. I could spend all my time and energy just plain coaching."

When the Rockets struggled as the 1972–73 season progressed, Patterson tried to force Tex's hand. "I had one player, Paul McCracken, whom I really liked," says Tex. "He was a minimum-salaried free agent who stood about six foot five, had long arms, and was a great defender. At one point Jimmy Walker's defense was so awful that I made up my mind to bench Walker and start McCracken. Patterson was upset about my plans. 'You can't do that,' he told me. 'Just watch me,' I said. And so the next day we had a practice session and McCracken wasn't there. Patterson had sold his contract to some league in Mexico. We had a meeting just before the All-Star break and I suggested to Patterson that he replace me with one of my players, Johnny Egan, and put me in charge of collegiate scouting for the rest of my contract, which ran through the end of the season. Which is exactly what happened."

It wasn't long before Tex was offered another coaching position, this one at Northwestern University. "The kids I was now working with were all good students who valued their education more than basketball," he says. "I'd have kids tell me that they couldn't make practice because they had to study for a test. But they loved playing the offense. Billy McKinney was my best player, and the others were mostly slow white guys. When I came to Northwestern, I had the third-highest winning percentage of any active coach. After five years I was down to fifteenth best. Even so, I liked working with those kids and I enjoyed coaching there."

By then, Tex had been elected to the National Association of Basketball Coaches' board of directors. "One of my duties was to run what was called 'The Past President's Room,' which used to be set up in a hotel suite during the Final Four. I used to take a shopping bag and go around buying the liquor and the snacks to supply the room for the whole week. A lot of the old coaches would stop by to shoot the breeze. Sometimes there'd be as many as forty of us in there, and I got a real insight into several of them. Johnny Wooden, for example, who has another side that most people don't know about. Among his colleagues, Wooden wasn't very popular, and he was never voted to the board of directors. That's because he was kind of arrogant. He'd never let his UCLA players participate in the Coaches All-Star game, and he never went out of his way to help anybody. Adolph Rupp was another conceited ass, a racist and a hypocrite from the word go, but a great storyteller. Hank Iba was a wonderful man who didn't have a jealous bone in his body. Clair Bee from LIU used to drink a lot, but he was another fabulous spinner of yarns. With all of the coaches and athletic directors I knew, I wasn't surprised to get another offer to coach."

Tex's next stop was the California State University-Long Beach, where he stayed for five years. After posting a record of 78–69, Tex was sixty-three years old and ready to retire. "And I *was* retired," says Tex, "until Dale Brown changed my mind. Brown was head coach at Louisiana State, and he wanted me to come in, be his consultant, and teach him my philosophy. Even though I was only listed as a part-time assistant coach, I was making more money than ever before."

The Tigers had great success under Tex's guidance, winning the Southeastern Conference and qualifying for two NCAA tournament appearances. Then, in 1985, the NCAA issued a ruling that effectively prohibited teams from having part-time assistants. Undeterred, Brown began angling for a way to keep Tex in Baton Rouge. "But Nancy and I had already bought a home in Salem Town, Oregon, which was a retirement community," said Tex, "and I believed I was done for good."

Tex and Nancy were in the process of packing up their apartment when he chanced to tune the TV to ESPN. "There was a press conference with a fellow named Jerry Reinsdorf talking about his recent purchase of the Chicago Bulls," said Tex. "And all of a sudden Reinsdorf was introducing Jerry Krause as the team's new general manager. I did a double-take. Then I told Nancy that Jerry would be calling me within the next twenty-four hours."

Tex's relationship with Krause dated back to the Kansas State days. "Jerry started out working for the old Baltimore Bullets," says Tex, "keeping stats and being a gofer. But he was a hard worker, so they eventually moved him into a scouting position, and that's when he started showing up at K State. Everybody always says that Jerry doesn't have good people skills, and I guess that's true. Anyway, he wasn't treated well by a lot of people, and he got kicked out of several colleges where he went to scout. But I befriended him, took him to dinner at the country club, and made sure he got good seats for the games. In the mornings after the games I'd be going over the tapes anyway, so I let him sit in with the staff. I also spent considerable time with Jerry one-on-one teaching him the philosophy of the Triangle. Jerry didn't have much of a background in basketball, but he liked the Triangle and he kept contact with me through the years. Jerry was an only child, so he spent a lot of time alone and had big dreams. And Jerry would always say to me, 'One day I'll be the general manager of an NBA team, and when I am, you gotta come and help me.' I'd say, 'Sure, Jerry. You bet.' But he was out of basketball at the time, and I never believed he'd get back into the NBA."

During Tex's last year at Northwestern, Krause was indeed named general manager of the Bulls. The story goes that as soon as Krause got the job, Ray Meyer (the legendary coach at DePaul University) let it be known that Krause had promised to hire him as the Bulls' head coach. Although Krause vehemently denied ever making such a commitment, Meyer was Mister Basketball in Chicago, and Krause was crucified in the local media. The inevitable result was that after only three months on the job, Krause had been fired. No wonder Tex was amazed to see Krause's resurrection.

Krause's first official act this time around was to fire the holdover coach, Kevin Loughery (who had been a star player at Baltimore when Krause was a gofer and had routinely ridiculed him). Krause's second official act was to call Tex and offer him an unspecified job.

Eventually Krause and Tex agreed on a salary, but Tex's job description remained vague. Tex wasn't keen on being a head coach, yet he still wonders why Krause never considered him for that capacity. "Jerry said that he'd be recommending me as an assistant to whomever he hired as head coach," Tex said, "but that he wasn't going to force me on anybody, and that was fine with me. Nor did I want any potential coach to promise to run the Triangle as a condition for getting the job. Of course I wasn't privy to what went on between Jerry and the coaches he interviewed, but I believe Jerry was straight with them and with me."

Krause eventually hired Stan Albeck, an experienced coach who'd enjoyed modest success with the San Antonio Spurs and the New Jersey Nets. And at age sixty-two, Tex began a new career as an NBA assistant coach.

At the time, PJ was coaching the Albany Patroons, and Krause had been keeping tabs on his progress. Krause was impressed with Phil's intelligence, motivational skills, and overall basketball acumen. However, because of what was generally perceived as his hippie lifestyle when he'd played for the Knicks, and his revelation of an acid trip in *Maverick*, the NBA establishment had indelibly branded Phil as an outlaw. Give Krause credit, then, for insisting that Albeck interview Phil for another vacancy on the coaching staff.

Meanwhile, Tex's return to the pro ranks was a mixed blessing: "Once I saw close up that Michael was such a great player, I began to salivate over how effective he'd be in the Triangle. When I expressed my opinion to Stan, I was more or less ignored. All season long I felt that I wasn't able to make the kind of contributions I was capable of."

Albeck's one and only season (1985–86) with the Bulls coincided with Michael Jordan's suffering a broken foot early in the season. Following numerous consultations with the Bulls' medical staff, both Reinsdorf and Krause advised Jordan to sit out the remainder of the year. I've always believed this advice was merely a ploy to deliberately toss the season onto the ash heap and thereby guarantee a prime draft choice come June. But after undergoing a vigorous rehab program in North Carolina, Jordan was convinced that he was ready to play again.

"So everybody eventually agreed that Michael could come back to the Bulls," says Tex, "with the stipulation that there'd be a strict limit on the number of minutes he'd play for each game. Then there was a game in Indiana where we had a chance to win, but Stan took

Michael out when that limit was reached. There was a big to-do about that. I'm not sure exactly what went down, but the Indiana game was mentioned by Reinsdorf and Krause in their decision to fire Stan."

The Bulls finished with a sorry record of 30–52, and Krause's enhanced draft pick turned out to be a lightweight forward from Ohio State named Brad Sellers. Then Krause turned his attention to hiring a new coach.

"I was delegated to conduct the initial interview with Doug Collins," says Tex. "Doug indicated that he'd studied my book and that he believed the Triangle could be an effective offense for the Bulls. But, like Stan, Doug had his own ideas, so I told him to go with what he knew best. Doug was concerned that Jerry would be disappointed because he didn't entirely embrace the Triangle and that maybe this would cost him a chance at the job. I told Doug not to worry, that I would handle Jerry. So anyway I did recommend Doug for the job, and I emphasized that Doug should be permitted to coach his own program. Jerry agreed, and Doug was eventually hired. In retrospect, however, I should never have agreed to be involved in the interviewing process."

In Collins's rookie year the Bulls employed three assistant coaches—Tex, Lanny Van Eman, and Johnny Bach. "Things went along fairly well," says Tex, "although we never did use the Triangle, which once again put me in the same frustrating position I'd been in with Stan. For some reason, though, Doug resented the fact that I was there on the scene before him, and he thought that I was operating as Jerry Krause's spy. Of course this was not the case at all. Never had, never would. In any event, Doug sort of divorced me from the day-to-day workings of the team. He didn't even want me to take an active part in the practice sessions, so I sat on the sidelines and kept notes. I wasn't trying to be negative. My aim was to point out what I liked about the practices and where improvements could be made. The term I used for my notes was 'critiquing.' I thought it was a pretty good term, but when I used it to him, Doug hit the ceiling. I think Doug's real problem was his insecurity about his ability to handle his job."

Chicago went 40–42 in Collins's rookie year, and after the season, Van Eman resigned to return to college ball. "That's when Jerry brought in Phil as an assistant," says Tex. "I know for a fact that Doug didn't want to hire him."

Before Phil became a co-worker, Tex had never met him. "Phil played with the Knicks when I was coaching the Rockets," says Tex, "and I respected him for being a very heady player. It was common knowledge that Phil was kind of a maverick, but Jerry told me that he was extremely intelligent, and it didn't take me long to discover that Jerry's scouting report was right on the money. I also knew Jerry well enough to believe that he already had some kind of agenda planned out when he brought Phil on board. In fact I'm sure that Jerry considered Phil his insurance policy in case Doug didn't work out."

Phil quickly joined Tex in Collins's doghouse. "Phil was very inquisitive about the Triangle," Tex says, "and when I gave him a copy of my book, he came back at me with all kinds of questions. But I never had any idea what his true feelings were until the summer after our second season together."

This was the summer of 1987, when Tex and Phil were ordered to coach Chicago's entry in the Los Angeles Summer League, a three-week program that comprised approximately seventy-five teams divided into several categories. Agents would enter teams consisting of players they represented in hopes that a good showing would result in either a big-time contract offer from a European team or an invitation to an NBA team's preseason camp. About a dozen NBA teams also used the Summer League to test the merits of their recent draft choices, the players at the end of their bench, and various free agents. To further legitimize the goings-on, all of the game officials were sponsored by the NBA. So the stands at Loyola Marymount University overflowed with NBA scouts and general managers, unemployed coaches and scouts, agents from wealthy teams from "across the water," plus CBA coaches like me.

"I'd told Doug that I was going to coach what I knew and understood," said Tex, "so that summer I taught the Triangle. During the games Phil handled the substitutions while I did the time-outs and called the plays. After he started getting the hang of it, Phil also got involved with teaching the offense in our practices. I believe that summer it became clear to Phil that the Triangle was the offense he'd been looking for. As he explained it to me, there were many similarities with what Red Holzman used to run with the Knicks. The spacing, the ball-and-player movement, and just the entire unselfish team concept."

According to Tex, Phil would occasionally fantasize about someday becoming a head coach. "He knew what he wanted to do defensively," says Tex. "In fact, what tickled me about Phil is that he used to say how much he hated to teach offense. And by the time he was the head coach, hell, we couldn't keep him off the offense."

Early in the 1988–89 season, Tex had a bulletin for Krause: "This is my last year, Jerry. I'm not making any kind of a contribution here, and I feel like I've been pushed aside."

When Collins was subsequently fired after the 1988–89 season, Tex felt a slight twinge of conscience: "I didn't want the fact of my resignation to be a factor in what would happen to Doug, but I'm sure my feelings helped influence Jerry's decision."

Not long after Phil was handed the head coaching job, he assured Tex of his total commitment to the Triangle. "Phil gave me the reins of the offense," says Tex, "and I was solely responsible for organizing the first forty-five minutes of every practice session. That's when I ran my drills and built the concept from the ground up. I've always been a fanatic on details, and I think in the first few years Phil saw me as being too meticulous because I kept repeating the same drills day after day. In my mind, once you start getting sloppy about details, then the mistakes start snowballing, and everything falls apart."

In Tex's mind, the primary obstacle to the implementation of the Triangle was Michael Jordan. "Phil and I thought Michael would immediately see the light and realize he couldn't carry the team by himself. Phil gave Michael a lot of rope, but unexpectedly, Michael just kept pulling. We maybe misjudged the depth of Michael's tenacity."

Compounding Michael's intransigence was Johnny Bach, another Bulls assistant, who was totally enamored of Jordan's extraordinary talent. Bach himself had never completely embraced the offense and would occasionally tell Jordan to "forget the Triangle."

"Phil did a great job selling Michael on the Triangle," says Tex. "Phil pitched it solely as an attempt to take some of the pressure off. Michael was trusting. He could easily have sabotaged the system if he wanted to."

Even so, after three championships, neither Tex nor Phil felt certain that Michael was entirely committed to the Triangle. In the spring of 1995, Michael's return to the Bulls from his abortive baseball career had culminated in a disappointing play-off loss to the Orlando Magic. The Chicago media was now doubting the effectiveness of Tex's system, and there was some question as to whether or not Jordan would return to the Bulls for the 1995–96 season if the Triangle remained in effect. Tex prompted Phil to confront Jordan about the situation.

"I certainly never wanted the Triangle to get in the way of the team," Tex says, "and I knew that Michael might not tell me how he really felt. I thought it best that Phil ask him. It worked out better than I anticipated—we finally got a real commitment from Michael to accept the system."

Three more championships followed, but the breakup of the team was inevitable. To many insiders, the bad angel was Jerry Krause, who publicly feuded with Horace Grant, Scottie Pippen, Michael Jordan, and Phil. In a foolish attempt to gain acceptance as the mastermind behind the Bulls' championships, Krause constantly downplayed the importance of his players and his coaching staff. "Organizations win championships" was one of Krause's more provocative statements.

Tex found himself in the middle—loyal to both Krause and Phil, he tried mediating their differences. "Jerry surrounds himself with capable people," Tex says. "As an evaluator of talent he's not bad. But he lacks the ability to relate in a positive manner. He's paranoid, suspicious, and negative—a real pain. That's the image he projects. Not many see his depth, compassion, or the goodness of his heart. You've got to work to get there."

In the end, Tex was unable to bridge the gap. "It's hard for some people to see why the Bulls' run couldn't last longer. But even success can't heal all wounds. Sometimes there isn't enough credit to go around, or it seems to only go to certain people. There's an awful lot of ego in an organization like the Bulls."

It was difficult for Tex to join Phil in Los Angeles. But, like Phil, he wanted to see how the Triangle would function with a dreadnaught pivotman like Shaq at its apex. Tex and Phil have won seven championships in ten seasons together, yet Tex professes to be unsure of exactly where he stands.

"After all these years," says Tex, "there are many times when I still don't know what Phil's thinking about. Maybe from the start he felt like I was forced on him."

More than anything, this is a testimony to Tex Winter's abiding modesty. In fact Tex and I had this conversation and others like it several times during the L.A. Summer League, in Chicago, and then again during his first season with the Lakers: "No, no, Tex," I insist, "Phil always loved the Triangle and he wanted to keep it going. Even now Phil has a great sense of continuing your legacy."

"Well," Tex says, "whether it's my legacy or Sam Barry's or whoever's it is, I believe that the Triangle is good for basketball."

Then Tex shifts in his seat and says, "Do you think Phil would mind if I drank a glass of his water?"

TEN

THE ROAD
TO LOS ANGELES

PHIL

In 1998, after forty-four years of being continuously involved with the game of basketball, I cashed in my chips and "retired" after winning my sixth championship with the Bulls. In the middle of the journey that is my life, I had lost my way. In a sense, it was fortuitous for me that the next season was delayed so long because of the lockout. I needed to be separated from the game for a while. I had no idea if I'd ever get back into it.

The NBA season finally got under way in February, and I was traveling one week per month speaking to various groups of corporate executives about leadership and teamwork. I managed to watch a few NBA games on TV, and it was with mixed feelings that I followed the struggles of "my" dismantled Bulls. Bill Cartwright, Frank Hamblen, and Tex Winter, my former assistant coaches, were still on Chicago's staff, and whenever they'd call I'd commiserate with them. It was no real surprise to any of us that the latest edition of the Bulls was built to fail. Jerry Reinsdorf, the Bulls' owner, had often stated that to be mediocre after "the fall" wouldn't get the team back on track very fast. If the Bulls went with "bad" players, however, they'd position themselves for top-flight draft picks. At the same time, they'd be way under the salary cap and could theoretically be very aggressive in next year's free-agent market. Having an inferior team for one or two seasons was exactly the game plan that the Bulls had opted for.

In March 1999 I was approached by the New Jersey Nets and asked to replace their recently fired coach, John Calipari. The Nets' organization had a new management team with several interesting ideas. There were plans to build a new arena in downtown Newark that would include theaters and museums and could revitalize the inner-city area. The Nets had already built a new practice facility and administrative offices and were well on their way to becoming a first-class organization. There was a lot of work to be done, but they were committed to making the Nets an important part of the community—something that had never been accomplished as long as the Nets played in the Meadowlands, an arena perched in marshland six miles from downtown Manhattan. The principals involved were moneyed people who understood that the organization had an image problem, and that the ball club's talent also had to be upgraded.

Ray Chambers was directing the search for a new coach and general manager, and I found him to be a thoroughly believable person, dedicated to the goal of rebuilding not only the Nets but Newark as well. Chambers and two of the organization's other leading lights presented some of their ideas as to how I could help them reach their goal. Obviously, they wanted me involved in the day-to-day running of the team, either as a coach, general manager, or VP in charge of basketball operations.

Then in April 1999, the Knicks' Dave Checketts arranged an interview with me to "explain" the Knicks' situation. There were ten days left in the regular season, and it looked as if the team might not qualify for the play-offs. General manager Ernie Grunfeld had been fired two weeks earlier, and the ball club seemed to be in complete disarray. Over the objections of the Knicks' coach, Jeff Van Gundy, Grunfeld had made several preseason roster moves that subtracted

John Starks and Charles Oakley, while adding Latrell Sprewell and Marcus Camby. Van Gundy had begun the season by keeping Camby on the long end of the bench and also limiting Sprewell's playing time. The firing of Grunfeld was widely considered to be the result of a power struggle that Van Gundy had won. In any case, the Knicks were obviously a house divided.

Checketts told me that once the distasteful season was over, the Knicks wanted to move in a new direction. He made no promises, no job offers, but he said that after the season he wanted me to allow him to make a presentation. I thanked him for his forthrightness. Then just before we parted, I told Checketts this: "If the Knicks make the play-offs, they have exactly the right combination of players to beat Miami. I say that with confidence because I know that you have built the team around the proposition that you MUST beat Miami. If that does happen, there isn't a lot of talent in the East, so your season might not be over until June."

That's precisely what happened—the Knicks reached the finals and lost in five games to the San Antonio Spurs.

Not long after my meeting with Checketts, I decided that neither a position in the Nets organization nor the unpromised offer of a job with the Knicks would be right for me. Both decisions were based more on intuition than on logic.

Even more than the absence of basketball, the root of my and my family's distress had to do with the relationship between my wife June and me. Our marriage had been a struggle over the previous two years, and we were working with a marriage counselor trying to discover how (or if) we could recommit ourselves to each other.

During my tenure coaching the Albany Patroons in the CBA, back in the mid-1980s, we'd rented various houses in Woodstock, and June and I had grown fond of the area. So during the fall of 1997 we found a house on the outskirts of town that appealed to both of us. There were certain renovations that had to be made before we could live there—a new kitchen, raising the doorways so I could safely pass from room to room—and our plan was to stay in Montana until the house in New York State was ready. June and I looked forward to returning to Woodstock, as we both believed that a new lifestyle would be good for us.

Even though the renovations weren't completed, we moved into the new house in mid-December 1998. Our reasoning was that we'd be able to enjoy the holiday season with our children. We also wanted to get reinvolved with the community as soon as possible, and generally to move forward with our lives. But living in the middle of construction, with so many workmen constantly on the scene, made for a very difficult transition.

During this time, I was very active in Bill Bradley's plan to run for president. I traveled to meetings with labor union representatives and also made appearances at fund-raising events on Bill's behalf. In lieu of any other career direction, I was inclined to accept an offer to help organize the Bradley primary campaign in Iowa. Also, Charley and I were dedicating three mornings a week to workouts at the Kingston YMCA, and in the process this book was taking seed.

The very fact that I entertained the prospect of joining the Nets in some capacity brought more tension into my relationship with June. We struggled with the reasons why I felt that I needed to reenlist in the NBA wars. It was a crucial issue. June felt that I was unable to commit to either my relationship or my family because my career was more important to me. My view was that I needed something in my life to keep me goal-directed and to satisfy my competitive nature. I also felt that coaching was a gift, and that if I didn't return to the NBA I would be hiding my God-given talent.

However, I certainly understood June's desire to live a more private life. Except for the prosperity it provides, and the access to high-profile people and events, the life of the wife of an NBA player or coach is not very attractive. There are the obvious pressures and overwhelming demands of an NBA season, but there's also the reality of giving up your partner for six to eight months of the year to a schedule that totally dominates every aspect of your lives. In addition, an NBA wife must deal with being mostly disregarded by the fans and the media. Prior to a "family" interview, the TV camera will typically show a shot of a player and his wife before zooming into a closeup of the player that totally ignores the wife. June had literally been trampled and/or shunted aside by fans on numerous occasions when we were out at restaurants or the movies, or on other public outings. There was no private life for June and me outside our home unless we were in Montana or traveling abroad.

June and I had dealt with this while I was playing with the Knicks. But the public interest in the Bulls' successes brought the violation of her privacy to a new level. Things came to a head during our last year in Chicago when our children were either away at college or had begun their professional careers. With me on the road so much and otherwise completely involved in coaching, the nest was as empty as could be. June has a master's degree in social work and had done hospice service for three years in Chicago. That was over, and she was wondering what to do with the rest of her life and whether her subsequent career would be inexorably tied to the whims of my career. To enjoy the freedom of a private life of her own, June had begun to travel by herself and live apart from me.

One night, before I'd informed either the Knicks or the Nets about my decision, June asked me to leave Woodstock and give her the space to create and live her own life. This led to another round of marriage counseling and late-night dialogues between us. June felt that our personal differences had become too great for us to find a place where we could truly respect each other. She liked to travel and valued new experiences. She saw me as mired in my fame and my day-to-day habits—a prisoner of my own past. Her way of being was to live life fully and wear her emotions on her sleeve. She felt that I was a hyperrational, intellectual person who "disdained" emotionalism as though it were a sign of weakness.

I heard all of June's opinions with a great deal of emotional distress. For twenty-five years she had been my best friend and my companion, but now there was no way I could reach her. I felt indescribable pain faced with what I perceived as the possibility of losing my entire family.

In May 1999 June and I made the separation. I would fulfill my last speaking engagement on the West Coast, then go to Montana while she remained in New York. It was a very emotional time for both of us.

I had one last motivational speech to make, so I drove cross-country to Pebble Beach, California. The long drive was a lonely experience for me, but it was also freeing. Somehow the trip was a bridge between one part of my life that was finished and another part that was yet to come.

I left Chicago during the NBA play-offs, just as the Lakers were squaring off against San Antonio in the Forum, and I listened to the game on the car radio. The Spurs were playing well, coming with quick double-teams on Shaq, and the Lakers' prospects looked bleak.

At halftime I stopped in a bar in Clinton, Iowa, to watch the lottery drawings that would determine the order of the coming draft. I was just sitting down at a table when the announcement was made that the Bulls would have the first overall pick. And there was a close-up of Bulls general manager Jerry Krause celebrating by pumping his chubby little fist. It made me laugh out loud. A mistake. Everybody at the bar turned to see who was making so much noise, and of course they recognized me. While Krause was being interviewed, people were buying me more beers than I could drink in a month, and then rushing home to fetch their kids and their Bulls paraphernalia. I slid out before the second half started.

The next day I reached Laramie, Wyoming, found a motel, and switched on the TV just in time to see the end of the fourth quarter of the fourth game of the Lakers-Spurs series—a sweep for San Antonio, and another play-off disaster for Los Angeles. Doug Collins was doing color commentary for NBC, and he went on about how the Lakers were chronic underachievers, how all their high hopes had once again ended in disappointment.

I was in Pebble Beach for three days, then I began the 1,500-mile drive to Montana. Along the way, I stopped in Coeur d'Alene, Idaho, to visit my ninety-two-year-old mom, who was in a retirement home. (My father had passed away in 1980.) Mom was living simply, and her presence touched my heart. What surprised me, though, was that she never asked about June. At this stage, Mom could only react to whatever was directly in front of her—what she couldn't see did not exist.

Back in Montana in early June, I got a call from my agent, Todd Musburger. It seemed that the Lakers had contacted him and wanted to talk to us. This time I was intrigued. Coaching the Lakers just might be the right job at the right time. And now that I was living life as a "single," going back to work in the NBA seemed more appealing. I told Todd to pursue the situation.

A few days later I left on an Alaskan fishing trip with my twin boys, Charley and Ben. It was a much-planned trip that had been delayed year after year because of the Bulls' participation in the NBA finals. But now the boys were nineteen, there was time to spare, and nothing could abort our plans. Along with a friend/guide and five other fishermen, we ended up in a lodge in Lake Illiamnu where we fly-fished for days and had an all-around terrific time. It was a wonderful experience for the boys and me. Perhaps I wouldn't be losing my entire family after all.

In Alaska, I was out of touch with "civilization," but I could be reached in any emergency. In any case, I trusted Todd to make whatever decision about the Lakers he thought appropriate.

While I was away up there, I discovered how fanatical the Alaskans were about their basketball teams. High school, junior high, boys, girls—every team in every town was totally supported. All of the away games could only be reached by plane, and a community's bush pilots would ferry the players and the fans back and forth across the wilderness. As we came out of the river on the last day of the trip, we passed by an Eskimo village. A little Eskimo boy wearing a Bulls jersey ran up to me and said, "Hey, you're Phil Jackson. Is it true that you're going to be the next Lakers coach?" I asked him where he'd heard the news, and he pointed to a satellite dish that was almost as big as his house. "It's on ESPN," he said, "so it must be the truth." I had a big laugh at that. Then he ran into the village and rounded up his friends. They met us at the river, where I signed autographs for them all.

June was waiting for us when the boys and I returned to Montana. She'd come to drop off our dog, Bo, and to take one of the boys, Charley, back to the University of Colorado, where he had a summer job. (Ben's plans were to stay with me for the summer.) If June was happy about the news, she was also cautiously concerned about how I would handle "all this," that is, making a life for myself in a new environment, finding a home and making it livable, continuing my new responsibilities as a single father, getting comfortable in a new organization, and taking on a team of outsized personalities and egos. But I did feel that the potential problems were in fact challenges that I'd be able to confront on my own. I had a new set of goals, and meeting them promised to inject a certain degree of passion back into my life—something I sorely needed.

I had two more months to spend in Montana before I was due in L.A., and there were many more changes in store for the Jacksons. All of my kids came out for their usual summertime visit. In July, my daughter Chelsea came with her boyfriend and suffered a nasty motorcycle accident that resulted in a broken leg. Pins had to be surgically implanted to hold her bones together while they healed. The recuperation period was eight weeks, which meant she had to forgo returning to New York and resuming her job in the entertainment division of NBA Productions. Since Ben was summering in Montana, he was able to help me care for Chelsea. I was still trying to overcome my own emotional setbacks, so it was an awkward time for us all.

In August, June and I met in Boulder as the family celebrated our younger daughter Brooke's graduation from the University of Colorado. I asked June if she would consider reconciliation therapy, if not now, then next year. She said that as long as I was coaching, she couldn't see any chance that we'd be able to reconcile. June had maintained that during our separation, we should each be free to develop relationships on our own. That had been an especially bitter pill for me. Despite my attempts to convince myself that I was "free," I discovered that I wasn't ready to look for another relationship.

Mindful of June's position, and feeling that I had to move on with my life, I filed for divorce at the end of the month. At the same time, I hoped that the divorce papers would never be signed. Perhaps in the coming months (or years?) we'd both evolve to the point where a reconciliation would at least be thinkable.

In September I returned to Woodstock with Chelsea, who was just out of her cast and tentatively walking without assistance. It was time to pack up my belongings and make the final break. On Labor

Day, my daughters helped me throw a party for our friends in Woodstock where we said our farewells. I played some of my old records from the 1960s and 1970s, and they brought fond memories back to all of us.

Charley Rosen had to lead the Eddie Mast Memorial Weekend at the Omega Institute that weekend alone while I made my preparations for departure. This was a program that Charley and I had undertaken together for the past five years to help raise funds for the surviving family of our dear friend, who had suffered a fatal heart attack while playing basketball in his hometown of Easton, Pennsylvania. Eddie had left his wife, Diane, and five children, without even the financial consolation of any kind of life insurance.

Charley and I did connect for a long phone conversation before I left for Los Angeles. Ten years earlier, when I was about to take over the Bulls, we'd had another conversation in which Charley predicted that I would coach Chicago to five NBA championships. His confidence in me was a wonderful boost. This time, Charley said that I'd win three championships in L.A.

I flew back to Montana to pack some more clothes and close up the house for the winter. Then on September 12, I began the long drive to Los Angeles. I'd been unable to bring my record collection with me, but my daughters had compiled a tape of my favorites. As I approached the Sierra Nevadas, I popped the tape into the deck. There was a definite message in the songs the girls had chosen—all about encouraging me to "live and love again." I pulled off the road and, surrounded by those majestic mountain peaks, I cried, overwhelmed with both sorrow and joy.

I'd been blessed with a wonderful opportunity to learn from my mistakes and go forward with my life. Suddenly, the future seemed to glow with golden opportunities. Healing was possible, renewal was possible.

Soon after I reached Los Angeles, I set about putting together my coaching staff. Charley was in a new and fulfilling relationship with a woman named Daia, and they were about to get married. Moreover, he had established himself as an outstanding writer who had an unequaled expertise on the subject of basketball. In fact, Charley was writing a new novel. So, the idea of jumping back into the madcap world of professional hoops now had little appeal to him. I don't know who was happier about his new life—Charley or me.

Anyway, I was assured by the front office that I could hire whichever assistants I wanted, but at the same time funds were limited. For many years one trademark of the Lakers organization was to have good coaches but to pay them lean salaries. It was a tight squeeze to accommodate the assistants I wanted within the team's budget. Fortunately for me, I was able to find room for everybody.

There were some disappointments: I'd known Jimmy Rodgers ever since North Dakota, when he'd been Bill Fitch's assistant. When Bill took over the Cleveland Cavaliers as an expansion team in 1970, Jimmy came along a year later. Bill also hired Jimmy when he moved to Boston in 1979. Jimmy was one of the finest assistant coaches ever to work in the NBA. He joined me in Chicago, leaving only when I quit the Bulls in 1998, and I was eager to add him to my Lakers staff. But by now he was happily retired in Florida. Another former assistant I was unsuccessful in recruiting was John Paxson, who'd also played for me for several years. Pax was doing color commentary for the Bulls' radio broadcasts, and he was also happy where he was. Someday, when the time is ripe for Pax, I think he's going to be an excellent head coach.

Jim Cleamons was unemployed at the time, and although Orlando was interested in bringing him in to assist Doc Rivers, Jim was eager to join me in Los Angeles. Bill Bertka had been a fixture on the Lakers coaching staff for nineteen years, and when I was asked to keep him onboard, I quickly gave my consent. Finally, both Tex Winter and Frank Hamblen agreed to leave the Bulls and move with me to the West Coast.

In Chicago I'd had productive associations with three of my Lakers assistants, and two of them (Jim and Tex) knew the offense from every angle. The only glitch was that everybody on the coaching staff was at least fifty years old. That's one reason why I'd wanted John Paxson.

Anyway, my agenda called for my assistants to be responsible for all of the advance scouting. Jim Cleamons had nine teams, Frank had nine, and Bill had ten. It was their job to watch game tapes, go on the road to scout their teams personally, and then prepare reports and game plans to present to the Lakers. Because of his age, Tex didn't travel any more than he had to and had no scouting responsibilities. Besides their scouting duties, each of my assistants had his own individual area of expertise.

Tex, of course, was the master of the Triangle and a great practice coach, so I could entrust all of the buildup drill work to him. During ball games, Tex sat beside me to chart every play and make suggestions. Tex doesn't always volunteer his opinion, but when he's asked, he's always brutally honest. Over the years, there have been many times when Tex has felt the need to take me to task, which is fine with me. Tex can also instantly spot a player who'll thrive in our offense, somebody like Steve Kerr or Jud Buechler—not supremely talented, large-minute players, but able to contribute to a team-oriented game in very subtle ways. When it comes to basketball, Tex has God's conscience.

Bill Bertka had a very considerable history with the Lakers. He'd been an assistant here from 1968 to 1974, leaving only when he was given the opportunity to head up the basketball operations for the New Orleans Jazz. Seven years later when the Jazz moved to Utah, Bill returned to L.A. and he's been with the Lakers ever since. His forte is personnel and scouting, and he loves statistics. He's always making noise and burrowing around, and you'd better get to the newspapers in a hurry before Bill cuts out all the interesting articles and stashes them in his files. Bill has a briefcase as big as Santa's bag that he carries with him everywhere. It contains all kinds of numbers and information going back as long as he's been in the league. Bill is definitely a facts man. In addition, he was a great help in getting the rest of us acclimated to the area. He knew where to eat, how to get from here to there, and where to go to get things done. Because the league only permitted three assistants to sit on the team bench, Bill sat behind us. But he was always a lively presence at practices and on the road.

A bachelor at age fifty-three, Frank is the kind of person commonly referred to as a man's man. He'd been a solid guard back at Syracuse University and became a scout with the San Diego Rockets immediately after his graduation. Then, when the team moved to Houston, Frank worked as an assistant to Tex. From Houston, Frank moved to Denver, then to Kansas City and Sacramento with the Kings, and on to Milwaukee. After Del Harris was fired in 1991, Frank coached the Bucks for sixty-five games and did a creditable job. With thirty-one years in the league, Frank knows everybody who was ever remotely connected with the NBA. His specialty is scouting, both individuals and teams, and he's very good at criticals. (These are the plays that a team will use coming out of a time-out, and in clutch situations.) Frank's been all over the NBA map and really knows what the pro game is all about.

Back in Chicago, Johnny Bach used to call Jim Cleamons "the Night Cat" because he was so quiet and private. It was all we could do to get Jim to join the rest of us for dinner on the road. He's not the type who'll blow his own horn, but he's a wonderful communicator whose observations are concise and always helpful, and he's very comfortable dealing with the younger players. Most importantly, his enthusiasm and dedication are contagious.

Of course, the Lakers' front office was already in place when I got here, and I've been comfortable working with them all. Jerry West was the executive vice-president of basketball operations. Jerry had been an all-time-great guard with the Lakers back when I was playing, and he also did an outstanding job coaching the team from 1976 to 1979. But unlike Jerry Krause, Jerry West was rarely around the team. He was usually on the road checking with his scouts—Ronnie Lester and Gene Tormohlen—or else secluded in a darkened room somewhere, poring over tapes of pro and college games. Jerry's a talent hound whose evaluations were always worthy of respect.

Jerry's assistant was another ex-player, Mitch Kupchak, whose official title was general manager. Mitch did the nuts and bolts work—paying bills, making sure the team stayed under the salary cap, and working with Jerry on personnel and players' contracts.

Before the 1999 college draft, I gave Jerry, Mitch, Ronnie, and Gene an idea of the kind of player that I was looking for. Footwork, passing ability, conceptualization—these were the aspects that I emphasized. I also gave them a basic idea of what the Triangle was all about. All four of them had played in the league, so they could appreciate my concern with fundamentals—and my dealings with them have been very satisfying.

Jerry Buss, the team's owner, was a very interesting man. He liked to discuss a ball game after it was over, but he gave me plenty of space to operate. Near the end of the season, Jerry sent me a note that pretty much revealed what our professional relationship was all about: "There are three things I'd like to suggest. One, that maybe you should monitor Shaq's playing time so that he doesn't get hurt, because without him we sure won't go far in the play-offs. Two, I'd like to see if we can't establish some value for the players that aren't being used too much. And three, I think the owner should shut up and keep his advice to himself."

Another personal priority was to find a place to live in the Los Angeles area. All of my children were either in college or out on their own, so I didn't have to worry about moving into a good school district.

Whereas Chicago was such an accessible city, L.A. is a massive sprawl. From mountains to canyons, from beaches to the desert, there are such a wide variety of environments to choose from. I made a couple of forays into the hills before I made a decision to live near the ocean.

There are other NBA cities close to water—New York, Boston, Miami, Seattle, Washington, and San Francisco. But L.A.'s beaches are unusually accessible, and the warm weather made beach living seem very enticing. I was also aware of the fact that having to drive to work (and to the airport) in a metropolitan area could be incredibly stressful. Otherwise, besides the freeway hassle and trying to avoid the rush hour, everything was very easy. Because I wanted my life to be as peaceful and unhurried as possible, I chose a house on the beach a short drive from the airport and close to our practice site.

I anticipated that dealing with the L.A. media would be another adjustment for me. According to Jerry West, the media has rarely been very fair-minded in their coverage of the Lakers. Maybe because I'm used to the New York and Chicago media, which are famously aggressive, I've been able to develop an evenhanded working relationship with the local news hounds.

Actually, the biggest problem I've had in this area has been the NBA and their media-friendly legislation. By decree, team practices have to be open to the media for a half hour, we have to meet with them for a fifteen-minute period an hour and a half prior to every game, and there are also mandatory postgame interview sessions.

For me, talking to the media before a game is incredibly distracting and requires too much energy. Also, open practices are as much of a hindrance to making progress as open therapy sessions would be. I agreed with Red Holzman's dictum that team practices should be private, safe havens where a coach can communicate with his players in whatever manner he deems suitable. Now, I'm not one to drop my drawers like Bobby Knight in order to demonstrate that my guys are playing like crap. Humiliation isn't in my coaching repertoire. But I do want to feel free to do something interesting or offbeat to get my players' attention.

Johnny Bach told me that once every season a coach should throw a tantrum in practice, kick all the balls into the stands, and tell the players to go on home. This is just to emphasize that a coach has certain standards, even in practice. And I've used this technique once here in L.A. It was in training camp, and I just stopped everybody in their tracks to say, "All of you guys are only thinking about how soon you can get out of here! Well, you can get out now! I'm sick and tired of seeing you guys loaf your way through practice! So get out of here and come back when you've thought it over and are prepared to play with intensity!" I certainly wouldn't want anything like that to wind up in the newspapers or on the evening news.

Practice is also a time for players to make the kind of mistakes that allow them to grow. And it should be a place where players feel secure enough to fight with one another. Especially in training camp where the guys are going head-to-head for weeks on end, a certain degree of hostility naturally builds up. Let's face it, basketball can be a violent undertaking, and sometimes the players' temperature boils over. Since I've been coaching I've seen perhaps five physical fights during practice sessions. It's normal, always embarrassing, and sometimes desirable. Almost all of the time, the guys who've been fighting calm down and subsequently form a tighter bond than before.

But with the media around, who knows how damaging that kind of situation could end up being?

But as of this writing there's still a hangover from the lockout season and the TV ratings are down, so the NBA is desperately using every possible means of cozying up to the media.

For me, playing in the new Staples Arena has been the quintessential Hollywood experience. The expensive courtside seats are always packed with movie stars, big-time producers and directors, rap stars, pop singers, everybody who is somebody. I can remember the first game we played there: the players and the refs were lined up and ready to go, and I said to myself, "Okay, let's douse the crowd lights, turn up the court lights, and play ball." But the crowd lights were never dimmed, and they were at least as bright as the court lights. The celebrities just didn't want to give up that spotlight. After considerable working behind the scenes, I put in my two cents and helped convince the right people that the celebrity grandstand lights should be dimmed just a touch to help bring the focus to the ball game.

There's also a lot of celebrity schmoozing that is expected to take place before games at the Staples Arena. But my job isn't to make friends with the Hollywood stars. Perhaps some of them think that I'm being arrogant or shy, but I'm only trying to keep my full attention on the game at hand. Being an NBA coach makes living a full life a difficult thing anyway. The traveling is so intense and the pressure so constant that any kind of relationship (superficial or otherwise) is almost impossible to maintain.

At the same time, being a celebrity here is much different than it was in New York and Chicago. In New York, if you don't sign an autograph for someone, they're likely to cuss you out. In Chicago, some sports fans are so starved for heroes that they approach local celebrities half expecting to be healed by a single touch. In L.A., people do gawk, but they're much less intrusive.

As a rule, people are much more open here than anywhere else I've ever played or coached. I think it's a function of the weather—the year-round sunshine. Nobody has to hide from the elements, and there's a lightness about the way people can move around in their lives.

And I do believe that there's a reason I've been given the chance to coach the Lakers: I'm convinced that I can play a part in helping to heal a community that's been through a series of jarring blows. From race riots to the O. J. trial, from Latino-Gringo antagonism to natural catastrophes, there've been a long series of devastating events centered around Los Angeles. I think that having a basketball team that's focused, poised, and successful, and that displays a certain amount of gratitude, love, and respect for one another can be a healing force. Especially given the multiethnicity of the community, the Lakers can provide a common ground. Sure, this may be an exalted idea, but it's still a viable one.

After all, the concept did work in Chicago, which is in some respects a city with an inferiority complex—Chicago, the Second City. Well, we had a Yugoslavian (Toni Kukoc) who was vital to our success and who helped bring the Croatian and Serbian population (which totaled about 250,000) of Chicago to a certain degree of harmony. We had Luc Longley, an Australian, white players like Steve Kerr and Jud Buechler, black Americans (Michael Jordan, Scottie Pippin, Dennis Rodman, John Salley) from rural areas as well as big cities—and their wonderful rapport with each other became an example for the Bulls fans that an ethnic mixture is healthy and productive.

A basketball squad that values teamwork and hard work can be inspirational to the community at large. In the Triangle, none of the players gets lost or stepped on. Every player has a part to play, and his contributions are prized. The Triangle can influence the way people live by showing that we are each important in our own way.

POINT TAKEN

CHARLEY

Surprisingly, Chicago's phenomenal success didn't spawn as many imitators as most NBA multi-champions usually do. (Think of Detroit's Bad Boys, which led to the thuggeries of Pat Riley's Nix, and ultimately to the creation and enforcement of the flagrant foul.) In fact, it wasn't until the 1993–94 season that a rookie coach, Quinn Buckner, set out to teach the Triangle to the lowly Dallas Mavericks.

Buckner had been a standout guard under Bobby Knight at Indiana University before enjoying nine solid years in the NBA. A quick-witted and unselfish player, Buckner included one NCAA title (1975) and an NBA championship (Boston in 1984) in his résumé. Subsequently, Buckner began a new career as a color commentator for the radiocasts of the Bulls' games, where he first became enamored of the Triangle.

These days, Buckner no longer has a lean and hungry look. Indeed, his business suits are custom rigged to conceal an expanding waistline, his cheeks are puffy, and he wears wire-rimmed spectacles. In the passing crowd, he could easily be mistaken for a college professor in the full bloom of his tenure, or a financial counselor riding the high tide of a bullish market. Only Buckner's smile has survived intact—gap-toothed, broad, and radiating intelligence and warmth. Surprisingly, Buckner betrays not a hint of bitterness as he discusses his brief tenure as an NBA head coach: "I was only thirty-nine years old, and I'd never even coached a high school team before. But I had a close personal relationship with the Mavericks' general manager, Rick Sund, and I expected that coaching pro ball would be challenging for sure, but also thoroughly enjoyable. What I didn't anticipate was just how much society had changed since I'd played the game. At Indiana, whatever Coach Knight said was the law, and that was the way it was supposed to be. The younger players on the Mavericks, however, had very little respect for any kind of authority, much less their coach's."

Immediately after signing up with Dallas, Buckner made an unsuccessful attempt to lure Tex Winter away from Chicago. "Tex was and still is the godfather of the Triangle," says Buckner. "But the Bulls were still in their glory, and Tex had no interest in moving along to a team that was in a rebuilding stage."

Although Tex's refusal was understandable, it doomed Buckner's plans to triangulate the Mavericks' offense. Instead of hiring experienced assistants, Buckner went with friends and ex-teammates who had already demonstrated an acceptable degree of loyalty to him. These were Tom Newell, Greg Ballard, and Randy Wittman. Buckner forthwith handed Wittman a copy of Tex Winter's book and placed him in charge of the offense.

"It was all a colossal mistake," Buckner says. "Without any personal credibility as an NBA coach, I should have developed a system to fit the Mavericks' holdover players instead of forcing them to learn the Triangle. The way things turned out, Jimmy Jackson and Jamal Mashburn were the young lions and were absolutely unwilling to accept what I was trying to teach them. I also had trouble with Jason Kidd because his game was still run-and-gun, and he wasn't yet comfortable in any kind of half-court set. In hindsight, I must confess that I really wasn't being fair to them. They were so young that my first priority should have been to help them establish their identities as NBA players. To keep them engaged, I should have kept some of the offensive sets they already knew and gradually introduced the Triangle, but I tried to do too much too quickly. Also, I was trying to teach a system that I myself hadn't fully mastered."

On the flip side, Buckner won't assume all of the blame for the Mavericks' disastrous record of 13–69: "If you break down the Triangle, what you have is simply the correct way to play basketball. Moving instinctively. Maintaining optimum spacing. Creating an advantage with every pass. Making every player a threat. My fundamental mistake was to assume that professional players know how to play basketball. In reality, most of them only know how to play either one-on-one or two-man basketball."

Buckner was also surprised by the players' immaturity. "One of the Mavericks was a twenty-three-year-old kid who'd been in the league for a couple of seasons," says Buckner. "When I tried getting him to move without the ball on offense, he was indignant. 'You're messing with my game,' he told me. 'I've been playing basketball since I was five, and nobody's gonna change the way I play.' Another time, we were on the bus heading for the airport after being waxed by the Denver Nuggets. We'd been down by twenty points with just seconds left in the game when one of my players got loose for a big-time dunk. On the bus, I overheard the dunker talking with another young player. 'Man,' the young player said, 'that dunk might make ESPN.' But the dunker disagreed. 'It wasn't one of my all-time bests,' he said, 'but I think it'll be good enough for CNN.' Leon Smith is another example of where these kids' heads are at. Leon was drafted by Dallas straight out of high school and then wound up in all kinds of trouble, including a suicide attempt. When Leon was asked why he wanted to turn pro, his answer was, 'All I want is to be on TV.' The point is that these kids are only interested in a quick fix, and they have no idea what it takes to win. In order to keep their jobs, most NBA coaches are willing to dumb down and cater to their players, something that I just couldn't do. And when I continued to insist that they play team ball, the kids took their complaints to management, and my goose was cooked."

In any event, Buckner is through with the NBA. "The pro game is all style and no substance," he observes. "I mean, look how hard the league is promoting the Sacramento Kings, one of the wildest, most undisciplined teams I've ever seen. And nobody gets it. The guys who make personnel decisions are still trying to put five All-Stars on the court. They don't understand that you can't win a championship without role players. I don't think there's any hope for the NBA until the game gets back to basics. Look, as far as I know, Phil Jackson and Tex Winter are the only current coaches who teach their players the proper footwork. But as disappointing as my one season in Dallas turned out to be, I still believe in the Triangle."

Buckner was replaced by Dick Motta, who lasted for two seasons. Then in 1996, Motta was succeeded by one of PJ's Chicago Bulls' assistants, Jimmy Cleamons. During his nine seasons in the NBA, JC played for the Lakers, Cavaliers, Knicks, and Washington Bullets. In 1976 he was named to the NBA All-Defensive second team, and although he never scored more than 12.2 ppg (with Cleveland in 1975–76), JC's game featured gangbusters defense and a deadly midrange lefty jumper.

I've always considered JC to have been one of the league's most underrated performers—and in my *God, Man and Basketball Jones* (1979), I evaluated the NBA's all-time backcourtsmen in fourteen categories (giving equal weight to ballhandling, passing, speed, creating own shot, spot shooting, shot selection, scoring, effectiveness without ball, defensive position, defensive anticipation, rebounding, consistency, versatility, and durability). Jerry West finished atop the chart (beating out Oscar Robertson primarily because he was better without the ball). Tied for thirteenth place (along with Bob Cousy and Slater Martin—and ahead of the likes of Pete Maravich and George Gervin) was Jimmy Cleamons.

I first became personally acquainted with JC during his stint with the Knicks, and somehow our cuts to the basket have crossed many times since then. He is an amiable yet highly competitive man, with a brilliant smile and a knack for the pressure points of the game. At age fifty-one, JC appears to be in game shape, still moving with the stealthy grace and kinetic power of a panther. He claims that he can still dunk when the wind is right.

When he was offered the Dallas job, Cleamons had earned four championship rings with the Bulls, and there were several cogent reasons why he should have refused Rick Sund's overtures: the Maverick players were still too young and spoiled to be corralled in the service of a team concept. Sund was rumored to be looking for greener pastures. "And," says Quinn Buckner, "the simple truth was that the city of Dallas wasn't ready for another black coach." Even though both PJ and Tex broadly hinted that he shouldn't accept the Dallas job, JC was anxious to run his own ship.

"Management told me that I couldn't use the Triangle," says Cleamons, "because the same unresponsive cast of players were there who had given Quinn such a hard time. So I ran Motta's stuff, which was mostly basic UCLA high-post sets. I gradually snuck in some terminology like 'reverse action' and 'blind pig,' but I never mentioned the word 'triangle.' Motta also encouraged three-point shots, and we must've taken at least thirty of them every game. We lived or died on our long-range shooting, but the guys didn't really want to do anything else. Practice sessions were another problem. Motta used to reward every win by not having practice. At the same time, the team chemistry was so bad that when the Mavericks lost, Motta would call off practice to keep the players away from each other. With the Bulls, all we did was practice. That's where players can make mistakes and learn how to play right."

Midway through Cleamons's first season, Don Nelson was named the Mavericks' general manager. "Nellie told the media that he didn't want to coach the team," says Cleamons, "and that he was only concerned with helping to make me a better coach. Nevertheless, Nellie and I had a total of only two meetings and the only help he offered was to criticize the way the team reacted to trapping defenses. Nellie did quiz me about the Triangle, but his lack of enthusiasm was clear. He said that Michael was the only reason we'd won in Chicago."

Nelson had barely settled into the command chair when he engineered a pair of trades: the first one sent guard Jason Kidd, forward Tony Dumas, and center Loren Meyer to Phoenix for guard/forward

Michael Finley, forward A. C. Green, and guard Sam Cassell. Six weeks later Nelson dealt center Eric Montross, guard Jimmy Jackson, forward/center Chris Gatling, forward/guard George McCloud, and guard Sam Cassell to the New Jersey Nets in exchange for a quartet of only moderately talented players—center Shawn Bradley, forward Ed O'Bannon, guard Khalid Reeves, and guard Robert Pack. "The Mavericks were only averaging ninety points per game," Cleamons notes, "and when the dust settled, Nellie had traded away guys who were scoring sixty points per game in return for guys who were only averaging forty per game. Where were the other twenty points supposed to come from? Nellie left me with only the shell of a team."

By Cleamons's reckoning, his altered roster contained only two players who were bona fide NBA starters—A. C. Green and Michael Finley. "The trouble was that Nellie insisted that I play Finley at the shooting guard position," says Cleamons, "even though he was much better at small forward. In addition, A. C. had a bad back, so he couldn't practice with the team, yet I needed him on the court so badly that I played him to death."

Cleamons was boxed into a corner. "I couldn't go and complain to Ross Perot, who was the owner of the team," he says, "because Perot didn't know anything about basketball and didn't even care about the game. Perot's purchase of the Mavericks had more to do with his real estate interests than anything else. He was hoping that owning the team would give him the inside track on building a new arena."

Yet Cleamons proceeded with his program: "When I instituted shooting drills as a regular part of our practices, the players complained loud and clear. They'd say that they already knew how to shoot. I also tried to install a sense of accountability by fining guys when they were late for practice, games, or team meetings. I wasn't taking *beaucoups* of dollars, and I even let them compete in shooting games where they could win back all of their fine money. But the players said I was being too hard on them."

During Cleamons's initial season in Dallas, twenty-seven players appeared on their roster. Yet despite the lack of continuity, the players' disgruntlement, and a slew of injuries, the team won twenty-four games, and among its fifty-eight losses were five games that were decided in overtime. "There were enough guys who played hard so that I was encouraged," says Cleamons.

During the off-season, Cleamons coached Dallas's entry in the Los Angeles Summer League, and finally introduced the Triangle. "Actually," he says, "we had mostly rookies and bench players in L.A., but we ran the offense well enough so that my chops were really up going into the season." Once the veterans reported to preseason camp, however, Cleamons was faced with the same old resistance: "The veterans wanted to run the pro set with three out and two in. But to use that successfully, a team needs a dominating center, players who can execute the screen/roll, plus plenty of shooters. Unfortunately, the Mavericks had none of the above."

The Mavericks began the 1997–98 season with three wins on the road before everything fell apart. "We had some injuries," says Cleamons, "and we didn't have enough depth to just go with the young guys. But with the vets getting more playing time than I'd been planning on, they became increasingly selfish. The Triangle is all about movement, but the older guys just didn't want to leave their personal comfort zones. All that concerned them was getting their stats. They couldn't see what the Triangle could do for them, so they sandbagged the offense. After our good start we lost twelve out of thirteen games, so Nellie fired me and took over the coaching job himself."

After the coup, Cleamons couldn't bear to watch the Mavericks play on TV. "The younger players were still my guys," he says, "so I didn't want to hold any negative energy toward the team. Then when Phil took the Lakers job and asked me to rejoin him, man, I couldn't get out here fast enough."

Cleamons is quite satisfied to be exactly where he is, yet he believes his number will come up again someday. "If I was ever again offered a head coaching job," he says, "I'd have to have more control over the roster. Hell, if my paycheck is in a player's mouth, I want to be able to determine who that player is. The way the cards were dealt in Dallas, man, I had no chance to succeed."

In the past, several NBA coaches used systems that approximate the Triangle: when Alex Hannum assumed control of the Syracuse

Nationals cum Philadelphia Warriors (1960–63, 1966–67), he reprised Sam Berry's center-opposite offense. Bill Sharman with the Lakers (1971–76) followed suit and added a squeeze action whenever the ball was passed into the pivot. According to Tex, Larry Costello (Milwaukee Bucks, 1968–76) and Jack Ramsey (Philadelphia, 1968–72) used the "basic structure of the Triangle without any of the details."

Phil was succeeded in Chicago by Tim Floyd, whom Jerry Krause plucked from Iowa State, and these days the Bulls are the only NBA team besides the Lakers to feature the Triangle. Floyd swears that he was under no obligation to adopt the Triangle as a condition of his employment. "There are several college coaches in the Midwest using the Triangle," says Floyd. "Most of them had been on Tex's coaching staffs somewhere along the line and became disciples. Jim Woolrich at Central Missouri State, for example. Also Gary Garner at Southeast Missouri. I always thought the Triangle was beautiful to watch. I loved the ball and the player movement, the fact that three players are always in position to attack the offensive boards, and the easy switch from offense to transition defense."

The affable Floyd considers himself fortunate that his rookie year as a pro coach coincided with the NBA's lockout season. "Phil sat out that season," says Floyd, "and Tex agreed to continue in Chicago and tutor me in the theory and practice of the triple-post offense. Because the season didn't begin until early February, I had four and a half extra months to do some intensive cramming."

When Tex was asked to conduct a clinic at Oregon College (an NAIA school), Floyd made sure that the entire clinic was taped. "I also went out on the court with the college kids," says Floyd, "just to see what it felt like to run the offense. And when the Bulls finally came into training camp, I knew enough to step back and let Tex and Bill Cartwright [another holdover assistant coach] teach the Triangle. I did much more listening than talking."

With Michael Jordan and Scottie Pippen replaced by the likes of Kornel David and Rusty LaRue, the Bulls' record for the short season was a paltry 13–37. The focus of the Bulls' offense was Toni

Kukoc, who shot first, never asked questions, and enjoyed not being scolded by his new coach every time he short-circuited the offense.

Even so, Floyd was happy with the Triangle, especially when he witnessed what the other teams were all about. "The Houston Rockets were the prime example of what was wrong with NBA basketball," Floyd believes. "Whenever Coach Tomjanovich called [Hakeem] Olajuwon's number, then Charles Barkley and Clyde Drexler raised hell."

Floyd reports that Tex totally supported Jerry Krause when he "blew up" the championship Bulls. "Tex said that the guys had stopped listening to the coaching staff," Floyd notes, "and he liked the idea of starting fresh with brand-new personnel. But the constant losing was more than Tex could bear. Even before Phil got the Lakers job, Tex knew he wouldn't be returning to Chicago. He told me that he had to go someplace where he could win."

In Floyd's sophomore season in Chicago, the Bulls' record was 17–65. "We went through twenty-two players last year," Floyd moans. "In one sense they were easy to coach because they were mostly role players who didn't have really strong personalities. But in order for the Triangle to succeed, you need shooters and post players. What we had was one post player in Eldon Brand and no consistent shooters. As a result, our offense was plain vanilla."

Sure, Floyd added several personal touches to the Triangle: cross-screens, down-screens, and flexlike sequences where Brand screened the screener. "In order to get shots," Floyd says, "not good shots, just shots, we also had to run more specialty plays than I wanted—mostly high screen/rolls and some single-double baseline action. And sometimes we just plugged Brand into the pivot and dumped the ball into him."

Through it all, Floyd remains provisionally committed to the Triangle. "We're about twenty-three million dollars under the salary cap going into the summer of 2000," he reports, "so we'll be able to make more lucrative offers to free agents than most other teams. Now, if a Hall of Fame–type player like Tim Duncan or Grant Hill says that he loves everything about Chicago except the offense, then I'll scrap the Triangle quick as a wish."

Should the Bulls ever abandon the Triangle, Jerry Reinsdorf will undoubtedly schedule a commemorative ceremony. A suitable pennant will be hoisted up to the rafters at the United Center, the big scoreboard above center court will show highlights, and t-shirts will be on sale in the lobby.

TWELVE

THE LAKERS' SEASON

PHIL

I remained in L.A. for about a week after I was announced as the Lakers' new coach (on June 16, 1999) to take a look at some of the team's holdover players. There was a rookie/free agent league about to start at Long Beach, and before Jimmy Cleamons took over the Lakers' entry, I was able to oversee four practice sessions. This provided an opportunity to determine who could and who could not adjust to the Triangle.

Probably the best player on hand was Ruben Patterson, who had played in twenty-four games with the Lakers during the 1998–99 season. He's a good defender, a hustler, and very effective in a fast-break situation. One of the problems with Ruben, however, was that he used to match up against Kobe Bryant in practice and play too ferociously, as though he had some kind of personal grudge against Kobe. In general, I liked Ruben's intensity, especially because I felt this was one aspect that my new team sorely lacked. In a ball club's normal practice sessions, the idea is for the coaches to push the players so that they work just one notch harder than they want to work. The players have to possess a certain level of maturity so that they can compete energetically, but also in a way that's fair and uncon-frontational. I believed that Ruben's practice habits were destructive to team harmony.

Another factor that led me to release Ruben was that he was a small forward who'd be playing behind Glen Rice, Rick Fox, and our top draft pick, Devean George. As it turned out, Ruben was signed by Seattle and became a starting player.

Sam Jacobson was an off-guard and former first-round draft selec-tion who had played in only two games during the previous season. I thought Sam was a very talented player, but one who didn't have the aptitude or the skills necessary to play in our system. I did, however, bring Sam into our preseason training camp, and I didn't cut him until the second week of the season.

Most players nowadays have learned how to play in a one-guard front, and they have what I call a point-guard mentality—"Here, give the ball to the little guy and let him get us into our offense." So, like Sam Jacobson, a lot of off-guards (also called two-guards, or big guards) come into the NBA without learning how to advance the ball, with an undeveloped left hand and poor overall court sense.

In the Triangle, we employ a two-guard front (as opposed to a sin-gle-guard front), and whenever a defensive player steps into a position to challenge the advancement of the ball, we identify this situation as "the moment of truth." This requires the other four players to make certain decisions. For the off-guard, or the guard who doesn't have the ball, he should move to a space fifteen feet laterally and five feet behind the ball. At the same time, the ballhandler should himself be fifteen feet from the sideline so that there's still room enough for him to negotiate his way around his defender or make a release pass to the other guard. Another option is for the off-guard to make a dive cut toward the basket on a forty-five-degree angle, which allows the lead guard to safely cross the court while dribbling with his outside hand. After his dive cut, the off-guard must then button hook and move to a position above the ball in order to make himself available for a lag pass should the lead guard be stymied by the defense.

While this two-guard rhythm is being established, the other three players are also reacting to the moment of truth. One of the wings might present himself for a wing entry pass, while the other wing might move to the opposite elbow for what we call a blind pig pass, a breakdown maneuver that creates wonderful opportunities to pass and cut. Depending upon the specific defense, another alternative would be for the center to come out to the top of the circle to receive a pass and then reverse the ball to the weak side. We like this center-release action a lot because the farther away the ball is from the basket, the more exposed the basket is. Whatever the first read may be, or whichever key pass is made, we're always looking to form some kind of strong-side triangle. So we needed players who could play with and without the ball, and I had to try to project what their learning aptitude might be. Would a player be able to recognize and execute what our system requires, and would he be able to do these things well enough for us to win?

It's the system that counts because: (1) it provides a clear purpose and direction, with implicit goals; (2) it trains and educates new people, who in turn learn how they can contribute; (3) it rewards unselfish behavior, which in turn renews the system; (4) it makes for easier transition through times of change; and (5) it provides a context within which a leader can integrate all the skills of the team.

Even before training camp got under way, I tried to anticipate how our holdover veteran players would fit into the Triangle: until I got to L.A., Shaquille had always played pro-set-type basketball in a three-out-two-in configuration. The normal action would have a point guard bringing the ball over the timeline, then passing to a wing and diagonaling through the middle. The wing would look into the low post (where Shaq would be), and if that wasn't available, pass to the other big man near the top of the key. There's usually an exchange on the weak side, with the point guard coming back to the ball at the wing and the center moving across the lane. There's a lot of room in the pro set and a lot of activity. Shaq had also run some screen/roll in Orlando and in L.A., but that wasn't the strength of his game.

Shaq has also been one of the NBA's best break centers, running what we call a post sprint from basket to basket and then posting up. If Shaq can catch the ball in the lane while he's on the move, it's almost impossible for the defense to form a wall that will keep him away from the basket. However, the Triangle doesn't provide many opportunities for Shaq to run a post sprint. Also, there isn't as much open court space as a standard pro set because we're always looking to overload one side of the court and then reverse the ball.

At the same time, I thought that putting Shaq at the apex of the Triangle would make him an unstoppable force. With his back to the basket, Shaq's most devastating weapon is a jump hook moving to the middle from the left box. He's also developed an effective turnaround jump shot from the baseline. Since he's been in the league, most of Shaq's game consisted of catching the ball and attacking the basket, or else throwing the ball back out, then either resetting or spinning away from his defender for a lob pass and a dunk.

I've always favored big centers who could hold their spots in the low post and present a good target for incoming passes—Bill Cartwright and then Luc Longley. But with Shaq, I now had a center who could score, or create a double-team situation. We played inside-out in Chicago, but with Shaq we could now play outside-in.

Yet as much as Shaq dominated the offensive end of the court, his defense was often passive. Other teams routinely tried to go at Shaq and get him into foul trouble, and he reacted by playing to avoid foul trouble. Nor was Shaq as good a rebounder as he might have been. There were occasions when he would make a one-time effort on the defensive boards and then leak out and be a post sprinter. The Lakers needed Shaq to become as much of a force on defense as he was on offense.

In midsummer I'd sent a letter to every player the Lakers had under contract, giving them introductory information about the Triangle and what to expect in training camp, and asking that they get themselves into good physical condition. Then, a few weeks later, Shaq was on a rap concert tour that had taken him to Kalispell, Montana, which was only a few miles from my home. While he was in the territory, Shaq paid me a visit, and I found him to be a polite young man and very eager to please. It was an encouraging sign.

At the power forward position, we acquired A. C. Green from Dallas in exchange for Sean Rooks. A. C. had played the Triangle in Dallas under Jim Cleamons. A fourteen-year veteran, A. C. was experienced, stable, and a very good defender. Because of his long tenure in the NBA, A. C. often got some slack from the referees when he was playing defense in the low post. Behind A. C. was Robert Horry, measuring six-ten, but a slender, run-and-jump type of player. When he first came into the NBA in 1992, Robert was an exceptional shooter with legitimate three-point range, but over the course of the last few seasons, his long-range accuracy had diminished. Here was a guy making around $5 million a year on a long-term contract and averaging less than five points per game. Robert had played on two championship teams with Houston and had experience as a starter, but the word around the league was that because he was strictly a finesse player, he could easily be overpowered. I wasn't quite sure, then, how Robert would fit into the system. In fact, my first take was that the power forward spot would be our weakest position.

At the small forward, we had Glen Rice, who'd been a workhorse and an All-Star player for the Charlotte Hornets before being dealt to the Lakers in March 1999. I'd seen Glen play with great effectiveness against Scottie Pippen, so I knew he was a radarlike jump shooter with wonderful form. I also knew that Glen was a fine defensive player who hadn't played energetic defense in several years. He wore some kind of metal prosthetic devices to protect his ankles, and perhaps they cut down on the quickness of his lateral movement. In any case, since the Triangle is essentially a shooter's offense, I expected Glen to thrive.

Rick Fox had a big body and could play both forward spots. I did have some input into the draft, and I liked Devean George, another small forward. But Devean was, after all, a rookie with maybe not much of an idea as to what the game was all about.

In the backcourt we had three small guards—Derek Harper, Derek Fisher, and Tyronn Lue—plus Kobe at the off guard. It looked to me like we needed a big guard who could handle the ball. We tried getting Scottie Pippen when he became available at Houston, but that didn't work out. We also took a couple of look-sees to find out if Penny Hardaway could be had, but that didn't lead anywhere either.

In any event, I had the notion that Kobe could play the lead guard. He was a pretty good defender face-to-face, and he did play hard. The trouble was his off-the-ball defense, where he recklessly chased the ball looking for steals. With Kobe at the point, though, we'd be a better rebounding team, and we'd be able to play a switching defense. Also, when you double-down with a smaller guard, the court vision of the player you're attacking is rarely impeded. But with Kobe anchoring a big backcourt, our double-teams would be much more effective. I wanted Kobe to play the point, but I didn't really know if he could do it.

Derek Harper had played well under the two previous Lakers coaches, Del Harris and Kurt Rambis, but last year's shortened season meant a lot of back-to-back games, and a dense schedule. Training camp had also been abbreviated, so many players weren't in game shape when the season began. Put all of these factors together, and the result was that Derek Harper, at the age of thirty-eight, had simply run out of gas.

Derek Fisher had started some games the previous season and had some difficulty with his shooting, but he had a great attitude.

Ron Harper had not been re-signed by the Bulls, and I was very interested in bringing him into training camp. We didn't want to use our two-million-dollar exemption, but Harp wouldn't come in for anything less. He was a savvy, long-armed guard who knew how to win, and who could help everybody else find the right rhythm.

John Salley was another training-camp player who'd been with me in Chicago, albeit for only half a season. He'd sat out the 1998–99 season, but he was another experienced player. We knew that, with his thirty-five-year-old legs, John could only play in short stretches, but he was a fine passer.

Another veteran center we had high hopes for was Benoit Benjamin, who could rebound and make a good outlet pass. We were concerned, though, about Benoit's ability to react to the ball, and this turned out to be his shortcoming. But while he was in camp, Benoit could at least bang Shaq around and make him work hard.

Travis Knight was a utility big man who'd originally been drafted in 1996 by Chicago as the twenty-ninth and last player in the first round. We had a stuffed roster at the time, so we were unable to sign Travis and he wound up first in L.A. and then in Boston. Rick Pitino liked him and surprised everybody by signing Travis to a high-end long-term contract. Then last season Jerry West traded Tony Battie to Boston and brought Travis back to the Lakers. Travis was a good shooter and adequate passer who could read the court pretty well. A hustle player, his biggest limitation was his lack of strength; he was capable of playing five to ten minutes at a time, and although he'd get hurt defensively because of his propensity to foul, Travis was frequently an effective player.

So, heading into training camp, I felt we needed a bigger backup for Shaquille, a younger power forward with real power, and another big guard.

As I prepared to introduce them to the Triangle, I was certainly expecting some degree of resistance from the players, especially since those Lakers who'd been together for a while really didn't seem to trust one another on the court. As Michael Jordan once said to me, "The Triangle is a community-oriented offense." So establishing a sense of community would be just as important as introducing the players to their new alphabet of Xs and Os.

Our first official meeting as a team was on Monday morning, October 4, just before the NBA-mandated "media day." After just a few words of general greeting, I sent the players out to the assembled media in groups about four minutes apart. First were the rookies, then the younger players, the vets, and lastly, Glen Rice, Kobe Bryant, and Shaq. After all of the players had their chance to shine in the media spotlight, I made my appearance.

Because I was supposed to be the Lakers' savior, I was the center of the media's attention. And I was bombarded with the same kind of questions: "How do you make these guys champions?" "What do you expect from this team?" "How is the Triangle going to work with a selfish team like this?" None of these questions could possibly have any meaningful answers until we were well into the season and I had learned the players' capabilities, so my responses were general and vague. Rather than trying to probe my answers, I think the local media was more interested in interacting with me and seeing me in action.

I did emphasize, however, that even with superstars like Kobe, Shaq, and Glen, I wanted to bring a certain kind of harmony to the team. The example I used was an orchestra playing something by Bach or Mozart, where all the instruments blended together. What I wouldn't accept was the kind of improvisational, individualistic jazz that a John Coltrane was famous for. Of course, I subsequently got a letter from an insulted fan who took me to task for saying that Coltrane couldn't play harmony.

After three hours of this media blitz, the team bused up to our training-camp site at the University of California–Santa Barbara (UCSB), one of the most beautiful college campuses in the country. We had dinner together and were formally welcomed by the most prominent members of the front office: Jerry Buss, the owner; Jerry West; and Mitch Kupchak, the general manager. Then I convened a team meeting, and we got down to business.

I told the players that for the Lakers to win a championship, we'd simply have to play better defense than they were used to playing. We'd have to concentrate on making quick transitions from offense to defense in order to prevent our opponents from getting easy scores in fast-break situations. We'd have to force teams to shoot over us, and Shaq needed to rebound and block shots like he'd never done before. From the get-go, the coaching staff would be zeroing in on the team's defensive intensity. At the other end of the court, we'd be running an offense in which everyone was going to participate, one in which ball and player movement would be our trademark. I talked for a considerable amount of time, then I went from player to player and challenged each of them individually.

I challenged Shaq to work hard and get himself into shape so that he could dominate the boards, be a defensive stopper in the middle, and be the leader of the team. He's a very endearing person who's nevertheless always given the impression that he's never having fun on the court. I told him that I expected his true personality to come to the fore.

Kobe was charged with maturing as a player. He'd been in the NBA for three years, and it was time for him to learn how to play within a team concept. Glen was coming off a below-par season, but still had All-Star potential. Like Shaq, he hadn't been in really top-notch physical condition for some time, and I expected him to work harder than he was used to working. Robert Horry represented nothing less than the difference between our being a good team and our being a great team, and I expected him to get back to the level he'd played when he was with Houston.

But while I was speaking, I gradually became aware of a problem that I'd never encountered with the Bulls: it was impossible for my new players to concentrate on what I was saying. There were blank looks on their faces, and their minds were obviously wandering. Some of them were tapping their feet in a very mindless way. Others were fiddling with their fingers. Some seemed almost embarrassed by the fact that they weren't able to pay attention.

"I know you guys are having trouble following all of this," I said. "Right now you may not be able to listen to me for more than five or ten minutes, but this is something that you're going to have to learn how to do. I want you to stop playing around with whatever's on the table in front of you, check your breath, and focus on what I'm saying."

I told them that learning the system wasn't going to be easy, but we weren't going to overload them. I expected that there'd be a normal learning curve, so I advised them to be patient, not to fret about their mistakes, and just to allow themselves to come together as a group.

Then I showed a short video of the Bulls in action that was essentially a training tape showing some of the key passes that would initiate the offense. This was something that they could deal with, and they began to demonstrate an enthusiasm that was normal for the beginning of training camp.

It was great to be back on the court after a year's absence. I was very concerned, though, about my left knee, which had been bothering me since the last time I'd gone one-on-one with Charley back in the Kingston YMCA. I began training camp wearing a neoprene sleeve to support my knee, yet my knee swelled up every night. (Once the season was over, arthroscopic surgery would be required to remove some torn cartilage.)

Another difficulty was that I didn't really know these players, and they didn't know me. Not having a basic understanding of each other's personalities certainly makes a difference. I had to learn which guys I could push and which I could pull. Robert Horry, for example, had a very lackadaisical attitude on the court. He had a gangly body type that resembled mine in my playing days, and he seemed to be very loose and nonchalant with the ball. But then something would go wrong and a bristling kind of anger would rise within him; I was left to wonder where it came from. Glen was a different case altogether—he had such a nice demeanor that I didn't know how hard I could ride him.

If a coach pushes his players too hard, they build up a certain edginess and lose their willingness to comply. Early in our training camp the coaches were doing more correcting than is normal because we had to stop and restart certain things to make sure the basics were correct. Also we had to spend so much time with the offense that I didn't get to teach defense as much as I would've liked.

The second day, we began to demonstrate how to break down a defense through penetration. We showed them how to accomplish this with passes (the preferred method), and also by dribbling (something that we rarely condone). With Tex taking the lead, they learned how to fill a corner and form a basic strong-side triangle.

One of Tex's seven principles of a sound offense is that a player must be able to initiate the offense by passing to any one of his four teammates. This requires a certain spacing that permits the players without the ball to be (or to move into) a position where they can receive the pass. Each of the four possible passes keys a specific action and creates a different series of sequences. One of the ways in which teams defend the Triangle is to deny certain of these key passes (under Pat Riley, for example, the Knicks would deny the wing passes). This tactic is successful in limiting the ways in which we can initiate our offense. That's why reading the defense was a crucial skill that the Lakers would have to learn in order for the Triangle to be successful. It meant being able to think on their feet, not just play like robots.

During the evening sessions we usually let them scrimmage, something that players always love to do. There were the expected lapses here and there, but their energy was pretty high. Still, my main focus was on getting them to keep building their intensity.

On Sunday, after only five full days of practice, we played an intrasquad game at UCSB. We were certainly well hosted in Santa

Barbara, and the gym was packed with excited fans. The players managed to maintain their concentration for longer than I'd anticipated, but things began to deteriorate in the second half. Midway through the fourth quarter, with the Gold team (featuring Kobe, Shaq, and Glen) ahead by twenty points, I was dissatisfied with the increasingly sloppy play, so I called it quits. We hung around long enough to sign some autographs (as per NBA requirements) and wave good-bye to the fans.

The following day we traveled to Little Rock, Arkansas, to begin our preseason schedule with a game against the Atlanta Hawks. The site was a brand-new arena that we would inaugurate in a game cosponsored by some Little Rock businessmen in conjunction with the Lakers' organization. Unfortunately, just as we were getting ready to board the bus and proceed to the arena, we were informed that some structural problems had been detected, and the game had to be canceled. Getting up for a game is a cumulative process, and to have it so suddenly canceled was very deflating. The loss of the game also cost the Lakers several hundred thousand dollars.

The following day in Kansas City, we finally got to take the court for real against the Washington Wizards. We played surprisingly well in the first half, and I was feeling good about our intensity, when Kobe was injured in a rebounding scrum. It turned out to be a broken finger on his shooting hand, and the prognosis was that he'd be out six to eight weeks. The kid was devastated, and I really felt bad for him. At the same time, I believed that Kobe's injury might be good for the team. Instead of relying on Kobe's incredible athleticism to create scoring opportunities, we'd have to run our offense with much more precision. We might be in for a tough time to start the season, but we'd be better off in the long run.

During the same game, Travis Knight also went down with a severely sprained ankle. Even so, we were up by fourteen points in the fourth quarter when I took out all of the surviving starters and we lost to the Wiz, 88–84. The truth is that I don't usually care about wins and losses in the exhibition season. It's more important to give everybody a chance to play and to discover what our rookies and free agents can do. The last two spots on an NBA twelve-man roster are very tough to fill and can sometimes make a big difference some-where down the line.

Fortunately, we were able to replace Kobe with a veteran big guard, Brian Shaw, who was a three-point threat and knew how to play defense. Brian was prone to turnovers, but he played with intel-ligence and he had the ability to up-tempo the game. Brian was also an easy fit because he'd played two seasons with Shaq in Orlando.

In our final preseason tune-up we were trounced by the Utah Jazz in Anaheim, to finish at 3–5 for the preseason. Since we opened up the regular season at Utah, I didn't want to show coach Jerry Sloan too much of where we were with our offense, and in fact I kind of set us up to fail by completely de-emphasizing the game. Even so, Glen Rice was 0–10 in that particular game, and I was beginning to have serious doubts about his ability to function in the Triangle. Nor did any other players function at an acceptable level. The Jazz handled us with ease, and despite my attempt to downplay that particular game, I wound up being quite concerned about our overall performance.

Tex and I had imagined that because of his shooting ability Glen would be very effective on a wing, in a corner, and especially sliding into the pinch-post position. We'd also anticipated him rub-cutting into a low-post spot in certain situations. We even instituted special isolation plays for Glen from the pinch post at the edge of the free-throw lane. But during the preseason Glen didn't show that he could easily adapt to the offense. He wanted either to pop out to the three-point line or to post up in the lane. Playing a midrange game, i.e., receiving the ball at the pinch post, didn't come naturally to him. His obvious discomfort made it difficult for Glen to find any kind of rhythm.

Old pro that he was, Ron Harper was trying to get everybody involved but also concentrated on passing the ball inside to Shaq. Meanwhile Shaq was trying to figure out how to position himself so that he could get the post-up angles he liked to use. Shaq had been in the league for seven seasons, and his favorite ploy was to simply back his defender toward the basket. Consequently Shaq was a good passer in a 3–2 offense—but the Triangle was another story. For the Triangle to work for us, Shaq would have to rearrange his priorities.

In the Triangle, if the ball was passed inside to Shaq and he didn't have an immediate opportunity to launch a turning hook or a power move, then we wanted him to become a passer. Once he'd made a pass, he'd be able to reset himself in a more advantageous position. So we were working on developing a triangle on the strong side, bringing it over to the weak side, then counteracting back to the strong side and finding Shaq reset in the pivot. We were able to make that initial pass into Shaq with ease, but we had trouble with all the counteraction, and I wasn't satisfied with the kind of low-percentage shots he was winding up with.

We didn't have much team speed, so we couldn't push the ball, and when Glen was on the court, we had only two players (Derek Fisher and Harp) who could handle in a broken field. Consequently it was vital for us to establish a slow pace to a ball game. That also meant no easy fast-break scores, and the indication was that we'd have to work hard to find good shots.

So it was with a great deal of trepidation that we prepared to open our season against the Utah Jazz. To add to my misgivings, I knew that the Lakers have always had a very bad time against Utah, and I was expecting that we would take our lumps early in the season. The Jazz had ousted the Lakers from the play-offs two years ago, and in last's year's shortened season Utah had beaten the Lakers three out of four games. But lo and behold, Glen had an excellent game (scoring twenty-eight), and we played with poise. Karl Malone played poorly, the Jazz players were not in very good physical shape, and we ended up winning the game quite handily. The following evening we played our home opener at the new Staples Arena against the Vancouver Grizzlies, a young, inexperienced team that we easily overpowered. So we were off to a good start.

Next up was the Portland Trail Blazers, a veteran squad with considerable depth. Scottie Pippen had recently been traded from Houston to Portland, and as one of the mainstays of the Bulls' championship run, he knew every twisting and turning of the Triangle. Portland had easily defeated us in an exhibition game played in Albuquerque, New Mexico, and after the game Scottie said that our Triangle looked more like a square. He also said that because

Portland could trap our guards, they could prevent us from getting into any kind of a flow.

We had a couple of practices before playing the Blazers, but I didn't feel we were prepared for the game, simply because we were still very unfamiliar with the Triangle. Portland put Scottie on Harp and Steve Smith on Glen. Smith overplayed Glen and prevented him from getting the ball, and Scottie generally harassed Harp so much that we did indeed have difficulty getting our offense in gear. And when Greg Anthony came into the game, there was even more pressure on our lead guard.

With Scottie leading the way, Portland was able to read and thoroughly disrupt our offense. Numerous passes were tipped and stolen, and Portland converted just about every turnover into an excellent scoring opportunity. But we managed to hang in—down eight, down ten, down twelve, back to eight. More than anything else, however, I was upset about the way the Trail Blazers were defending against Shaq.

"Defending" isn't the correct word—what they were really doing was attacking him. They just wrapped Shaq up and tried to foul him every time he got the ball. They weren't playing the ball or playing the shot, just indiscriminantly fouling him hard on the first touch. Against any other player in the league, the same fouls would have been called flagrant, but when you're Goliath, the rules seem to be different. The problem, of course, was that Shaq was only shooting maybe 33 percent from the foul line. The way I interpret the original rules of basketball is that committing a foul is not supposed to profit the defense. But with Shaq hitting only one of three free throws, Portland's tactics showed a clear advantage.

Early in the game, after Shaq had been fouled in an especially rough fashion, he'd retaliated by shoving his defender and been whistled for a technical foul. One more T meant automatic banishment. With about nine minutes left in the game, we were down by eight, and we had possession when Shaq received a pass and was once again assaulted as he started his shooting motion. The culprit this time was young Jermaine O'Neal (no relation), and Shaq freaked and pushed the ball into the youngster's face. A second technical was immediately assessed, and Shaq was out of the game. To make a bad situation even worse, the referees ruled that Shaq had not been in the act of shooting, so we didn't even have the consolation of two free throws. With Shaq gone, Portland aimed their offense at seven-foot-three Arvydas Sabonis. We had no answer for this, and so the game was lost.

I could see that Portland was going to be a problem team for us all season long. With their size, and the length of their bench, they had the ability to confound our offense.

Afterward I expressed my unhappiness with the refereeing, and the NBA eventually fined me $10,000. Jerry West told me that although the organization was unhappy about the fine, he realized that my comments about the referees proved to Shaq that I was going to stand up for him. At the same time, another message to Shaq was that he had to make his free throws in order for us to really think about challenging for the championship.

The next night we were set to play the Dallas Mavericks at home, and before the game Don Nelson—bless his heart—came up to me and said, "You know, Phil, we'll probably be fouling Shaq intentionally, so don't take it personally." Sure enough, at the end of each quarter, when Dallas was over the foul limit, their strategy was what the media called "Hack-a-Shaq." And it worked out well for Dallas; Shaq shot something like five for fifteen from the line. The difference in the game, however, was that Shaq recognized the double-teams early enough to make the appropriate passes to our good shooters, and we were able to maintain a comfortable lead throughout.

We were scheduled to play the Mavericks down in Dallas two days later, and once the season began, practice time was very valuable. Our new practice facility, the Healthcenter, wouldn't be ready for us until the end of February, so until then we were a team without a home. We never got to practice in the Staples Center, and we sometimes practiced in the "old" Forum. So our primary practice site was Southwest Los Angeles Community College, which was at the confluence of several freeways and therefore very accessible, but otherwise an unacceptable venue for a professional basketball team. There was only one cramped room available for our team meetings and video sessions. A series of clear windows were set high above the basketball court, and in the morning light streamed into the gym and into the players' eyes. The weight lifting facility was decent, but the showers were not. Most of the guys would show up already dressed in their practice gear and then shower at home. All in all, our practice situation made us feel like orphans and was very damaging to the communal feeling I was trying to establish.

Tex spent considerable time after practice working with Shaq on his free throws. "Don't worry," Shaq said, "I'm going to make my free throws in the clutch."

When we got down to Dallas, their defensive tactics were the same—foul Shaq hard as soon as he touched the ball. Shaq only made three of twelve free throws in the first half, and as his frustration began to increase, I was afraid that he'd go off again. Sure enough, when I followed the players into the locker room during the halftime break, the place was already a shambles. Tables had been overturned, a TV had been torn off its wall rack, and just about everything else that wasn't bolted down had also been tossed around the room.

"What the hell's going on here?" I said. "Who's responsible for this?"

And the guys said it was Ty Lue, who's just about five-eleven and 180 pounds and would need a crowbar to do the job.

It was clear to me that Shaq was responsible for the damage, and I went off: "Doing something like this is just stupid! Destroying property is not only a silly way of expressing anger, it's also a waste of energy! It's harmful, abusive, and other people have to clean up the mess and pay the price! The next time any of you feels like trashing somebody else's property, you'd be much better off banging your head against a cement wall!"

Then I said to Shaq, "Make your free throws and quit making a mess for yourself."

When the team took the floor for the second half, Kobe lingered behind to tell me of the time Shaq had gotten so angry last season that he'd ripped a steel door off its hinges. "Oh," I said, "so it was Shaq who wrecked the room."

"I didn't say that," was Kobe's response. "I'm just telling you that Shaq is the strongest person I've ever seen when he goes wacko."

I was astounded by two things: Shaq's incredible strength, and the rage that seemed to be smoldering inside him. He kept it bottled up most of the time, but it came out with intensity, and I was afraid that someday he'd hurt himself.

In any case, Shaq went out and had a great second half. Dallas played small ball at the end of the game and they had a six-three guard, Eric Strickland, defending Shaq. But releasing his anger seemed to make Shaq free and loose, *and* he made his foul shots.

In the NBA, any win on the road is especially sweet. Beating Dallas put our record at four and one, but this was definitely misleading; our offense was functioning at a fairly low level, and we were averaging maybe eighty-five points per game. What was carrying us was the intensity of our defense.

From Dallas we traveled to Houston to play the Rockets, who I thought were very beatable. Neither Hakeem Olajuwon nor Charles Barkley were in the best of shape; they had young players in the backcourt; and Shannon Anderson was new to the team and still getting adjusted. The Lakers had great success against the Rockets last season, sweeping all four games. But Rudy Tomjanovich, Houston's coach, had played the Triangle when Tex coached the Rockets, and consequently his teams had always done a good job against the Bulls. Rudy tried to jam up the Triangle by sinking his defense around the center. Occasionally he'd also double-team the center, usually on the dribble, and usually from the top—anything to make our center feel uncomfortable. Houston also had a big kid in the middle, Kelvin Cato, a very active shot blocker who could even challenge Shaq's jump hook. In fact, Cato's presence tended to force Shaq to turn baseline rather than swing into the middle.

And, of course, going against Charles Barkley was always an adventure, and that game was no exception. Early on, there was some extracurricular contact under the basket, and Barkley decided to throw the ball at Shaq, who reacted by swinging (and missing) an open hand at Sir Charles. It definitely wasn't a punch, because Shaq never made a fist. Not to be outdone, Barkley tackled Shaq, lifted up his legs, and threw him down. Naturally, the refs kicked both of them out of the game.

We definitely missed Shaq more than the Rockets missed Barkley, but we were able to compensate by doing a lot of little things—setting solid picks, making crisp cuts, passing unselfishly, executing the offense, and of course playing good defense. Salley came in and did a good job fronting Olajuwon at critical junctures, and we pulled the game out of the fire.

Now we were five and one, and things were cooking. Two days later we were due for a return match with Houston at the Staples Center, and we knew they were going to be ready for us.

Playing at the Staples Center didn't give us the same substantial home court advantage that other teams enjoyed. No matter how much noise the hometown L.A. fans made, it's all sucked up into the ceiling, so the arena actually seemed kind of dead. There were also too many lights on even while the game was being played, so it seemed that the ball game was kind of an afterthought or sideshow. As in all the newer arenas around the league, the backboards are set on a long cantilevered beam, which means that the rims were much too bouncy. Whenever a ball hit the front of the rim, it vaulted like it'd hit a diving board. Consequently a lot of rebounds would bounce out of reach of the big men and had to be contested by the guards.

Anyway, because Shaq was judged to have thrown a punch at Barkley, he was suspended for the second Houston game. This time, we just didn't play hard enough to fill the space. They played a zone defense against the Triangle all night long, and we couldn't hit a shot. I kept at the refs to call their illegal defense, until finally one of the refs did make the call. Another ref, Joe Forte, was standing right beside me, and when I said, "At least somebody can make the right call," he whistled me for a technical. I retaliated by calling him a name, and he tossed me. So I had to watch the rest of the game on TV in the locker room. Houston had little trouble beating us, but getting tossed was a message to my players that I was very unhappy about their lack of effort. So we had two losses in the first two weeks of the season, and both losses were directly attributable to Shaq's absence. Obviously this situation short-circuited the sense of team harmony I was trying to promote. But the greatest thing about an NBA season is that there's always another game on the horizon.

After blowing a twenty-seven-point lead and narrowly defeating Atlanta at home, we headed into Phoenix to play the Suns, a really quick team who'd beaten us twice in the preseason. The way Phoenix usually defended the Triangle was to get up on the wings and force the guards to initiate the offense with a dribble-entry. After dribbling into position, the guards would then pick up their dribble and be dead on the wings—unable to penetrate, and left with only two options, shoot or pass. This tactic successfully stifled the free flow of the Triangle and made it highly predictable. But we used our automatic releases; Shaq had an overpowering game (thirty-four points, eighteen rebounds, and eight blocked shots); and we came away with a very satisfying win against a superior ball club.

Next we flew up to Denver where—surprise! surprise!—we were beaten by a decidedly mediocre squad. Denver was very active on defense and destroyed whatever momentum we were able to generate by using a one-two-two half-court trap that forced us to take early shots. They also had a rookie small forward named James Posey overplay Glen Rice and keep him away from the ball. Still, Glen made Posey's task easier by not moving very much without the ball, so he spent much of the game on the bench, and wound up scoring only four points. With Kobe still on the injured list, Shaq scored thirty-six but just couldn't carry us by himself. Nick Van Exel got hot, Shaq shot a miserable 2–14 from the foul line, and we lost by eleven points.

After the game I met with the media as always, and the L.A. writers were anxious about Glen Rice, who would be a free agent next year. They wanted to know why Glen hadn't played much. "Maybe he doesn't deserve to play," I told them. "He doesn't seem capable of playing without the ball, so he's just not doing the job."

Glen was a little stung by this exchange, but I certainly didn't mean to hurt him. I just wanted him to get the message that he had to fight his way through all the difficulties of learning a new system. "Some guys have more early success than others," I told Glen, "but you've got to keep on plugging away."

We came back from Denver to face the Chicago Bulls at home. Under Tim Floyd, they also played the Triangle and they certainly had more flow to their game than we did. They ran great dribble weaves and were able to reverse the ball very effectively.

Elton Brand had been the first pick in the 1999 draft, and with twenty-nine inside points and seventeen rebounds, he was impressive.

On defense the Bulls picked up our guards at three-quarter court, which forced our front line to move farther away from their natural spots. But we managed to cope. Our big advantage was that the Bulls had no answer to Shaquille, so they fouled him just about every time he touched the ball. Shaq went to the free-throw line thirty-one times (making nineteen) and ended up with forty-one total points.

Now, all this Hack-a-Shaq business was really getting him angry. Shaq has a tattoo on his arm of the Superman logo, and at practice one day the guys were kidding him about being fouled so hard so often. They said that only a kryptonite foul could hurt him. So Shaq went over to another player and pinched his arm. "Ow!" the player yelped. "That hurts, huh?" Shaq said. "Well, it hurts me just the same."

He was just letting his teammates know that even though he's so big, he had the same pain threshold as everybody else. And just because the fouls he'd been absorbing hadn't knocked him ass over teakettle didn't mean they didn't hurt.

I was very sympathetic to what he was suffering, and very desirous of getting his free-throw inadequacies straightened out; because if Shaq kept on floundering in that aspect of his game, then he was going to continue getting fouled and fouled hard, and his frustration level was bound to rise into a danger zone.

As it was, his problems at the line were embarrassing and brought a certain tension to the entire team.

I put in a call to Leonard Armato, Shaq's agent, a onetime ballplayer himself at the University of Southern California. Armato said that Shaq was going to hire a free-throw specialist to help him out, and I thought that was a great idea.

We lost a home game to Toronto, playing atrocious defense, yielding a blizzard of three-point shots and a total of 111 points. Vince Carter scorched us for 34 points on a variety of acrobatic shots, and I felt that his potential was just about unlimited. The game underlined just how crucial Kobe's presence was against really athletic teams. But we came back with a good effort to beat Utah at Staples.

During this particular game against the Jazz, A. C. showed that he could play very effective defense against Karl Malone. While it's also true that A. C. didn't match up as well against younger players like Portland's Rasheed Wallace, I still felt that maybe we had enough stuff at the power forward position to be in the hunt for a championship. Supplementing A. C., of course, was Robert Horry, who had certainly stepped up his game. The only trouble with Robert was that whenever he got off to a bad start in a game, I could count on him to compound his errors by passing up good shots and sometimes gambling on defense. But when he got off on the right foot, Robert made a difference. Given that I could also use Rick Fox or Travis Knight at the four-spot, I didn't consider power forward to be a problem anymore.

Two days later we had an easy win over New Jersey, and it looked like we might be finding a little bit of a rhythm.

At this point, we'd played fourteen games (winning ten of them), and I tried to step back and take another look at my team: teaching a new system is always difficult when a team is loaded with veteran players because a coach has to eliminate the veterans' bad habits before he can begin to implement the way he wants things done. We had several players who routinely passed the ball while their feet were off the floor; we had players whose footwork was totally inadequate; and we had players who didn't know how to execute simple passes with speed or accuracy. Even worse, most of them didn't understand what the function of an offense was supposed to be, and the concept of coordinated team movement was a total mystery.

One morning before practice, the coaching staff was watching game tapes, and we saw that all the players seemed to be kind of frantic and confused when the defense sent a double-team after Shaq in the pivot. In the Triangle, we actually invited double-teams because we could easily counter them by overloading the offense and thereby creating open lanes for cuts and easy shots behind those cuts. Bill Bertka had been a longtime assistant coach with the Lakers, and I asked him what was going on. "We spent the last three years teaching them just to spread out when Shaq is doubled," said Bill. "They have no idea that there's any way to aggressively attack a double-team."

Coaching veteran players can also be difficult because they don't want to hear a coach constantly chirping at them after every botched assignment. Vets will invariably resist any suggestion that there are inadequacies in their games. Even when their bad habits are revealed again and again as they watch game tapes, the vets refuse to claim their own frailties and prefer to blame somebody else. It's a delicate situation for a coach; you have to work in a territory that doesn't threaten the veteran players and put them on the defensive. With the Lakers, I had to register the veteran players' errors in a nonverbal but unmistakable fashion. I call this style of coaching "I-know-that-you-know-that-I-know." By this process, the team understood that certain players had been dealt with in a way that upheld my standards.

I certainly felt that the players were cooperative and showed an earnest desire to satisfy my demands. At the same time, they were frustrated because they didn't understand the basic concepts of the Triangle, so their performance lacked genuine commitment and consistency. As a result, I found my own frustration on the rise. I didn't quite know what to do with these guys. At one point, I even considered allowing their bad habits to go uncorrected in the hope that they'd learn by repetition and some vague process of osmosis.

Then I realized that there was so much nonverbal communication going on that the players needed some kind of voice inside their heads to constantly remind them of the terminology we needed to use. A specific terminology is absolutely necessary—there has to be one unmistakable definition of the relevant action, be it "blind pig," "speed cut," "rebound cut," "pinch post," or "line of deployment." For the time being, that voice inside their heads had to be mine.

So we were in the middle of a game in New Jersey, running what we called a five-up series. Simply put, this involves bringing the weak-side wing into the low post and then interchanging him with our high-post player. A whole sequence of options evolves out of this rotation, but each option is triggered by a verbal call, so I shouted out the one I wanted—"guard quickie." But one of the players didn't hear me, the play disintegrated, and Glen was forced to take (and miss) a bad shot.

I decided to address the issue in the locker room at halftime and as is my wont, I found a biblical equivalent. "You guys have to be tuned to my voice," I said. "It's all about recognizing the master's voice and responding to his calling."

Well, they sure called me out on that one. John Salley said, "PJ, do you want to further explain that politically incorrect statement?" So I told them about the parable in the Bible where Jesus spoke about the sheep knowing their master's voice. What Jesus was getting at had to do with his disciples knowing the will of God.

The players got the drift, but they also had some fun at my expense: for the next couple of weeks some of the guys would baa like sheep whenever I called the "guard quickie."

Another thing I wanted to emphasize was the rhythm of our offense. Their lack of synchronicity created confusion, forced shots, and then resentment. It was very interesting to watch how their timing gradually improved as the season progressed. In fact, they were on the verge of getting used to each other's movements within the context of the offense when Kobe came back off the injured list and started practicing with the team. Because Kobe is such a dynamic and idiosyncratic player, suddenly everybody's sense of rhythm was broken. While we knew that we'd eventually be a better team with Kobe integrated into the Triangle, it was a painful process to see the players lose what they'd worked so hard to gain.

We finished up November with a game in Seattle that turned out to be very important for our development. We were down by sixteen points in the second quarter when we made some defensive adjustments and just ripped through the rest of the ball game. We showed courage, the ability to adapt, and resilience—all of the qualities necessary to win a championship.

We beat Golden State handily in Kobe's first game back (he scored nineteen), then came home for another shot at our nemesis, the Portland Trail Blazers. Kobe was playing with a plastic guard on his injured right hand, and I was using him off the bench mostly at the point guard position. Even though he was playing mostly left-handed, Kobe made a spectacular difference in our team. Suddenly we could get out and run a little bit, and he was the only player on the team who could break down a defense with his dribble. So Kobe had a couple of dunk shots, and he even blocked Scottie Pippen's shot at the end of the game to seal the win for us.

As talented as Kobe was, he had an especially difficult time adjusting to the system. The biggest problem was that Kobe liked to penetrate a defense off the dribble. When he received the ball at the top and was supposed to make a reversal pass and then cut to the basket, his first impulse was to drive the ball by himself. He wanted to dribble, screen/roll, do anything that would let him threaten the defense, take it to the hoop, and dunk on somebody. He wanted to force the action instead of letting the game come to him. As a result, defenses simply collapsed on him as he approached the basket, and even when he beat his own man, there were another two or sometimes three defenders coming at him.

But I really enjoyed working with this young man, and I thought he was making some strides in the right direction. He still got impulsive once in a while, but he always worked hard, and he's all about winning.

After beating Dallas and Washington at home, we lost to the Kings in Sacramento (a sign of things to come!) on December 8, then rolled off sixteen consecutive wins. One of our most important wins came on Christmas Day at home against the defending champions, the San Antonio Spurs. The Spurs' game plan was to bang around whomever was playing on the weak side and to deny the reverse pass by overplaying our topside guard. But again we won with defense, limiting Tim Duncan and David Robinson to a combined 10–31 from the field.

Even so, throughout our streak I never thought we were playing that well. Our offense continued to be stilted. We could get in the right spots and throw the ball in to Shaq, and he'd throw it back out, reset, and then receive the ball again, looking to score. If the defense recovered enough to continually double-team Shaq, then Kobe could penetrate and create something, or Glen could find an open shot from the perimeter. But the flow wasn't quite satisfactory. Sometimes a player wouldn't fill a corner to form a triangle, so we'd end up with a solo situation and the ball would get stuck somewhere. This lack of balance also affected our retreat defense, and we were susceptible to fast-breaking teams.

The only purely positive aspect of our offense was that Shaq's work with his free-throw coach was paying dividends. He had developed a ritual at the foul line of bending his knees, setting the ball on his hand, and focusing on the front of the rim.

But I couldn't seem to convince the team in general that we had to swing the ball and re-form a triangle on the weak side. It was too easy for them to toss the ball in to Shaq and become spectators. It was our defense that kept our streak alive—we were funneling guys baseline and sideline, and overplaying everybody so they'd be forced to deal with Shaq in the lane. As always, A. C. played exceptional post-up defense, while Glen was moving better laterally and had become a solid defender. Harp, of course, knew how to mess with the guys he guarded—poking at them from the side, the back, and generally making them uncomfortable. Kobe was very active and coming up with steals. We rarely doubled anybody, and we were able to push screen/rolls to the sideline too. High screen/rolls had been tough for Shaq to defend, but now he was showing once in a while and pressuring the ball on the other side of the screen. Shaq's willingness to play defense so far away from his comfort zone near the basket clearly inspired his teammates.

On January 12, we beat the Bucks in Milwaukee, but Robert Horry suffered a broken nose. For the next four weeks or so Robert played with a protective mask, and his shooting percentages went down the drain. He had trouble breathing with the mask on, and his field of vision was severely curtailed. Sometimes he'd come out of a game disgusted with the way he'd played, and he'd tear the mask off and throw it to the floor. Our trainer, Gary Vitti, couldn't convince Robert to play without the mask. "What if I get hit there again?" was Robert's response. And Gary would say, "How many times have you ever been hit there before? Once in five hundred games?" But Robert didn't want to take any chances until he felt his nose was completely healed.

Anyway, our run came to an end on January 14 in Indiana. This was the first game in the entire season where Shaq wasn't dominating. He was something like eleven of twenty-five from the field, and he only shot a couple of free throws. Another bad thing that happened was that we let a late lead slip away by allowing them to score thirty-five points in the fourth quarter.

From there we went to Minnesota, and after being tied after three quarters, we were able to turn up our defense and hold the Wolves to only eleven points in the fourth quarter—a good win for us, because Minnesota was a formidable team on their home court.

We flew back to L.A. right after the game, took the next day off (which was a Sunday), and played Seattle at noon on Martin Luther King Day. This was a game that I'm convinced I messed up.

Okay, we had a one-point lead going down the stretch, and Shaq was fouled in the act of shooting. Before Shaq took his position on the foul line, Seattle substituted a small lineup into the game. I should have called a time-out after Shaq's first free throw (a make) and set our defense. Seattle had been playing high screen/roll, and I wasn't happy with the way we'd been attacking it, but I didn't call the time-out because I was reluctant to ice Shaq and also have him miss his second shot. I mean, we already had the lead, so playing the right defense was more important than whether or not Shaq would make his free throws. When Shaq missed the second shot, our lead was two.

What happened was that with Seattle playing small ball, Shaq ended up guarding Ruben Patterson, who set a high screen for Gary Payton. Shaq didn't come out to challenge Payton, Harp went under the screen, and we got stung when Payton made a three-point shot. We did get a last-ditch chance to win when Kobe drove to the baseline, didn't get a call when he was clearly fouled, and lost the ball out of bounds. There was less than a second left in the game, and we trapped the inbounds pass effectively enough for Glen to intercept the ball. But there wasn't enough clock left for Glen to get off a shot, and we lost by one. It was an awful way to lose a game.

Two days later we played Cleveland at home, and we were atrocious. I went off on them at halftime about their lack of enthusiasm.

"What the hell's going on with you guys? We're going to have a meeting tomorrow because I want to get to the bottom of this." We did rally in the fourth quarter to win the game, but I was still unhappy with the way we'd been playing.

Before the players came in the next morning, the coaches went over the game tape, and the only unusual glitch that we found was one particular fast break where Kobe and Shaq were moving out in fine fashion, and then Shaq just stopped running.

At the meeting, I spoke to the players about the roles of the team captains, Harp and Shaquille, who were responsible for bringing any internal disagreements to me. Then Shaq said, "I have something to say. I think that Kobe is playing too selfishly for us to win."

Naturally, this created quite a stir. I would rather Shaq had approached me privately to say his piece. Then I could have sat down with both of them and hashed it out by ourselves. But by exposing his feelings to the entire team, Shaq really put Kobe on the hot seat and threatened to create a division that could be very destructive. Some of the guys spoke up to support Shaq's view, and some spoke up in defense of Kobe. Then Kobe said a few words about how much he cared about the guys and how much he wanted to be part of a winning situation.

It was important for Kobe to speak on his own behalf, as the youngest player on the team and very much an individualist. He lifted weights by himself and never hung out with the guys between games. The trouble was that Kobe wanted to be a leader, and nobody wanted to follow him. At the same time, he wouldn't follow anybody else. It was kind of a stalemate, and my idea was to convince Kobe to go along with the program until he matured into a leadership role.

I think Kobe's situation went back to his father, Joe "Jelly Bean" Bryant, a talented six-ten forward who played for Philadelphia, San Diego, and Houston. Joe wanted to put the ball on the floor, play a one-on-one creative type of game, and he was an exciting player to watch. During his eight years in the NBA, his career average was a respectable 8.7 ppg. His best season was '81–'82 with the San Diego Rockets, when he tallied 11.8 ppg. For Kobe, navigating between his father's influence and his need to define his own game led him to develop his unique intensity. I wonder how old Kobe was the first time he beat his old man one-on-one? People forget how young Kobe was when he turned pro in 1996, aged eighteen and fresh out of Lower Merion (PA) High School—and how much room he still has in which to grow. As hard as it is to imagine him getting better than he already is, he will.

Besides his considerable talents, I loved Kobe's intensity, his competitive nature, and his desire to succeed. And I had to be careful not to stifle his will or work him over too hard. But it was his mental attitude that bothered me. He simply had to find a way to involve himself with his teammates, trust them, and give them credit where credit was due. I knew that young players had a different way of regarding their elders, emphasizing the veterans' weaknesses while overlooking their strengths; but if we were ever going to establish the sense of true community that we needed to make our system function, then we had to resolve this problem.

When everybody had their say, I told the team this: "I'm afraid that what just happened in this meeting will jeopardize our ability to beat Portland when we play them on Sunday. I think it's self-defeating to go through something like this. I hope you guys will prove me wrong."

Then I made sure to have breakfast with Shaq, and lunch with Kobe, to try to lower everybody's temperature.

Despite our recent sixteen-game streak, Portland had kept the pace and trailed us by only two games. It turned out to be a wonderful contest between two excellent ball clubs. Kobe made a costly play at the end of the third quarter when he tried to overpenetrate, got the ball taken away from him, and reacted by committing a silly foul, his *fourth* of the game. Scottie's experience took its toll once again— it was a continuing struggle just to get our offense set up properly because we were still running such an elementary form of the Triangle, and he could easily anticipate what we were trying to do. Even so, we had a six-point lead with seven minutes to go when they just put the clamps on our offense. In addition, Kobe picked up his fifth foul and had to sit. Also, Shaq was tired at this point, and Brian Grant was able to push him off his space and prevent him from moving across the lane. We had a chance to even the score as the clock ran out, but Derek Fisher took a difficult three-pointer (an air ball), and that was our last gasp.

Next for us was Utah on the road. We actually played a good game, but we lost in double-overtime. Shaq had to play fifty-five minutes, and we were all exhausted when the final buzzer sounded.

Driving to practice the morning after, I was in an awful mood. Things had sure looked rosy when we ripped off those sixteen consecutive wins. But now we'd suffered three losses in eight days. It was clear to me that not executing the small, simple parts of our offense—the solid picks, timely cuts, and so on—had caught up to us at last. My only hope was that a few more losses would make the players more coachable.

What I really didn't like was that some of the players were starting to play the blame game. My job now was to mend some fences and convince them of the need for taking responsibility for their own actions. They were finding out already that every time you pointed a finger at someone else, there'd be three fingers pointing back at you.

Whenever any of my Bulls teams played against Shaq, our aim had been to control the auxiliary players and make Shaq work hard for his points. By not double-teaming Shaq, he got into a one-on-one mode of play while his teammates stood around and watched him. It's also noteworthy that several of Shaq's teams had been swept in the play-offs—against Indiana in a first-round series in 1994, a year later in the finals against Houston; in 1996 versus the Bulls in the Eastern Conference finals; after he'd moved to L.A., when the Lakers were blanked by Utah in the 1998 Western Conference finals; and by San Antonio in the 1999 conference semifinals.

What did all of this signify? Perhaps that Shaq's trust in his teammates was very fragile and disintegrated in adversity? Or maybe he was unable to stay positive about himself?

So one Sunday morning I had breakfast with Shaq and talked to him about what being a team leader really means. I told him about a miserable play-off game that Michael had had against Cleveland in 1989. The Cavaliers had beaten us all six times we'd played in the regular season, and we couldn't seem to find a way to overcome them. We were up two games to one in a best-of-five series, and game four was played in Chicago. Well, in the stretch run of that game, Michael missed four of six free throws that ultimately cost us the ball game. Yet on the morning of the fifth and deciding game, Michael was totally confident that we would win. Not only was he confident in himself, but he was positive that his teammates would also pick up the gauntlet. And that's exactly what happened—Michael made the so-called miracle shot at the buzzer, and we won the game by a single point.

The message was that Shaq shouldn't be afraid to let his natural buoyancy show—not just a blind optimism, but a real belief in his own abilities, no matter what the situation. Well-grounded confidence is contagious and a very powerful positive force. Faultfinding is the other side of the coin and buys only disharmony and failure. Rather than tearing his teammates down, a team leader always lifts them up.

Now, I'm sure that Shaq had heard this kind of spiel before without really modifying his behavior. So why would he be receptive to me? Because I had won six championships.

We beat Milwaukee at home, then were off on a Texas tour—a game in Houston, then one in San Antonio. The Houston game was to be played at noon (ten a.m. L.A. time), and we planned to leave at four o'clock the day before. But there was a problem with our plane, and we didn't get to the hotel in Houston until ten o'clock. The guys had to go out and get something to eat, and all of a sudden it was midnight. Because of the early game, we had our pregame meeting at eight a.m.

After a guy's played about thirty-five minutes in a game, he's used up about four thousand calories and is almost dehydrated. (Just to keep them in game shape, we'll have all the guys who've played less than twenty minutes work out for twenty minutes on an aerobic machine once the game is over.) After they drink their liquids and ice their sore joints, they're still juiced up, and it takes about two or three hours for them to calm down. So they're walking out of the locker room at about ten-thirty, and because they haven't eaten much, they're now very hungry and ready for their major meal of the day.

They don't finish eating until around one o'clock in the morning; then because they're still vibrating from the ball game, they'll stay up until three or so. Shaq rarely gets to bed before four in the morning, and then he sleeps for six hours. I'd much rather have the guys eat a lighter meal after games and be in bed by two o'clock at the latest.

Whenever we have to play an early game, it really destroys the players' biorhythms. Throw in the radical time changes when we move eastward, and the early games are a tremendous advantage for the home teams. Moreover, guys are much more susceptible to injuries when they're tired. That's why playing in the Pacific Division is so tough. And it's all done for the sake of television ratings.

So, there's a two-hour time difference between Houston and L.A., and since the game at hand was one of those noon-timers, we didn't have a lot of energy. The Rockets were a rather weak defensive team, yet we could only manage eighty-two points, and we were never seriously in the game in the stretch run.

Robert Horry's family lived in Houston, and his wife had just given birth to a little girl. During the game, Robert was notified that there were some serious problems with his infant daughter, and he was a mess. Right after the game, he passed on a shower, jumped into his clothes, and said, "I won't be on the plane because I've got to go to the hospital."

Shaq also stayed behind in Houston because he had children living there, so the rest of us flew to San Antonio and arrived at the hotel in time to watch the Super Bowl.

Several of the coaches came up to my suite to see what turned out to be a very interesting game. Football is a sobering game because of the constant possibility of serious injuries. We saw the big hit that knocked out one of the Tennessee players for a full twenty minutes. It was dreadful. The med squad rushed out with their neck braces and stretchers and carted the poor guy off the field. Even though they eventually lost the game, it was amazing to see how the Tennessee players could get their chops back up and compete with such reckless abandon.

And there we were in San Antonio where Sean Elliot was working his way back onto the court after having a kidney transplant. It cer-

tainly seemed very risky, especially since basketball players are so vulnerable in that area, and unlike football and hockey players wear no
protective devices. Most basketball players, present and past, have
suffered some serious injury to one joint or another, but they want to
play ball no matter what. And bang! On any given play, a guy can go
down and blow out a knee.

Anyway, we didn't practice on Monday, but I gathered whichever
players were there to tell them how poorly we had played in
Houston. Fortunately, San Antonio was in the middle of a bad
stretch, so we had a real chance to turn our game around. Then my
coaching staff and I went over to Steve Kerr's house for a wonderful
dinner. Steve had opted to leave Chicago when I did, and he'd signed
on with the Spurs for a very healthy contract. He turned out to be
the fifth guard in their rotation, so he didn't get much game time,
and since he still had that competitive fire, he was anguishing on the
bench. But Steve was also going on thirty-four years old, his wife and
kids loved San Antonio, and he was grateful for the security.

In San Antonio, the team stays in the Marriott Rivercenter, which
represents the latest type of hotels that NBA ball clubs look for. The
larger, more traditional hotels are always swarming with tourists and
conventioneers, and when the guys walk through the lobby they feel
like aliens. Places like the Rivercenter are smaller, more luxurious situations that are designed to accommodate business conferences
more than tourists. There's a residential atmosphere at the
Rivercenter, and it has several outstanding restaurants. It's also located right on the River Walk, one of the historic areas of the city, and
staying there is very comfortable and relaxing.

In any case, we had a ball game to play. I had thought that the last
Houston game had been our worst of the season, but we played twice
as badly against the Spurs. The score was 105–81, and we were really on the skids.

We returned home and prepared to play the Jazz, who'd beaten us
in that exhausting double-overtime game in Utah only ten days ago.
I gave the guys a day off, then when we reconvened, I told them this:
"It's time to analyze exactly what each one of you wants to get out of
this season. If it's a championship, then you have to take a good look

at yourself in the mirror and figure out what you can do to help us get there. We've got to rededicate ourselves to learning the offense and to playing together. And we've got to understand *why* we need to play together."

Then I decided to take my own advice, and I really opened myself to them. "I'm a stranger in L.A.," I said, "living alone and without my family. My life has dramatically changed, and I don't really feel as close to you guys as I have been with my other teams. I've given you books to read, but I haven't exposed much about my personal life. I think I've been hiding behind my reputation, and I need to tighten it up with all of you. For example, my mother is ninety-two, and she's led a very satisfying life, but she's been hospitalized for several weeks now, and there's a possibility that she may pass away at any time. I'm going through a lot of self-analysis about my relationship with my mother, and it's a process that's been very draining."

And they responded with interest and compassion. Their parents were my age, and their grandparents were my mother's age, so now they had another way of relating to me. Then we talked about Robert Horry's daughter, and Shaq's new baby, and Jimmy Cleamons's infant daughter.

The next day we played our best game so far. The guys got down and dirty, played awesome defense, and we walloped Utah by the amazing score of 113 to 67! From there we went on a roll—beating Denver and Minnesota (by thirty-three points) at home. The All-Star break followed, and we would hook up again in Chicago.

Before we split up, I told them not to think of the break as a vacation. They should take care of their bodies and prepare themselves mentally and emotionally for the drive to the play-offs.

Because we had the best record in the Western Conference on a certain Sunday evening at the end of January, I was to be the coach of the Western All-Stars. This was the case, even though Portland had jumped ahead of us when we went zero-for-Texas. I didn't like being the All-Star coach with only the second-best record in the conference. It just didn't seem logical.

At the time, I mentioned to the L.A. media that I didn't really want to attend the All-Star game because the whole deal is to honor the players, not the coaches. The only function of the All-Star coaches is to handle the substitutions, and so much can happen between the All-Star game and the end of the season that having the best record by a certain date can be a fluke. Doug Collins, for example, was the East's coach in 1997, and his Detroit Pistons eventually ended the season in fourth place.

The only way that coaching an All-Star game would be meaningful is to duplicate the procedure used by major-league baseball—honoring the coaches of the two teams who played each other in the previous season's championship series. (Or else have former players who've been MVP in previous All-Star contests return as coaches.) This way, you'd know beforehand that you'd be going to the All-Star game and you could plan ahead. For me, I always looked forward to the All-Star weekend as a chance to hang out at home with my family, or else go to a health spa with my wife, June. It was a time to catch my breath and get reacquainted with my loved ones.

To make matters worse, the All-Star break caught the Lakers at the beginning of a road trip. The fact that I had to be in San Francisco for three days just made the trip that much longer.

Anyway, I had coached the All-Star game twice before, in 1992 and again in 1996, and my approach was to have a good time with the players and help them to enjoy each other's company. I made sure to stay out of their territory, I kept a low profile in the media, and I took care to connect with each player on an individual basis.

So, the schedule called for the coaches to attend an obligatory media function on Friday afternoon at two o'clock, followed by an open practice on Saturday morning. Well, there was a lot of fog and rain in L.A. that Friday morning, and I had to sit in the airport for four hours. By the time I landed in San Francisco, the rush hour was in full bloom, and it took me an hour and a half to get to the hotel. The upshot was that I arrived five hours after the media free-for-all was scheduled.

My opposite number for the All-Star game was Jeff Van Gundy, coach of the New York Knicks, and the two of us have had quite a contentious history. Our latest antagonism occurred when an L.A. writer asked me what book I would give to Van Gundy. My suggestion was Tex Winter's *Triple-Post Offense*. Then the writer said, "How about *Good Things Happen to Bad People*?" I really didn't react to this, but then it came out that *I* was the one who suggested it, and Van Gundy was peeved.

Actually, my thing with Van Gundy was rooted in my relationship with Pat Riley: because we played against each other so many times when he was with the Lakers and then Phoenix, Pat and I respected one another and got along very well. We even competed head-to-head in the finals in 1972 and 1973. After he retired, Pat got into broadcasting and then became an assistant coach for the Lakers under Jack McKinney. Then at the beginning of the 1979–80 season, McKinney had a serious accident while riding his bicycle, and Paul Westhead took over the job, retaining Pat as an assistant. Just about two years later, Westhead had some ideas about changing Magic's role and wound up getting fired. All at once, Pat was put in charge of a highly successful franchise that featured Magic and Kareem, two of the greatest players in the history of the game. Pat did a great job, and he led the Lakers to four championships.

But over the years with more and more young players joining the team, Pat's method of pushing his guys harder and harder was meeting increased resistance. At the same time, Pat was allegedly maneuvering to gather more power within the Lakers' organization. Anyway, the players' resistance grew more pronounced, and Pat saw that the time had come to return to the broadcasting booth. Pat stayed out for a year, then came back to coach the Knicks.

In May 1992, the Bulls were the defending champs and bound for our repeat title when we first squared off against Pat's Knicks in the play-offs. Pat was still learning how to coach his team, guys like Patrick Ewing, Charles Oakley, Xavier McDaniel, and CBA survivors like Anthony Mason and John Starks. Some of these guys were marginal NBA players, but Pat found a system in which they could operate successfully. From the showtime, high-powered offense he'd employed with the Lakers, Pat was now using a goon squad.

So the Knicks had defeated the Pistons in a brutal series and came into Chicago to engage us. But before the series was under way, Pat started talking to the media about how many offensive fouls and ballhandling violations the referees let Michael Jordan get away with. I thought it was highly ironic because to this day Ewing doesn't make a move in the post without palming the ball, or else holding the ball so long between dribbles that he should be called for discontinued dribbling—to say nothing of his favorite move, the Georgetown Gallop, where he takes an extra two or sometimes three steps.

Obviously, Pat was trying to influence the referees, but there's an old axiom about people who live in glass houses being careful not to throw stones. Anyway, I just let the whole business slide.

Once the series began, however, the Knicks just ruthlessly pounded away at my players—making harmful contact after the whistle had already blown, taking cheap shots, and playing muscle ball. Then when Starks just slammed Scottie to the floor hard enough to injure Scottie's ankle, I decided that if Pat was out to manipulate the media, I was going to try to even the playing field. So I told the media that I thought the NBA was finished with the Pistons and their Bad Boy style of basketball. Of course Pat immediately retaliated, calling me a whiner and worse. My retort was to say that a onetime NBA player like Pat Riley should know better than to encourage his players to endanger another player's livelihood.

Twenty years ago, the only way that coaches would talk about each other or about players on opposing teams was in totally complimentary terms: So and so is a great player (or a great coach), and we're going to have to do a great job..., etc. Whatever real criticism they had in mind was kept private. But Pat Riley and I found ourselves in a running battle in the early 1990s, when the Bulls and the Knicks routinely had very competitive play-off series. Pat and I tweaked one another as a way of motivating our teams, and it was kind of fun. Then Pat left New York and landed in Miami. Van Gundy had been one of Pat's assistants for several years, and when Pat took a powder, he became the Knicks' head coach.

From the start of Van Gundy's tenure, I just laughed him off. It was like, "Hey, little fellow, if you want to pick a fight, you'd better go home, get your big brother, and send him over here, because I'm not going to bother with you." The truth is that Pat built the Knicks—the defense is Pat's, and so is the offense. Jeff's done a good job in continuing what Pat had started, and has certainly shown the ability to successfully coach NBA players (even beating Miami in the play-offs three times in the last three years).

Of course, one of Jeff's problems with me is that he believes that I went after his job in the spring of 1999 when the Knicks were floundering. But Jeff doesn't know anything about what really happened.

I had met with the Knicks' president, Dave Checketts, several months before the 1999 season began, when we commiserated with each other after Red Holzman passed away. Then Checketts called in April after he'd fired Ernie, asking to have an informal meeting; out of professional courtesy, I agreed. At the meeting Checketts said that he wanted me to be a part of the Knicks organization in some way that would help perpetuate Red's legacy. I told Checketts that I would speak with him after the season, but that never happened. Checketts never offered me a job, and I didn't solicit one.

The entire Knicks situation stemmed from Jeff's power struggle with Ernie. Well, Jeff won the war, and for whatever it's worth, he also won the backing of the New York media. But Jeff has no bone to pick with me. My meeting with Checketts had nothing to do with him. In fact, Jeff owes me a big thank-you; my rather vague and innocent meeting with his boss served to galvanize the Knicks players, fans, and New York media into his corner.

I was coaching the West team, and Jeff was coaching the East team. And if he insisted on referring to me as "Big Chief Triangle," I couldn't care less. I do have a mischievous streak in me, though, and sometimes I would call Jeff "Van Gumby."

Even though the All-Star game is more of an exhibition than a true game, I'm sure that Jeff was unhappy about the disparity between our squads: we had a tremendous advantage in size with three seven-footers (Shaq, Tim Duncan, and Kevin Garnett) in our starting front line. Jeff could counter with speed, but his biggest player was six-foot-ten Alonzo Mourning, and most of his other front-court guys were six-eight or smaller.

Now, the game may not count in the standings, but as long as you have to be there, you want to win it. I was on the wrong side of the

Magic Johnson Show in 1992, so I know firsthand that losing isn't very enjoyable. That was the year the NBA permitted Magic to play in the All-Star game after a positive HIV test had forced him into an early retirement. He hadn't played at all that season, and it was unbelievable that the league would allow such a thing to happen. There was a great outpouring of love for Magic, but there was also a circus atmosphere. I talked to my players before the game and asked if anyone wanted to be the stooge who'd guard Magic. Isiah Thomas could never refuse being in the spotlight, so he volunteered. Magic was about nine inches taller than Isiah, and he wound up having a great game and winning the MVP award.

The game itself was boring. We were down by twenty at halftime and lost by the absurd score of 153–113! I had two players, Brad Daugherty and Mark Price, who weren't feeling well enough to play a fair share of minutes. Plus, Dennis Rodman was a defensive specialist in a game that traditionally ignored defense, so he didn't even want to play. The West was coached by Don Nelson, so they played what I call "Nellie Ball," which was mostly isolations, and a lot of two- and three-man stuff—the kind of loose, individual play that most guys enjoy, especially in a game like that.

If I was sincerely motivated to win All-Star Game 2000, there were a number of other distractions that I had to deal with. First off, Karl Malone had announced that he was hurt and was going to skip the All-Star game. Well, the league wasn't too happy about that, and they basically forced him to play. The reality was that Karl has two children (a boy and a girl) with a former girlfriend living in Louisiana. Both of the kids were basketball players, one in high school and the other in college, and Karl had never had the opportunity to see either of them play. As a result, Karl missed the media session and the practice and showed up just for the All-Star game itself. I took it upon myself to cover for Karl during his absence: "We all know what a great competitor Karl is ..." Blah, blah, and blah. And when Karl finally arrived, it was clear that he really didn't want to play at all. After talking it over with him, we decided he'd play for only five minutes. David Robinson showed up with a stiff back, so I didn't play him much either.

Before the game, Jason Kidd and Kobe told me that Jason and Gary Payton had grown up playing in the same schoolyard in Oakland, so the hometown crowd would really love to see them play together. Well, there were only approximately five thousand hometown fans there anyway, because the NBA always takes over about three-quarters of the All-Star game tickets to distribute to their corporate sponsors. (At any All-Star game, the season ticket holders are routinely x'ed out.) Since Kobe and Jason had been voted as the starting backcourt, it was a nice gesture for Kobe to voluntarily give up a big chunk of his playing time to Payton. This was a far cry from Kobe's first All-Star appearance at Madison Square Garden in 1998. In that game, Kobe was so totally focused on outdueling Michael Jordan that late in the game he'd dribbled the ball into the front court and waved Karl Malone out of the pivot so that he'd have the space to try to drive and dunk on MJ. A nineteen-year-old kid telling a future Hall of Famer to get out of his way! Karl was irritated, and understandably so, but had long since gotten over the insult. So Kobe's deferring to Gary Payton was an important sign of the young man's growth. Of course, Jason and Gary got to play together for nearly seven minutes in the first quarter and had a wonderful time.

After the game, I had dinner with my three daughters, Elizabeth, Chelsea, and Brooke, then I took the first flight out the next morning to meet the Lakers in Chicago.

This was my first return to Chicago, and I had John Black, the Lakers' director of public relations, set up a press conference so that I could deal with all the media demands at the same time and there was quite a turnout. Then someone asked me about next season's crop of free agents, which featured Tim Duncan and Grant Hill. The only teams that had salary-cap room for both of them were Chicago and Orlando, and a sportswriter asked me if I thought the Bulls had a chance to sign either Duncan or Hill or maybe both. Doc Rivers, the Magic's coach, had already been lobbying for Orlando, emphasizing the sunny weather, the chance to play golf all year round, and the absence of a state income tax in Florida. "The Bulls have a great chance," I said, "because Chicago is such a wonderful city. It's a hundred and fifty years old, and it has wonderful architecture, museums, and the lake. Chicago also has the opera, an NFL team, two baseball teams, lots of clubs where you can hear some old-timers play the blues, plus the influence of several major colleges. I don't think that players are going to avoid Chicago because of Jerry Krause or because they don't want to play with a team that's rebuilding. There's some grist to Chicago. It's a city with heart and soul. Orlando doesn't have a heart. It's a plastic city."

At game time, I wasn't sure how I'd be received by the Chicago fans, but they gave me a standing ovation that really touched my heart. The Lakers got off to a very slow start and only scored thirty-six points in the first half. We were very sluggish, and our execution of the offense had regressed over the break. Despite not shooting well, we managed to win by 88–76.

We flew to Charlotte for a game the very next night, and we were behind until the fourth quarter. The Hornets were a good ball club that always gave us trouble. But another twist to the game was the rivalry that existed between Eddie Jones and Kobe. Eddie had been a Laker when Kobe first joined the team in 1996, and since they both played the same position, they went head-to-head in practice for almost three years. Of course, Eddie was then traded to Charlotte along with Elden Campbell for Glen Rice (and a pair of alphabetical throw-ins—J. R. Reid and B. J. Armstrong) in March 1999. Jones was a three-time All-Star and had just started for the East in San Francisco, so he and Kobe were more competitive than ever. Kobe finished with twenty-six points, and we came from behind to win the game by 92–86.

Wouldn't you know that our next stop was in Orlando? It turned out that my press conference in Chicago had been shown live in Orlando, and when we came to town, the press was all fired up. There were headlines all over the place—Jackson Calls Orlando Plastic City! I've always had a good relationship with the Orlando Magic's organization. I'd coached the All-Star game there in 1992, and the Bulls were treated well during a play-off series there four years later. I was kind of irked at the media for focusing on what I'd just said in Chicago, but I did say it, so I had to eat my own words.

It's strange the way things sometimes turn out. Shaq had begun his pro career with the Magic and played there for four years before signing with the Lakers as a free agent in 1996. The Orlando media, as well as the fans, still resented what they regarded as Shaq's defection. So everybody started saying that I had deliberately made my "plastic city" remark to deflect all of the abuse that Shaq is usually faced with whenever he returns to Orlando. Another brilliant coaching move!

Doc Rivers was doing an outstanding coaching job, and the Magic pressed, trapped, and always played their hearts out, so we had trouble establishing an offensive rhythm in the ensuing ball game. But Shaq was incredible. He scored thirty-nine points, had fourteen rebounds, and with only seventeen seconds left in regulation, he also stole an inbounds pass and went the length of the court for a dunk that tied the score and gave us the opportunity to win in overtime.

Our next game, in Philadelphia, was highlighted by the way that Kobe defended Allen Iverson. Our game plan was to force Iverson left and then jump him with our big guys. Iverson was only about six feet tall, and his tendency was to try to make precision passes while he was still in the air, so being two-timed by a couple of bigs cut down on Iverson's field of vision and often created turnovers. This left us vulnerable to some offensive rebounds, but it was well worth the trade. After a close first half, Kobe held Iverson scoreless from the field, and we won going away. This was the game that made people around the league start to realize that Kobe could be a stopper on the defensive end.

The game in Philadelphia was also interesting because the trading deadline had just passed, and the Sixers had dealt for a player that we wanted—Toni Kukoc. There had been some talk between the Lakers and the Bulls, but we couldn't reach an agreement.

The weeks and days leading up to the trading deadline can create tensions in a ball club. When a guy's name is bandied about as being on the trading block, he understandably gets the idea that his current team doesn't want him anymore. That's why, except for saying that Kukoc was a great player, I avoided any public dialogue about any potential trades we were seeking.

In reality we were looking to find a backup center, because John Salley and Travis Knight were both rather lightweight centers. And we also needed another long-range shooter who could take advantage of Shaq's being constantly double-teamed. But nothing worked out for us, and barring any injuries, we were fairly well satisfied with what we already had.

The Nets were next, and Stephon Marbury was the story. New Jersey had just come back from an emotional win in Minnesota, which marked the first time Marbury had played there since forcing the Timberwolves to trade him. Marbury had scored thirty-nine against his former team, and he was riding high. We only beat the Nets by 97–89, but the game was more of a cruise for us than the score indicated. Marbury had a seventeen-point third quarter, and no matter what we tried against him, we couldn't even slow him down.

It was back-to-back time, and we flew into Cleveland to play the following evening. Shaq had some early foul trouble against the Cavaliers and wasn't his normal dominating self. What bailed us out, however, was Robert Horry coming off the bench to hit five three-pointers. The final score was 116–98 and aside from Robert's performance, it was the Cavaliers' rookie guard, Andre Miller, who impressed me the most. I think Miller is as good as any guard who's come into the league for a long time. He plays with terrific poise and control, and he knows how to get to his favorite spaces on the floor. Miller probably won't threaten anybody for the NBA's scoring title, but he'll develop into an outstanding player who can help his team get to the next level.

There are several guards who I would consider to be great ballplayers but who couldn't play in the Triangle. Guys who play with their heads up so that they can see the floor, who aren't interested in hogging the ball, and who have multiple skills—those are the kind of guards I like to have on my side. If their shots aren't falling during a ball game, they can contribute by making intelligent passes, playing defense, rebounding, and/or moving without the ball to create space for their teammates to score.

After playing in Cleveland, we had a short stretch at home where we defeated the Celtics and then the Rockets before traveling up to Portland for a showdown with the Trail Blazers. Both Portland and the Lakers had an identical record (46–11); each was riding an eleven-game winning streak, and both were light-years ahead of the next best team in the Western Conference.

At the time, our point of emphasis in the offense was to shift the triangle from one side to the other. We'd build our triangle, bring the ball in to Shaq, see what the defense was doing, then pass it back out, swing the ball to the weak side, rebuild another triangle there, and look for Shaq as he crossed the lane. Sometimes we'd go with Shaq in the solo post and find him there. We weren't playing weak-side ball as well as I would have liked to, so I wasn't quite sure if we were ready to handle the Blazers in such a big game on their home court.

Before the game I made an offhanded remark to one of the L.A. sportswriters: "I think the team that wins this game will develop enough momentum to probably not only win the division and the conference, but to wind up with the best record in the league as well."

As much as we had progressed since last playing Portland five weeks before, Scottie was still able to periodically disrupt our offense. The difference this time was twofold—our defense, and Shaq's newfound ability to make his free throws (shooting 9–13). Arvydas Sabonis had a good game against Shaq, but we were able to corral both Damon Stoudamire and Rasheed Wallace, both of whom had gotten out of our control in the previous games. Another difference was the fact that when Sabonis got himself into foul trouble (which he usually does against Shaq), Wallace moved into the center spot, and Shaq manhandled him. Scottie had nineteen points but missed a desperate three-pointer down the stretch, whereas Robert canned an important three-pointer for us. So we came away with a gutsy 90–87 victory. Afterward Portland managed to hang with us for about a week before slowly fading.

Aside from our mounting another winning streak, there was another important development during this particular part of the season that boded well for the Lakers. It was the difference in Kobe. With so many games on the road, he started to socialize more and more with his teammates. A bunch of them even went to a movie together.

Back home to play the Vancouver Grizzlies. Again, Robert had a big game off the bench to the tune of ten points, seven rebounds, and three assists, and we won by 103–91. We followed this up with a pair of one-sided home wins against first Indiana, and then Miami. The L.A. Clippers were our next opponent in a "road" game at the Staples Arena. Well, Shaq went to town, scoring sixty-one as his own twenty-eighth birthday present to himself. We had another big win at Golden State before a wild win at home versus the Sacramento Kings. The Kings were a dangerous team with lots of firepower throughout their lineup. They were up by twelve to start the fourth quarter, but Shaq and Kobe combined for seventy points and thirty rebounds, and we pulled out the game by 109–106.

Sacramento had a second-year guard named Jason Williams, who attracted a lot of attention with his behind-the-back-no-lookers and his full repertoire of passing fancies. I'm sure that somebody in NBA Entertainment saw Williams play and said, "This kid's great! This kid's great! Right?" Then somebody else said, "He's real exciting, and he does all kinds of tricks!" And I think the NBA just jumped the gun by promoting Williams as part of the new wave of players. The Kings' coach, Rick Adelman, did a great job trying to let Williams develop by giving him the first and third quarters and letting him play a speed game. The rest of the time, the Kings used a more balanced unit keyed by Tony Delk at the point and using Predrag Stojakovic and Jon Barry as their featured scorers.

But despite Adelman's good intentions, the hype definitely hurt Williams's growth. Of course, after the NBA started ballyhooing the kid, whichever sneaker company he was tied to made things even worse. Look at all of the sneaker commercials, and what do you see? Guys beating somebody one-on-one and then pounding on their chests or making grotesque faces by way of celebration. The whole thing's over the edge, and it encourages the worst kind of on-court hijinks. Most of the players on my teams haven't gotten into that kind of ego-indulgent behavior, because they know where the emphasis has to be—on the team.

Anyway, we went into Denver and escaped with a ten-point victory when Brian Shaw hit two consecutive three-pointers to keep the

Nuggets from catching us. The win moved our latest streak to nineteen games.

I felt that during this streak, we played on a much higher level than we had in December–January. Our ball reversal was improved, and our defense was more consistent. On an individual basis, Shaq was confident that he had mastered the system, and he even wanted to play the lead guard position. This was actually an idea that I was seriously considering, and I remembered that when Don Nelson coached the Knicks, he had experimented with Anthony Mason by making him a point forward. (It remains totally possible that someday I'll let Shaq play point center.) What I did, however, was to install more high-post action so that Shaq could handle the ball about eighteen feet away from the basket.

As for the rest of the team: Glen was still not comfortable moving without the ball. He also continued to resist vacating those spaces on the court where he'd historically scored his points. Kobe was still aborting plays and going off on his own too much to suit me. Robert had great basketball intelligence, and once he ditched his protective mask, he was a player who could make good things happen on both ends of the court. A. C. was thriving. Brian Shaw was still feeling his way around the offense a little bit. Derek Fisher was a natural in the system.

So there we were, riding high and arriving in Washington to play the Wizards, a lottery team for the past several seasons. Well, Kobe was in foul trouble early, and that was the key to the game. Kobe was matched up against Mitch Richmond, and there were at least three unbelievable calls that went the Wizards' way. Kobe never argued with the refs no matter how the calls went, so he was just dumbfounded. There was one obvious foul against Richmond that was never called—and then late in the game, after Glen had led us back from a twenty-one-point deficit, Richmond drove to the basket and was obviously tripped by Harp. We were all baffled when the ref whistled Kobe for his sixth foul. Nothing really worked for us that night, and our winning streak was history.

Our next opponent was the Detroit Pistons, who ranked only behind the Kings in team offense. The Pistons were on a modest four-game win streak and were playing very well under new head coach George Irvine. But we played terrific defense and trounced them by twenty-eight points.

On to New York, where Shaq had his way with Ewing to the tune of forty-three points. Again, our defense was sharp and although our winning margin was only eight points, we successfully controlled the tempo of the game. The next game at Miami was our fourth road game in five days. There was always the chance of a letdown after playing the Knicks on national television, and we were pretty much burned out. Indeed, we trailed by thirteen at the half (57–44) before turning up the screws on the defensive end and winning by 100–89. Glen and Shaq each had twenty-eight points, and the Heats' total of only thirty-two rebounds was crucial. It would have been easy for us to lose the game, but we gutted it out. Looking back over the season, I came to believe that this particular game was the turning point for us, the one that proved we were capable of winning the championship.

Returning to friendly L.A., we blew out Golden State. Next up was Phoenix, also at home, and on the day between these two games, Rick Fox stopped by the office to speak to me.

Rick told me about how erratic his play had been, not only this season but ever since he'd been in the league. Some of the things he did on the court were absolutely nonsensical, and the players had a name for it—"Rick Ball." Rick believed that he could trace the source of his difficulties to his final game as a collegian at North Carolina against Kansas in the Hoosier Dome during the NCAA tournament. Rick had felt primed for the ball game—this would be his opportunity to establish himself as one of the best college players in the country, and all of his dreams would be fulfilled. But he was unnerved when his coach, the legendary Dean Smith, had a disagreement with a referee and was thrown off the bench. Anyway, Rick shot poorly, and UNC had basically fumbled the game away. Rick believed that this game created some sort of mental block that he still needed to overcome.

Rick had been drafted by the Boston Celtics and had had a very frustrating rookie season under coach Chris Ford. It's okay for coaches to be tough on rookies, but Rick got there when Boston was falling from prominence after many years among the NBA's elite; and it seems that he was subjected to a lot of abuse in practices and in huddles. So he'd go out on the floor and compound whatever mistakes he'd already been making. Even now, Rick would get into some kind of a zone where crazy things would happen to him.

As a direct result of our discussion, I decided to let Rick play significant minutes against Phoenix at both forward positions. And sure enough, he was involved in several weird sequences. Basically, Rick had five turnovers in the last two minutes of the game, but only one counted in the score book. One time, he drove the lane and tripped on his way to the basket. On his way down, he threw a wild pass to the wing that the defensive player tried to grab but only managed to bat the ball into the air. Of course the ball fell back into Rick's hands just as he was climbing to his feet. Rick caught the batted ball, shot it at the basket, and bingo! In it went. On another occasion, Rick threw an errant pass that hit a defensive player in the shoulder and once again bounced back to him. Then there was the wounded duck pass that Rick tossed to nobody, and Cliff Robinson was about to intercept—except that Robinson ran into a referee and lost the ball out of bounds, so we retained possession.

Meanwhile, on the bench, Tex's reaction was, "Take him out! Take him out!"

Poor Rick. Sometimes he just closed down on the court and got so rigid that he couldn't get a handle on the game. We squeezed out a victory, and Rick came to me after the game to thank me for staying with him. The truth was that I believed in Rick because he's a big-time shot maker, a sound defender, and he understood the offense.

After that, we went up to Sacramento to play the Kings, and it was one of the darnedest ball games of the year. The score was tight throughout, but we really couldn't get any rhythm in our game. Chris Webber had a monster first half, scoring twenty-two points and routinely hitting his jumper. He's a little too quick for A. C., but Robert succeeded in slowing him down in the second half. Nothing else that I tried seemed to work. I ran some screen/rolls for Kobe on the wing, but they chased him to the baseline, and he lost the ball a few times. Anyway, we were scratching and biting and down by three with the game ticking down when Kobe made a layup to cut our deficit to one point with twenty seconds to go. Of course we had to foul, so Adelman put five guards on the floor, who were presumably his team's best free-throw shooters. So we fouled Derek Martin, an 85 percent shooter from the line. After he made the first shot, I called a time-out and diagrammed a play. The second shot was a miss, and since I'd already called the play, we took the ball right down the court. Webber had fouled out, and except for Vlade Divac, the Kings still had a small lineup on the floor, probably to protect against a three-point shot. Anyway, Kobe rubbed off a big pick by Shaq, and Divac stepped too far toward Kobe, leaving Shaq open under the basket. The pass, the catch, the dunk, and a foul on Martin. Shaq made the free throw, and we were up by one with four seconds left—plenty of time for the Kings to run a play. Williams drove hard to the middle, made Shaq commit, then pitched the ball back out to Divac for the shot that would either win or lose the game. Now, there wasn't enough time left for Divac to do anything but catch and shoot, and there was Shaq, running from the shadow of the basket to jump and block Divac's shot. It was a remarkable play, because Shaq had covered at least twenty feet.

It was a big win for us; Sacramento had played us tough all season long.

This was followed by a surprisingly difficult win on the road in Vancouver. Rick Fox had a fine ball game in place of Glen, who was out with a stomach virus, and Kobe led us with twenty-eight points.

Next on the agenda were a Friday-night game against the Sixers and a Sunday-afternoon date with the Knicks—both at the Staples Arena. I told the local reporters that there was no way we'd win both games. Philly was on a streak, having just beaten Indiana, Minnesota, and Seattle on the road, and the Knicks figured to be sky-high and out for revenge.

Under Larry Brown's leadership, the Sixers had become a very solid ball club. Larry's strategy against us was to play their center, Matt Geiger, away from the basket and try to draw Shaq out. Geiger did have twenty points, mostly on outside jumpers, but he needed twenty-two shots, so I still considered his output to be a victory for the defense. Once again, the difference was our team defense (headed by Kobe) on Iverson, forcing him left and jumping him with a big man. Iverson finished with fifteen points while shooting only 6–20 from the floor.

The Knicks game was a total surprise. We were their fifth road opponent in eight days, and teams usually get their chops up for their final game on a road trip. We were in control of the action, leading by eleven late in the third quarter, when Kobe got into a tussle with Chris Childs. Kobe was standing there with his hands down, and Childs butted Kobe's chin, then threw two quick sucker punches at Kobe's head before Kobe reacted by flipping an elbow into Childs's chest. They were both ejected, and I'd never seen Kobe so riled up. He felt like he'd been totally chumped, and he even wanted to chase Childs into the locker room. "I'm sorry I didn't get in the first punch," Kobe said. (For their scuffle, Kobe was suspended for one game, and Childs for two games.)

Glen hit several important baskets, and Shaq once again overpowered Ewing in the low post. He was quick and active, and he was able to anticipate Ewing's moves to the hoop. The final score was 106–82, the Knicks' worst beating of the season.

Back-to-back road games against Phoenix and Golden State were our next obstacles. Being able to win in back-to-back situations is one mark of a superior team. Conditioning is a factor; so is having young, sprightly players. Power helps, too, and being able to play a slow-down game is another plus. Up until that point in the season, our record in back-to-back games was 23–1. We'd lost the front end of one sequence, but never the second game.

I'd been planning to give Harp some rest starting with the Phoenix game, but with Kobe suspended, Harp had to lace them up.

The Suns' Penny Hardaway always gave us some trouble, but without Kobe we expected at least a migraine headache. In addition, Phoenix's trademark was having active, quick players and playing an uptempo pace. To make our plight even worse, Shaq had twinged a hamstring muscle against Miami, and he hadn't been as active on the defensive end ever since. Even though Shaq only captured four rebounds for the game, Robert contributed eleven points and eleven rebounds, and we escaped Phoenix with a one-point victory.

The next night, Shaq was the only player who could get anything accomplished against Golden State. The Warriors kept sending big bodies to the boards, and they decimated us in the rebounding department. We had hoped for an easy game, considering Golden State's poor record, but we were forced to play hard from tip to buzzer. Fortunately, Shaq scored forty-nine points, and his hamstring seemed to have been cured overnight. Unfortunately, Shaq turned up the next morning at practice with a slightly sprained ankle.

I knew that Shaq had turned the ankle, but I was used to Michael playing every night come hell or high water, so I didn't give the injury much thought. The X rays and MRI were negative, but we decided to be cautious with the play-offs on tap. Also, Shaq was wearing down some, and we'd actually been looking for an excuse to give him some time off.

We needed to finish off the season by winning all of our remaining six games to bring our season's total to seventy. In truth, winning seventy meant nothing, but I told the guys it was important only as a way to try to keep their juices flowing. In fact, it had been several weeks since we'd clinched having the league's best record and enjoying the home-court advantage throughout the play-offs. And the guys really hadn't let up.

San Antonio was our opponent, and I wanted to beat them even without Shaq. I always felt that the Spurs were one of the teams that could easily upset our applecart in postseason play.

There was also some bad blood between the Spurs and me because of something I'd said about last season's championship. In point of fact they had been the best team in the NBA, but the season itself had been different, lasting only fifty games after the lockout was resolved. When thirty-two games are missing, that adds up to two and a half months of play; so the Spurs were never challenged over the long haul. On the other hand, teams with older players got wasted by having to play four games every week. The Utah Jazz, for example, had to play sixteen games in the last twenty-seven days of the season, and they were totally burned out. I was only trying to have some fun with the Spurs when I said they were the champions of an asterisk season.

Anyway, without our big man in the middle, we just didn't have enough energy or size to challenge the Spurs for more than one quarter. We made too many mistakes at too many critical junctures. Until I found out that Robert and Fish were nursing injuries, I was very disappointed with the way our second unit performed. Kobe also went retro—playing hard, but forcing his dribble into traffic.

All in all, our execution of the Triangle was poor, and the way they played told me that the guys really didn't trust the system. They took quick shots and subsequently weren't in good rebounding position or retreat defense. Even though we only had nine turnovers for the game, the Spurs converted them into eighteen points—and that was the ball game. Had we run the offense, we would have gotten decent shots and would have prevented the Spurs from running out. I wasn't very happy.

Of course, we had the excuse that Shaq hadn't played, but it was a crutch that I didn't care to use. The game was important to us as a chance to see which of our players would step up and put their hearts on the line. A. C. was one, and so was Harp.

So we went back to the drawing board at practice the next day. I told them that champions always compete, regardless of who is or isn't playing. We had an hour-long video session, which I thought went very well. They seemed to be focused and willing to admit their own errors.

Shaq was still out, so Seattle at home was another big test for us, an opportunity to reestablish the validity of our entire system. And most of the guys did pick up the challenge. John Salley was effective, and Kobe was mostly under control. We went into the fourth quarter up by thirteen points, but then our second unit let the Sonics back into the game. We needed a last-ditch shot by Glen to get us into overtime, where we eventually prevailed.

Next for us was a Sunday-afternoon home game against the Minnesota Timberwolves, a rapidly improving team under the direction of Flip Saunders, one of the best young coaches in the league. Flip had also served his apprenticeship in the CBA, and I'd coached against him a couple of times at the end of my tenure there. I thought so highly of him that we interviewed him in Chicago when we had to replace Johnny Bach on the coaching staff. Ultimately I had decided on Jimmy Rodgers, but Flip was very impressive.

I'm likewise impressed with Flip's offensive system. Basically it's an adaptation of what Hubie Brown did in Atlanta in the late 1970s, so it's called the Hawk series. The offense is initiated by the two-guard making a diagonal cut off a high post (which can be either the power forward or the center), then either posting, moving to the wing, or coming back and setting a rip screen for the player at the high post. There are two screeners on the weak side and the opportunity for all kinds of screen/roll action, plus post-ups, pop-ups, and a lot of fluid motion. The Timberwolves work the offense on both sides of the floor, which isn't normally done in the Hawk Series. The offense is perfectly suited to the quickness and multiple skills of Kevin Garnett. On defense, Flip runs a variety of half-court traps and an excellent half-court zone.

Shaq was ready to play again, and we were coming into the last three games of the season with the possibility of winning sixty-nine games, a total that would match the team record set by Bill Sharman's Lakers in 1972, but the guys were somewhat worn-out. I had hoped to rest Harper at the end of the season, but that hadn't been possible because Derek Fisher had to go on the injured list with some bone spurs in his ankle. We were definitely up for the game, though, because of the possibility that we'd have to face the Timberwolves in the upcoming play-offs.

It turned out that Minnesota really played us well. They were able to establish the kind of quick tempo that they liked, and they were very active on defense (being particularly quick and efficient in doubling Shaq). At the other end, we had some trouble with their high screen/rolls; then Terrell Brandon and Garnett had a couple of hot streaks, so we really had to screw up our defense. Eventually we were able to win the game on defense when Kobe came up with a last-second steal.

So we headed down to Texas to finish the regular season with back-to-back games in Dallas and San Antonio. Even though the

Mavericks hadn't beaten the Lakers in eighteen consecutive games, they'd come on in a rush during the last thirty games of the season and were now one of the top three or four teams in the West. Don Nelson was famous for what we called Nellie-Ball, which featured a small lineup and a series of pinch-post moves that created switches that the Mavericks could exploit. Nelson had already announced his retirement (he later signed a new three-year extension), and the game was heralded as his farewell. Another flip to the game was that Del Harris, who'd coached the Lakers for five seasons before being fired in 1998, was now one of Nelson's assistants. Moreover, Dallas was one of the teams that Bill Bertka was responsible for scouting, and he really wanted to win the game. Before the players took the court, Bill reemphasized the desirability of winning sixty-nine games and thereby stepping up to an historic level of accomplishment.

Our guys played hard up to a point. I thought they were secretly thinking that since we'd already clinched the best record in the league and would have home-court advantage throughout the play-offs, the game wasn't really too important. How many of them knew and/or cared about the 1972 Lakers? So the game was close for most of the first half, but the guys were unwilling to find a way to fight to the bitter end, so they ultimately gave it up, and we took our lumps. I wasn't too upset because over the course of any season there are just too many games in too many cities, and sometimes you just can't get it done.

On to San Antonio to close out the "first season." The Spurs were a ball club that we'd struggled against all year, and there was a good chance we'd be facing them in the second round of the play-offs. Tim Duncan was out with a knee injury. At the time, the injury was considered to be a day-to-day situation, and everybody expected Duncan to be ready for the postseason. I told my starters that none of them would be playing more than thirty minutes, but I still believed it was important for us to win the game.

The San Antonio fans were still incensed about my disparaging comments concerning the Spurs' championship in last year's lockout season. But our starters played well enough to gain a fifteen-point lead going into the fourth quarter. I kept Kobe out there because he had missed some games and needed some conditioning work. Otherwise, the outcome rested strictly in the hands of the bench players. I thought this would be an opportunity for these guys to gear up their games and get ready for the play-offs. But the roof caved in. Travis Knight couldn't handle Duncan's replacement, Samaki Walker, and the game went into overtime. I put Shaq back in to try to win the tip-off, but David Robinson outjumped him. Once play began, the clock didn't stop, so I couldn't get Shaq out as quickly as I wanted to. It turned out that Robinson simply outplayed Shaq by a wide margin, and we got blown away. There was one touchy situation when Shaq very nearly got a flagrant foul, so I burned a quick time-out and sat him down.

The team's mood was somber in the locker room. The starters knew that the bench had let them down, and because of them, the team would be going into the play-offs on a down note. I knew that I had to pick them up in a hurry.

"Let it go," I said. "Don't get yourselves into a snit because we lost two games in a row. It's only the third time we've done that this season. Shrug it off. We've just finished one season, and the play-offs are another separate season. There's no continuity, no carryover, from one to the other. We have the best record in the NBA, and home-court advantage against everybody. This is something we've worked hard to accomplish, so we have every reason to feel positive about ourselves."

Indeed, I felt good about the current status of the team, and on the long flight home, I mentally reviewed how much we'd progressed throughout the season: they still didn't play as consistently hard as the Bulls—that level of concentration was beyond them—but they did compete with all their might for short stretches. On the plus side, they'd certainly learned how to play contain defense and force opponents to shoot from the outside. They'd also learned how to play transition defense, something that was absolutely necessary for any team with championship aspirations. They knew a variety of ways to initially format their offense and deliver the ball to Shaq, but there were certain nuances of the Triangle that they were still struggling with.

The most important aspects of the Triangle that they lacked were the counteractions—swinging the ball and re-forming the triangle on the weak side. The first two key passes would happen smoothly, but they'd have difficulty with the four and the five passes, so the offense would get stuck on one side of the floor. They were also grappling with creating and maintaining the proper spacing needed for isolations. Neither had they quite mastered the use of screen/rolls within the context of the offense.

Overall, I couldn't help being pleased with our season. We'd won sixty-seven games on Shaq's back, and I was looking forward to the play-offs. We'd proved that we could shoot well from the perimeter, that (disregarding our last loss to San Antonio) our bench play was more than adequate, that we had much more of a community consciousness than we did at the start of the season, and that we were physically strong enough to win a championship. But the one trait of this team that made me believe that a title was truly within our grasp was their heart.

III. BEYOND WINNING

THIRTEEN

ON THE SCENE

CHARLEY

During the process of coauthoring this book, I made five separate trips to Los Angeles. It was interesting to see Phil in his new world. He seemed still to be trying to define himself without his family. Paradoxically, L.A. seemed at first to be a more claustrophobic environment for Phil than Chicago had been. Sure, he went out in public to dine just about every night, yet now he was assuming a persona I hadn't seen before—more aware of himself as a public figure and therefore more zealous in defense of his privacy. Phil was also much more formal with the local media than he'd been in Chicago, keeping his distance as though still trying to figure out who were the good guys and who were the bad guys. Some things hadn't changed: underneath the facade, Phil was still compassionate in his own spartan fashion and unimpressed by celebrity, including his own. So I wondered if his subtle discomfort didn't stem from his missing the ring-around-the-blue-collar Bulls fans.

I was very much surprised at how lenient Phil was with his players. It was incredible, for example, how casually the Lakers approached practice sessions. Even though Shaq was the nominal captain, he didn't always show the competitive drive that had defined Michael Jordan's genius and that had compelled the Bulls to play balls-out whenever somebody kept score.

Was Phil—mirroring his new team or influenced by the incessant sunshine—becoming too much of a mellow fellow?

I watched the Lakers play in late April as the regular season was coming to an end—and I wasn't confident about their ability to elevate their game to a championship level. Phil, of course, knew them far better than I did, so I trusted his trust in them.

As I traveled around and about L.A. with Phil, I interviewed several players and coaches, and I also kept track of whatever I observed that revealed something about the city, the Lakers fans, the game, and/or myself. Everything I saw seemed connected in some way—as if I were looking into a kaleidoscope—to the onward momentum of Phil and the team....

Zooming along eastward on a ten-lane speedway on our way to a ball game, bumper-to-bumper at seventy miles per hour, the traffic moving in the opposite direction just as swiftly—until just before the Pico Street exit, one of the westbound lanes is backed up behind a rusty gray VW van. Two young Chicano men are standing outside the van, stripped to their waists, their backs, chests, and arms displaying numerous tattoos of unfamiliar geometric shapes and symbols. Laughing all the while, both young men are blatantly peeing in the middle of the freeway as several of their friends cheer them on from inside the van.

With their penises dangling in the breeze and the sunshine glittering on the gushing streams of their urine, the young men's faces glow with power. *Here! Look at us! We're strong enough to piss where you live, and you can't do shit!* And the motorists stacked up behind them are indeed intimidated. Instead of leaning on their horns or shouting curses, they quietly try to change lanes.

The rage of the young men is frightening. At the same time, there is something gutsy about what they are doing. What would happen if a cop showed up? *Who cares? Fuck them too!* Their freedom is on the line, yet the act of inviting danger—*bring it on*—is a source of pride to them.

And I can't help but admire their spirited reaction to the racism and economic oppression that blight their lives. How much better than to sit passively in front of a TV set and mindlessly gulp down all the fantasy and propaganda that passes for entertainment.

It's midway through the first quarter of a late-season game against the Minnesota Timberwolves, and an Elvis impersonator is sitting in a two-hundred-dollar seat near the end zone. He wears a white jumpsuit, dark sunglasses, and a glitzy gold-colored medallion that hangs around his neck. His black hair is slicked back, and a pair of phony black sideburns are glued to the sides of his face. During a time out, he jumps into the aisle and starts gyrating his pelvis as he holds a Let's Go, Lakers! sign above his head. The crowd, used to much slicker forgeries, blithely ignores him. During every time-out and after each quarter, the ersatz Elvis repeats his act. No matter how many times he pumps his hands to encourage a response, his practiced hysteria is utterly disregarded. Undeterred, he repeats his act perhaps two dozen times during the course of the game.

A. C. GREEN: "The Triangle brings a sense of having to pay attention to details, which I enjoy. I had a taste of it in Dallas when JC coached there. For me, the Triangle is just the way basketball is supposed to be played. You pass the ball, you cut and pick, until somebody gets a good shot. It's also reassuring to be in a certain format at all times, and understand the synergy."

The walls in Phil's office at the Healthcenter where the Lakers practice are mostly decorated the way they were at the Berto Center in Chicago, with artifacts sacred to Native Americans: a Hopi ax, a war bonnet, a tobacco pouch, a bear claw necklace. Other objects that have been sent by fans and admirers include a "Welcome to L.A. Earthquake Kit" courtesy of the local Red Cross, which contains a flashlight, radio batteries, blankets, a bottle of water, and a small box of first-aid supplies. Also on Phil's desk are two Shinto porcelain kittens that have been blessed by Japanese masters; a cluster of origami swans; several dozen mechanical apparatuses meant to improve Shaq's free-throw shooting (arm braces, rubber devices, and various springs); a carton of Korean ginseng tea; a small yet extremely heavy piece of meteorite.

There's also a framed piece of parchment upon which someone named "D. Gerch" has hand-printed an inspirational free verse:

> Meekness in itself
> is nothing else
> than true knowing and feeling
> of a man's self as he is.
> Any man who truly
> sees and feels himself as he is
> must surely be meek indeed.
> —Anon

HORACE GRANT: "I played the Triangle under PJ for five years in Chicago. It took me a year to get comfortable in it, but I eventually started making the proper reads. The trouble with the Triangle is that if one player misreads, then the whole thing gets messed up. On the other hand, the Triangle is very hard to defend because there are so many available options. In the long run, the Triangle is also much easier on a player's body because you're constantly moving away from pressure and just sailing around the court. After the Triangle, regular offenses seem too simple and too inefficient. You're either bumping and grinding against the defense or else you're standing around and waiting your turn. The physicalness wears you down, and the waiting takes the edge off your game. Somewhere, sometime, I would love to play the Triangle again."

Just before a practice session, Shaq is tossing around a football with a ball boy. Shaq throws perfect spirals, and his passes are on the mark. On the receiving end, he runs surprisingly quick-footed patterns and makes one-handed catches as easily as an outfielder flagging down fly balls.

What a tight end he would've made (so long as nobody tackled him below his knees)!

Vlade Divac is playing with one technical foul when he reacts to another call against him by throwing the ball wide and hard in the general vicinity of the offending referee, Jimmy Clark. The home-towns Laker fans are aroused, and Clark plays along with them, holding one thumb up and cupping his ear to hear the crowd's reaction, then doing the same thing with one thumb down.

What a grandstanding buffoon! Why does Clark go out of his way to embarrass Divac?

The crowd clamors for the T and Divac's subsequent banishment, but Clark won't make the call.

Sitting in the coaches' office and telling Rick Barry stories:

Even though he was the first All-Star player to jump from the NBA to the fledgling American Basketball Association, Barry always disdained the new league. Once, when he was playing with the New York Nets, he let his teammates know in no uncertain terms that he was the best player in the league. When the other Nets players bristled, Barry challenged them to a one-on-one tournament—he would go through the entire roster, and should anyone defeat him, he'd pay them each one hundred dollars. One after another, Barry trounced his teammates, laughing all the while.

Later, when Barry returned to the NBA, he played with the Houston Rockets under coach Del Harris. There was a lot of conflict on the team, and Del Harris called the team together one day. Harris was a fervent believer in the power of visualization, and he told the players to visualize the source of all the conflict being placed into a black leather bag. Then they were to visualize themselves walking out onto the middle of a bridge, where they would throw the bag into the water, and as the black bag sank below the surface of the water, all of the conflicts would vanish. Harris repeated this scenario a few times, embellishing all the details, and then he told everybody to come back to the here and now. Billy Paultz opened his eyes, turned to face Rick Barry, blinked once, and said, "Rick, how come you're still here?"

To keep Phil away from the media hordes in the Staples Center's press room, his dinner is delivered to the coaches' office about an hour and a half before game time. These semiprivate meals are always simple—some kind of broiled fish with rice, a steamed vegetable, a bountiful salad, and a basketful of dark, crusty bread. When Phil has eaten, he stacks the tray, plates, silverware, and metal food warmers on the floor near the door. Phil rarely touches his bread.

Meanwhile, Tex feeds for free in the "Chick Hearn Press Room," a chancy undertaking that tonight offers cold cuts, white bread, salad, and brownies. A child of the Great Depression, Tex eats with a rapacious two-handed quickness. In the heyday of the Bulls, whenever Tex chowed down with Jerry "Crumbs" Krause, any other tablemates would keep their distance so as not to get caught in the crossfire.

The subsequent game is a feverish overtime victory over Seattle, and by the time the Lakers coaches have rehashed the game and Phil has addressed the media, smoked a cigar, and packed up his black leather briefcase for his exit stage left, the remains of his dinner are still waiting to be collected. Before Tex leaves the office, he carefully rummages through the basket of untouched bread and extracts several pieces, which he stuffs into his own briefcase.

The coaches will convene tomorrow morning at the Healthcenter at ten a.m., an hour before the players are due.

STEVE KERR: "It used to be easy to double-team Shaq. Now that he's playing in the Triangle, however, all of the offensive players are in constant motion, so the defense can't use a designated double-teamer anymore."

For the June 1997 issue of *Sport* magazine I wrote a story called "The Portland Jailblazers," documenting the arrest records of Isaiah Rider (drug possession, possession of stolen goods, assault), Jermaine O'Neal (assault), Dontonio Wingfield (assault), and Rasheed Wallace (assault). The Portland organization has a reputation around the NBA for paranoia and was rumored to be unhappy with my story.

Nearly three years later, the Blazers are in L.A., and I seek to visit their pregame locker room to question Scottie Pippen about what it felt like to defend the Triangle after so many seasons in Chicago. In the corridor just outside the locker room I encounter coach Mike Dunleavy and pause to greet him and perhaps ask a few questions.

"Charley," Dunleavy says, "I'll answer anything you want, but I'd appreciate it if you didn't go into the locker room until after the game. Because of your relationship with Phil, I'd just rather not have you see the scouting report that's written on the board."

"Sure," I say. Then I ask him what he thinks of the Triangle and how he defends against it.

Dunleavy offers that while he admires the system for its "good spacing," there are several other teams that feature similar offenses: the Houston Rockets, which run "a wing-crossing transition pattern" that moves into a "post-fill forward triangle." Also the Utah Jazz, which employs a "power triangle." Everybody's been playing against the Triangle for so long that most teams run some aspect of it.

"To be honest," says Dunleavy (did this mean he's been lying up till now?), "the Triangle tends to use up a lot of clock and needs a dominant player who can create something when the clock is short. Shaq and Kobe certainly fit the bill, except that Kobe sometimes causes problems by going off on his own and taking quick shots."

Although Dunleavy never mentions his game plan in defense of the Triangle, he does say this: "We do use similar sets, but it's the

kind of system where to do it justice, a team should make a full commitment and run it all the time. Even though it doesn't really suit my
own philosophy, I feel like I know the Triangle well enough to run it
myself."

"Thanks, Mike. And good luck."

"No problem, Charley."

"So I'll be able to speak to Scottie after the game?"

"No problem."

We'll see.

After the game—a Portland victory—I am surprised to be barred
from the visitors' locker room. But here's my media pass! "Sorry,"
says the security guard, "my instructions are to keep you out."

After a forty-five-minute wait, Scottie Pippen comes bustling out
into the corridor.

"Scottie!"

"I'm in a rush, Charley," he says.

As he strides down the corridor toward the team bus, I have about
fifteen seconds to scurry along beside him and ask my questions:

Yes, Scottie misses playing in the Triangle. At the same time, he's
comfortable in Portland's offensive scheme because there's "a lot of
movement that's almost similar to the Triangle." And, yes, if he
ever coached an NBA team, he would "certainly" teach the
Triangle.

JIMMY CLEAMONS: "Guys who were born in California don't want to
practice hard. They'd much rather be outside in the sunshine. Back
East, coming in from the cold to a warm gym is much more con-
ducive to working hard in practice. That's why teams have to be very
careful when they want to draft players from California because no
matter how important a game might be, their general attitude is,
'Hey, it's just another game.'"

The Cleveland Cavaliers are in town, and according to what's written on their pregame board, this is how they plan to defend the Triangle:

1. Transition defense—Sprint back—Get one foot in the lane
2. Come together on splits—talk
3. Go quick on Shaq—don't let him turn on his left shoulder into the lane

Rather than addressing the specifics of the Triangle, these are strictly generic stratagems.

TEX WINTER: "Everybody thinks they know the Triangle, but few really do. Phil thinks he knows it, but he only knows his version of it."

Whenever the game clock is dead and there isn't some kind of to-do transpiring on the court—the Lakers Girls prancing about and smiling as hard as they can, or a fan attempting a half-court shot that might win a free airline ticket, or two kids matching foul shots, or some other kind of vaudevillian family fun—the huge four-sided screen above the scoreboard flashes images of apparently random fans dancing, singing, and bopping in time to the loud Muzak. The lucky fans wave their hands in a frenzy when the camera catches them in the act. In La La Land, five seconds of fame is good enough.

Of course, the only fans who make the cut are wearing some kind of official Lakers apparel.

There's a hugely pregnant woman in a Lakers t-shirt wiggling her hips and clapping her hands. Upon seeing her image on the screen, she lifts her shirt to reveal an orange basketball painted on her distended belly.

SHAQUILLE O'NEAL: "I like playing for PJ because he has great communication with the players. He's prepared for every situation, he's fair, and he means what he says. And I also like the Triangle because

I'm the kind of player who likes to give the ball up. Traditional offenses are boring."

I watch the game from a press table situated behind one of the base-lines. One of the game officials is Kenny Mauer, a CBA graduate. During a time-out, I salute Mauer as he assumes the referees' stan-dard hands-on-hips dead-ball pose and casually scans the nearby crowd. He's a small, slender man with black hair slicked back à la Pat Riley, and his gaunt face lights up when he sees me.

"Charley," he calls out, "what're you doing here?"

"I'm working on a book with Phil."

But he can't hear me, so he beckons me to the apron of the court. I lean over the head of one of the courtside luminaries (Goldie Hawn) as I repeat my answer.

"Good to see you," Mauer says, extending his right hand, which I grasp lightly.

Why am I doing this? Actually going out of my way to talk to a referee, and an unusually arrogant one at that? "Fine," I say. And despite myself, I seem to be enjoying the glow of my momentary celebrity. Perhaps even Goldie Hawn will be impressed.

Mauer and I stare at each other, waiting for the game to resume, searching for something else to say. The best I can come up with is this: "You were the first one who ever kicked me out of a game."

"Get up here," he says with a friendly sneer, "and I'll toss you again."

Ha. Ha.

My five seconds of fame are terminated by a loud horn, the game restarts, Goldie Hawn never turns her head, and I return to my seat.

RON HARPER: "Playing the Triangle is fun. If the Bulls were graduate students, we're still at a third-grade level here."

What's it like learning the Triangle from the beginning again? Are you learning anything that you may have missed the first time around?

HARPER: "I ain't missed shit. I know the Triangle like the back of my hand. I know what PJ's gonna call before he opens his mouth."

In Phil's office at the Healthcenter, we're watching Pete Maravich's famous how-to video on the intricacies of dribbling when Tex sticks his head into the room.

"Who's that?" Tex asks.

Pistol Pete, with his Beatles haircut and floppy socks. "What do you mean, who's that?" Phil says.

Tex stares at the video and talks to Maravich: "Keep your head up, son. You can't survey the damn court." When Maravich lifts his gaze from the ball, Tex says, "That's good."

Phil shakes his head. "Look at all that stuff he can do without ever palming the ball. Guys today don't need this kind of instruction. They just palm the ball while the refs suck on their whistles."

"It's a disgrace," says Tex.

The halls of the Healthcenter are lined with photos of famous Lakers—Kareem, Magic, Big Game, Stumpy, Zeke from Cabin Creek, and Uncle Wiltie. Also the rarest picture in the history of the NBA—Elgin Baylor shooting with his *left* hand.

JOHN SALLEY: "I love the Triangle, but Tex's terminology has to change. 'Line of Deployment'? It's too warlike. And the guys don't even ask themselves what 'deployment' means. 'Moment of truth?' Where I grew up in Brooklyn, that's what happens every time you unlock your front door."

After practice the morning after the Seattle game, Tex gets his free lunch from the snack room near the coaches' office—a small box of cold cereal, a pint of milk, and a container of fruit-flavored yogurt.

For his dessert, Tex pulls a plastic bag from his briefcase and unwraps a crusty chunk of last night's brown bread.

"That's good bread," says Bill Bertka.

Tex nods. "That's why I'm eating it."

A pair of Sacramento Assistant coaches on the Triangle:

PETE CARRIL: "I like the Triangle because of all the passing and cutting. A guy never gets stuck out there, because there's always a place for him to go. But players have to be able to focus. Like I used to tell my guys when I coached at Princeton, 'You've got to concenfuckingtrate!'"

JOHN WETZEL: "My coach at Virginia Tech was Howard Shannon, who played for Tex at Kansas State and later was an assistant coach under him. We ran the Triangle, except that it wasn't dressed up as much. All it is is playing basketball. Heck, we even used it against zone defenses. There are several reasons why more NBA teams don't use the Triangle. First, because it's so foreign to the way pro players have learned the game. Second, it's usually a scramble while players try to learn it, and while that's going on, a coach's job is at risk. Third, you need a dominant player—like Michael or Shaq—to buy into a system that requires everybody to play so much without the ball. But if I had a long-term guaranteed contract as a head coach, I would definitely use the Triangle."

Periodically during a break in the game, the screens above the scoreboard are filled with a Sound-O-Meter, which ostensibly measures the decibel level of the crowd noise. Egged on by a close-up of Mickey Mouse's gloved hands clapping, the very appearance of the meter induces a Pavlovian response from the assembled multitude. And even though a full roar produces a decibel level of approximately 95, the Sound-O-Meter invariably tops out at 999.99, a measurement that would instantly deafen everybody in the building.

After the Minnesota game, there's a hubbub in the coaches' office. As I push through the door, a ruddy middle-aged man is opening a stainless-steel gold-colored suitcase and setting it down on a table in the middle of the room. The suitcase's inner lid is cushioned with plump black leather, and at the bottom two sheets of paper are set under glass. The man's name is Ian Naismith, and the papers contain the original thirteen rules of "Basket Ball" (typed along with some handwritten corrections) that his grandfather, the original Doctor J, posted on the door of the Springfield YMCA early in the morning of December 21, 1891!

1. The ball may be thrown in any direction with one or both hands.

2. The ball may be batted in any direction with one or both hands (never with the fist).

3. A player cannot run with the ball. The player must throw it from the spot on which he catches it; allowance to be made for a man who catches the ball when running at a good speed.

4. The ball must be held in or between the hands; the arms or body must not be used for holding it.

5. No shouldering, holding, pushing, tripping or striking, in any way the person of an opponent shall be allowed; the first infringement of this rule by any person shall count as a foul, the second shall disqualify him until the next goal is made; or, if there was evident intent to injure the person for the whole of the game, no substitute shall be allowed.

6. A foul is striking the ball with the fist, violation of Rules 3, 4, and such as described in Rule 5.

7. If either side makes three consecutive fouls, it shall count a goal for the opponents. (Consecutive means without the opponents in the meantime making a foul.)

8. A goal shall be made when the ball is thrown or batted from the ground into the basket and stays there, providing those defending the goal do not touch or disturb the goal. If the ball rests on the edge and the opponent moves the basket, it shall count as a goal.

9. When the ball goes out of bounds, it shall be thrown into the field and played by the person first touching it. In case of a dis-

pute, the umpire shall throw it straight into the field. The thrower-in is allowed five seconds. If he holds it longer, it shall go to the opponent. If any side persists in delaying the game, the umpire shall call a foul on them.

10. The umpire shall be judge of the men and shall note the fouls and notify the referee when three consecutive fouls have been made. He shall have the power to disqualify men according to Rule 5.

11. The referee shall be judge of the ball and shall decide when the ball is in play, in bounds, to which side it belongs, and shall keep the time. He shall decide when a goal has been made, and keep account of the goals, with any other duties that are usually performed by a referee.

12. The time shall be two fifteen-minute halves, with five minutes rest between.

13. The side making the most goals in that time shall be declared the winners. In case of a draw, the game may, by agreement of the captains, be continued until another goal is made.

The source!

A small edge of each page sticks out at the bottom of the glass, and I ask Naismith if I can touch them. After announcing that the pages are worth ten million dollars, he says, "Sure."

YESSS!

I have touched the Holy Grail, and I am blessed beyond measure!

FOURTEEN

THE "SECOND SEASON"

PHIL

As a rule, play-off basketball is a much different game from the type of contest played in the regular season. During a regular-season game there's a period somewhere between the last two minutes of the first quarter and the first five or six minutes of the second quarter where the bench players of both teams are on the floor and the game presents some open-court opportunities. Ten-point leads and ten-point deficits aren't very significant, because there's plenty of game time remaining in which to make the necessary adjustments. This kind of loose play simply doesn't exist in postseason play because each possession is so critical and every mistake is amplified. Since so much is at stake, play-off basketball tends to be more conservative.

When teams compete in best-of-five or best-of-seven series, there's so much time available to study the game tapes that both teams become totally familiar with the nuances of each other's game plans. This familiarity forces teams into the third or sometimes fourth options on their favorite plays, so the unfolding of each offensive sequence takes more time. This also serves to increase the physical nature of play-off games.

Our initial "second-season" opponent was Sacramento, a dangerous team, especially in a short five-game series. We'd beaten the Kings three out of four games during the regular season, but most of those games had been closely contested.

Sacramento's coach, Rick Adelman, is an excellent tactician who gives his team a lot of confidence about playing an open-floor game. Most up-tempo teams will initially look to fast-break, but if nothing beneficial develops, they'll pull the ball back out, call a number, and move into a half-court set. Adelman's style is to flow directly from a fast break right into a high-intensity motion offense. A lot of credit for this quick-hitting passing attack goes to assistant coach Pete Carril, who'd brought much of the concept with him from Princeton. The Kings' high-octane offense put a lot of pressure on a defense and made double-teaming difficult.

But the Kings were far from being a one-dimensional ball club. High-scoring teams are normally very weak defensively, but this wasn't the case with the Kings. On the contrary, they had fast hands up and down their lineup.

The Kings worried me because of their overall talent, and because several of the matchups actually favored them. Vlade Divac, for example, presented a series of unique problems for us. At seven-one and 260 pounds, Vlade can dribble and pass like a guard, run the lanes, operate effectively in a screen/roll situation, and shoot three-pointers. Vlade also has the ability to apply enough leverage to Shaq's left shoulder that Shaq can't turn so easily to the middle and is forced to swing toward the baseline for his little push shots.

Chris Webber is an exceptional power forward who, on the basis of his season-long consistency, I'd rank as being one of the top three players in the league. He can run the court, post up, and hit three-point shots. A. C. Green and Robert Horry tag-teamed the power forward spot for us, but Webber can easily overpower both of them. The Kings' offense ran through Webber, and to win the series we'd have to find an answer for him.

Jason Williams was the starting point guard, a wild talent whom Adelman managed to control as much as possible. Jason is just as capable of hitting five three-pointers in succession as missing ten, of completing five consecutive dipsy-doo passes for layups as tossing five out of bounds.

Nick Anderson is an offensive-minded small forward capable of scoring a flurry of points. Corliss Williamson is a tough customer at the small forward slot, tough inside and on the boards.

Their bench was very potent, starting with Predrag Stojakovic, who is a deadly outside shooter, on through another fine shooter, Jon Barry, and point guard Tony Delk, who always played well against us.

Every play-off series is like solving a puzzle, and the key to beating Sacramento was in slowing the pace. To do this, we needed to create (and make) good shots, play good transition defense, and make them play half-court basketball. On the other hand, the Kings did not always hustle back on defense, so we felt we might be able to run on them and possibly go to Shaq before they could collect their defense.

We also felt that having the home-court edge was a significant advantage for us. Because of their racehorse style, the Kings were much more comfortable playing at home, where their devoted fans helped energize them, and where the shooting background and the rims were totally familiar. Younger players like Williams, Barry, Delk, Stojakovic, and even Webber don't yet have the resilience necessary to stand up to a hostile crowd and win road games.

In preparing my teams for play-off opponents, I've always spliced some form of popular movie into my scouting tapes. For the Kings I used *American History X*, which starred Ed Norton as the leader of a group of skinhead pseudo-Nazis. For me, the film addressed the mistaken belief that one's existence is totally influenced by external forces. Specifically, the view raised by the movie is that white Americans are losing their jobs because people of color are coming into the country and supplanting them. Norton's character is a young man who goes over the edge and is sent to prison. That's where he's befriended by an African American who forces him to come to terms with his prejudice and to take charge of his own life. My message to my players was this: "The play-offs are not about the Lakers' recent history of disappointments. It's not about how the referees will treat us. It's easy to blame outside forces. But the play-offs are all about controlling our own destiny."

Somehow, though, a media hound found out about the film. Because Adelman's mustache gives him a certain facial resemblance to Adolf Hitler, and Jason Williams has numerous tattoos and a clean head, the charge was made that I was out to brand both of them as being fascists. Nothing could have been farther from the truth. Williams is just a young ballplayer searching for his niche in the league, and I don't know, and don't care, about his politics. As for Adelman, well, he's one of the nicest guys around.

Anyway, we had a pair of easy games in L.A. to start the series. And sure enough, in the first game, Webber got into early foul trouble, lost his composure, and got himself bounced by one of the referees.

The third game was up in Sacramento, and they just came out and blitzed us. We turned to putty in the second half, but part of our failure was an adjustment that Adelman and his staff had made in an attempt to control Shaq. Webber made no pretense of guarding A. C. and just sagged back into Shaq's lap, so we couldn't make an entry pass. It was blatantly illegal, but the refs wouldn't make the call.

Everything seemed to go wrong for us: Shaq was in foul trouble, he was whistled for several three-second violations, and he couldn't make his free throws. In fact, Shaq was scoreless in the fourth quarter. As the game wore on, I could see the guys getting stiff and tense out on the court. We tried going to Kobe for some dribble penetration off screen/roll situations, but to no avail. Kobe either had the ball ripped out of his hands, had his shot blocked, committed an offensive foul, or was hammered without a foul being called his way. And every time something went awry, the Kings got runouts that eventually broke the game open. Give the Kings all the credit: their three-point shooting was incredibly accurate, and their bench outplayed ours by a wide margin. Even worse was the fact that once the game started getting away from us, my guys stopped executing the Triangle.

All of this was going on in the noisiest arena I've ever been in. The hometown fan corps were totally supportive of their team, as well they should be. But aside from the crowd noise, the decibel level was boosted by so many buzzers and electronic noisemakers being detonated behind our bench that communication with my players during time-outs was very difficult. To further stoke the fans, Lakers' jerseys were set on fire.

After the game, a local reporter asked me if the Kings fans were the most energetic I'd ever seen. And I said, "No. The fans down in Puerto Rico were much more rabid. But I do have to assume that the fans in Sacramento are at least semicultured, even though they might be rednecks."

Perhaps my comments could be considered rude and insulting, but that's exactly what I said. Sometimes I'm not as diplomatic as I should be, but I had to take the heat and, right or wrong, assume total responsibility for my public remarks.

For game four (the second in Sacramento), we adjusted the Triangle by inverting A. C. with the guard who was normally positioned at the top of the circle. What we hoped to accomplish was to make Webber's failure to defend A. C. so obvious that the refs would be forced to blow their whistles. Unfortunately, this never happened. Webber continued to play a one-man zone without having to pay the price.

Once again their bench dominated ours, their three-point shooting was uncanny, and we had to play from behind from the get-go. We did manage to control Williams, but Delk, Barry, and Stojakovic ran wild. The Kings went to a two-man game with Webber and Stojakovic that we couldn't deal with. Webber had a breakout game, and Divac drove the ball right at Shaq. Whenever he picked up quick fouls, Shaq's tendency was to be less aggressive on defense. I had to convince him to keep on playing all-out even if it risked his fouling out. That's why I deliberately kept Shaq in the game even when he was saddled with foul trouble.

The series was now tied at two games each, and the media had a field day. Their operative theory is that whichever team has lost the most recent game will never win again. As far as the media was concerned, the Lakers were falling apart, all of our weaknesses were revealed, and we were doomed to lose game five.

Obviously, I didn't like having to go the limit; anything can happen in the deciding game of a play-off series—an injury, foul trouble for a key player, a hot streak by a bench player. At the same time, I really believed that playing in such a crucial game would be good for us, and I believed that we would rise to the occasion. We had to learn how to get hardened to extreme pressure, how to play under the increased scrutiny of the officials, how not to be discouraged when Shaq missed his free throws, how to stick with the Triangle under duress.

Before the game I told the players, "If you don't win this one, then you don't deserve to move into the next round. You've got to play to win, not play to avoid losing. Be aggressive."

We came out with fire in our eyes. We were also the beneficiaries of two quick illegal defense calls against Webber (and a third one later on), which freed up some space for our offense to work, and the game was over early in the third quarter.

The media wasn't satisfied, of course. They said the Sacramento series proved that the Lakers weren't "invincible." But winning a championship isn't about being invincible. It's about winning the last game of the season.

The Phoenix Suns were on tap for the second round. We'd beaten them four-of-four during the regular season, but both games in Phoenix had been tight ones. The Suns had an offense-first mentality and were one of the most talented basketball clubs in the NBA. Their coach, Scott Skiles, had never been an accomplished defensive player during his NBA career, yet he'd evolved into a highly respected defensive coach. He'd taken over the team at midterm (replacing Danny Ainge) and survived several injuries to important players. Tom Gugliatta had a seizure, then a broken foot; Jason Kidd suffered a broken foot; Sean Marion had knee surgery; Luc Longley and Penny Hardaway also spent significant portions of the season on the injured list. The only big-minute players who remained healthy throughout were Rodney Rogers and Cliff Robinson.

But the Suns were fresh off an impressive series against San Antonio, which remained an excellent squad despite the lingering injury to Tim Duncan. David Robinson was still an outstanding defender, and the Spurs still played with grit and hustle. Scoring was their number-one challenge, and in the first couple of games neither the Suns nor the Spurs topped eighty points. By any measure, Phoenix was another team that was capable of upending us.

The Suns wanted to run the ball down our throats, and they had the extraordinary quickness and athleticism to succeed. They liked to play small ball, and they'd sink or swim with their three-point shooting. When transition buckets weren't available, Skiles's philosophy was to run isolations for any one of several players, chief among these being Penny Hardaway. With Jason Kidd assuming the point-guard responsibilities, Hardaway was free to post up or run isos from either wing. Kidd, of course, had gotten healthy just in time to play against us, and although he's not a consistent shooter, he's quick with the ball and smart enough to break down any defense.

Cliff Robinson was having a banner year—a six-foot-ten frontline player who could score in the pivot, beyond the three-point arc, and all stations in between. Sean Marion was a rookie, a pogo-stick kid who liked to defend and jump all over the offensive boards. Marion had young legs, and his special joy was to run the court. His love of the game was infectious, providing an enormous infusion of energy for his team. Rodney Rogers was the Suns' sixth man, a terrific college scorer at Wake Forest who'd had several so-so seasons with Denver and the Clippers. The desert climate had revived him to the point where Rogers was a 44 percent three-point shooter. Luc Longley played about twenty-five minutes in the center spot and was remarkably athletic considering that he measured about seven-foot-two and 300 pounds. One of the reasons why I had been sold on Luc when he was with the Bulls was that he had the strength, the size, and the heart to stop Shaq's initial burst into the lane. If Shaq couldn't simply overpower the first line of defense, there was enough time for help to arrive on the scene. So the Suns were loaded, and the series promised to be a difficult one.

The key to this particular puzzle was to successfully defend the screen/roll situations that the Suns would use to set up their isolations. The singular problem was that for at least half of the game

Shaq would be paired against either Robinson or Rogers and would therefore have to move out of his comfort zone when the Suns ran high screen/rolls. If Shaq was going to have to go out to cover the screen/roll, then hurry to the boards to rebound, he'd be worn to a nub by the fourth quarter. Our counter to this was to try to cross-match Shaq as much as possible, that is, have A. C. or Robert Horry jump out to guard the screener and keep Shaq attached to whichever big man remained on the weak side. Another difficulty was that since Hardaway was a devastating post-up player, Skiles's offensive scheme usually had one of his big men acting as the feeder. This meant that Shaq would have to challenge the entry pass, then if he stayed home with either Robinson or Rogers, or even Longley, Hardaway would be working one-on-one close to the hoop. If Shaq dropped down to help, a quick return pass would create open shots for the shooters. The only solution was for Shaq to be all-out aggressive and for me to consider shortening his playing time.

The opening game in L.A. was a dead ringer for the first game against Sacramento—Shaq had a field day, and we cruised to an easy win. I wasn't overly impressed by our victory because I knew that Skiles and his staff would make adjustments.

Sure enough, in the second game, Phoenix sagged off of A. C. and Harp, then quickly doubled Shaq with either Kidd or Hardaway, a pair of big guards. On offense, Skiles realized that we didn't like to double-team in isolation situations, so he one-on-oned us to death. Another tactic they adopted was to drive the ball right at Shaq whenever possible, hoping to hang some early foul trouble on him.

Anyway, we played a solid all-around game. The guys were starting to get the hang of the Triangle's counteraction, so we had a lot of success getting the ball to Shaq as he came across the lane. We were up by twelve in the last few seconds of the third quarter, and the game seemed to be well in hand. The Suns had the ball, and we had a foul to give, so I yelled out to Rick Fox to deliberately foul Hardaway. While Rick glanced up at the scoreboard to check out the team fouls and the time remaining, Hardaway drove the ball right by him. Horry had to move away from Robinson and step into the middle to prevent a layup. Hardaway kicked the ball to Robinson, who knocked down a three-pointer. So now instead of a twelve-point lead to start the fourth quarter, our margin was suddenly down to nine.

We had possession to start the quarter, and in the huddle I reminded the guys that Phoenix liked to pressure the inbounds pass. And that's exactly what happened. Rogers charged up from half-court and succeeded in tipping the ball away from Brian Shaw. Bang! Hardaway hit a jumper. On the ensuing sequence, Horry tried to bring the ball upcourt on his own and dribbled it out of bounds. Wouldn't you know it? Phoenix scored again, and within the space of just over one minute our lead was cut from twelve to five.

Now Phoenix was feeling confident. They'd found a great rhythm in their offense and were beating us badly on isolations and screen/rolls. Then Kidd, who's not a reliable shooter, hit a big three-pointer over Glen Rice, and coming down the stretch the game was up for grabs.

The situation was this: we were down by one, Shaq had fouled out, and we were down to our last possession. During the subsequent time-out, we decided not to inbound the ball in our frontcourt to prevent Phoenix from stacking up their defense right away. So we went with Kobe in a full-court, middle-of-the court-situation that just about prohibited a double-team. Kobe took the ball where he wanted to and hit the big jumper to win the game. It was a huge confidence booster for the young man.

A win is a win is a win, and we'd eked out a two-to-nothing lead in the series.

The next two games were in Phoenix, where the fans were very much anti-L.A. Throughout the late 1980s and early '90s the Suns and the Lakers had hooked up in several combative play-off series and the rivalry was still going strong. Also, Phoenix and Los Angeles were always being paired as the two major cities in the Southwest, and Phoenix usually came out with the short straw—L.A.'s little-sister city.

Going back several years, the Suns were forever touted as being a team on the come, but in reality they were a team that had never arrived. The upshot was that the Suns' fans didn't totally believe in their team.

I was concerned about playing in Phoenix, since both of our regular-season games there had been tight ones. But game three was a good one for us, and our 3–0 lead basically sealed the series.

For some reason, the referees seem to be more responsive to the home standing coach, and Skiles's campaign was to get three-second violations called on Shaq. (In the Sacramento series, Adelman had filibustered for offensive fouls on Shaq, and Portland's Mike Dunleavy would nag the refs about illegal defenses.) But I don't think Skiles ever got what he wanted.

We had a mini-practice the day after game three, and I wasn't happy with the guys' ability to concentrate on what we were doing. Later that same night a producer from Los Angeles set up a private viewing for us of a new movie, *Gladiator*, in a theater right across the street from our hotel. "Okay," I said to the players. "Bring a guest or two. This is an opportunity to do something together as a team." I showed up with my coaching staff, the trainers, and George Mumford, the team's psychologist—and only five players were there: Rice, Shaw, Fisher, Knight, and Devean George. Shaq went to an WNBA exhibition game and then to some kid's birthday party. Harper didn't come. Kobe's a recluse who never goes anywhere. I was very disappointed; the no-shows contradicted the sense of community and shared time that I thought were at the heart of what we were trying to accomplish.

So I wasn't totally surprised when game four on a Sunday afternoon was a total blowout. Jason Kidd banked in a half-court three-pointer to conclude the first quarter, and they just cracked us open. We allowed the Suns to score seventy-two points in the first half, which I thought was a humiliating exhibition of how not to play defense.

There was a published report that I didn't talk to the team during the halftime intermission, but that's not true. I did let them stew by themselves until two minutes before they were due out on the court. While I was outside the locker room, I heard them barking at each other and expressing their unhappiness. Rather than being angry myself, I kind of empathized with them. They just didn't understand what it took to win an NBA title.

When I entered the locker room I became very demonstrative. I threw a bottle of Gatorload hard against the wall and chewed them out big time. Going off on the team is something that has to be done carefully and at the appropriate time. I knew we didn't have much of a chance to win the game, but it was important for them to understand how upset I was.

Just about the only player who responded was Rick Fox, who had been having a hard time throughout the play-offs. His wife, Vanessa Williams, had given birth to a baby girl while we were in Sacramento during the Kings series, and Rick had to shuttle back and forth to Los Angeles whenever he could. As a result, he'd been pretty much out of sync ever since.

Rick had made several careless defensive mistakes in the first half that contributed to our pitiful performance, so as our deficit mounted in the second half, I put Devean George in the game ahead of him. With about four minutes to go in the game, I finally let Rick escape from the bench. Almost immediately, he expressed his irritation by committing a hard foul on Cliff Robinson, which somehow earned him a technical foul. I was puzzled by the referees' overreaction, but I only issued a pro forma complaint. On the next sequence, Rick fouled Robinson as soon as he touched the ball. Okay, I thought, Robinson will shoot two, and that'll be that. To my surprise, Rick was thrown out of the game. Again I didn't understand what the refs were doing. The whole Hack-a-Shaq routine featured quick fouls, and nobody'd ever been tossed. Why now? I couldn't get a straight answer from any of the refs, but once again I was irked at their inconsistency.

After the disaster was finally completed (the score was 117–98), this was my postgame speech: "You guys are a little tired of each other and don't want to work together as a cohesive unit. All of this is understandable at this stage of a long season. To win a championship, however, you've got to find a way to match each other's energy and to match your opponent's energy. You've just got to figure out what it takes to win night after night. Let's learn from this game and not let it happen again."

We came back on Tuesday night in L.A. in a different frame of mind. Even though we wound up on the long end, game five proved to be extremely ugly, with Phoenix scoring only eight points in the third quarter. The Suns were clearly embarrassed by their lack of proficiency and we just snowballed them by 87–65 to close out the series. In two consecutive games we'd gone from a nineteen-point loss to a twenty-two-point victory, an outrageous swing of forty-one points!

There's been much comment in the media about how schizophrenic the Lakers are. How could we look like champs one night and chumps the next? Why didn't we have the killer instinct necessary to close out a series?

I think some of our inconsistency is due to youth. But a lot of it also has to do with Shaq's performance at the free-throw line. When Shaq has one of his four-for-fourteen nights from the line, it's almost like we're committing five turnovers. We know that our offense can generate free throws, and whenever Shaq gets fouled in the act of shooting, it's easy to believe that we're getting something positive accomplished. Then Tex will say, "We haven't scored the last four times down the court."

To compound the problem, bad free-throw shooting is contagious. The other guys feel they have to shoot a hundred percent to make up for Shaq's misses, so they get all tight and start missing, too.

Anyway, we moved on to the Western Conference finals against the Portland Trail Blazers, who had just defeated the Utah Jazz in five games. We'd split our four regular season games with Portland, and now we had to gear up against the team we expected we'd have to go through to get out of the West. Portland had come through the play-offs in very good shape, losing only one game to Minnesota and one to Utah. They were undefeated on their home court and were at the top of their game.

Even though Portland had won fifty-nine games during the regular season I believed that they were underachievers. They got testy when I said this to the media, and it gave them some ammunition in the coming war against us, but I didn't mean it as a slur. In truth, I have a certain affinity for this team, and I like the way they play the game. But with their depth and their level of talent, I thought they easily should have won sixty-plus games.

This was a team that regularly pressured the ball in the backcourt and tried taking you out of your offense. Scottie Pippen's defense covered the entire floor, and Rasheed Wallace was athletic enough at six-eleven to trap in the backcourt. They tried to keep Steve Smith and his bad knees at home, while Arvydas Sabonis lingered in the lane.

At seven-foot-three and approximately 320 pounds, Sabonis was even bigger than Shaq. He wasn't a shot blocker per se, but big enough to bother anyone who got to the basket. Like Longley, Sabonis could absorb that first shock when Shaq tried to move into the middle, and hold him up until a double-teamer got there. A couple of years ago, Sabonis's chronically injured legs severely limited his playing time and his lateral movement. He's still not a flash when moving from side to side, but Dunleavy nursed him through the season, and the big guy had solid legs underneath him for the first time in many years. Although Sabonis didn't score for a high average, he could hit three-pointers and he was a wonderful passer, which was why the offense ran through him.

Damon Stoudamire was a quick left-handed point guard who was extremely dangerous when allowed to penetrate. Steve Smith was an outstanding spot shooter with incredible range, and at six-eight, also an effective post-up player. If Rasheed Wallace could see the basket, he could fill it. Inside, outside, he was a young man with a lot of firepower. The only problem with Wallace was his tendency to lose his composure and overreact whenever calls went against him.

Bonzie Wells came off the bench and could really light up a scoreboard. He'd even had a couple of twenty-point quarters during the regular season. Greg Anthony specialized in defense as Stoudamire's backup. Detlef Schrempf was an experienced six-foot-ten swingman who used to be a high-caliber scorer and still retained his smarts and his ability to pass the ball. Backing up both power spots was Brian Grant, a hustle player who ate up offensive rebounds. Stacey Augmon was another defensive specialist, and young Jermaine O'Neal was a quick-jumping frontline player who longed for more playing time.

I believed, however, that Scottie Pippen was the key to Portland's fortunes. It was Pippen who was responsible for getting the ball in to the post, for regulating the team's tempo, and for executing all the subtle moves that made Portland so effective defensively. Of course, Pippen also had the wherewithal to disrupt the functioning of our Triangle. Pippen had to be the spark plug in order for the Trail Blazers to beat us. And I did make a public statement to this effect.

Mike Dunleavy was a very clever coach, and he had a zillion and one things that he could do on offense. He could field a variety of lineups—big guards, small guards, speed players, power players. What he aimed to do was run guys in and out until he could create a dramatic mismatch somewhere, then pound away at that mismatch until you started bleeding. This tactic worked so well because he had ten players at his disposal who had been starters in the league. Right from the tip-off, the Blazers would push the basketball right at you, with Stoudamire scampering around screen/rolls and creating open floor situations. Smith could score on kickouts or inside, and Wallace was a very high-percentage shooter in the paint. After Stoudamire did his ten-to-twelve-minute stint in the first quarter, Pippen took over and generated the team's offense by operating as a point forward.

To open up the series, I did make a few adjustments to try to keep Pippen from jamming our offense. I put Horry in the backcourt and ran Harper away down the floor hoping he'd take Pippen with him. Or else I had Kobe bring the ball upcourt in a one-guard front while Harper again ran to the baseline. This meant that if Pippen tried to harass Horry, then the five-foot-ten Stoudamire would have to defend either Harper or Kobe, and we could take the little guy right into the pivot. I was gambling on two things—that Portland wouldn't try to trap Horry in the backcourt, and that Stoudamire's full-court defense wouldn't bother Kobe. As it turned out, both situations were resolved in our favor. I also wanted Shaq to stay up on Sabonis and try to deny him the ball, even at the three-point line.

Early in game one, Scottie had a couple of dunks and gave us a hard time on both ends of the floor. But for the most part he was content to kind of sit back and let the game roll along. Then we got a huge second quarter out of our bench, and we blew the game wide open. Sabonis wound up with zero points, Shaq had forty-one, and the outcome was never in doubt.

The only real surprise Dunleavy showed us was to shorten Greg Anthony's rotation. Up till then, Anthony normally had a ten-minute run in the second quarter and would also play most of the last quarter. But Anthony was recovering from a leg injury, so when Stoudamire was out, Portland went with a big lineup—Wells, Smith, Pippen, Wallace, and either Grant or Sabonis. We hadn't seen much of that lineup during the regular season, and it gave us some trouble. I liked playing my small guard, Derek Fisher, but he got mismatched against Bonzie Wells, and we had to scramble. When Wells, or any other of the Trail Blazers, set up in the pivot, they'd look to drive the ball hard to the basket—no turnaround jumpers for them.

The most interesting facet of that first game was Dunleavy's going into a Hack-a-Shaq mode midway through the fourth quarter after the Blazers managed to squeeze our twenty-point lead down to twelve. Whenever we inbounded the ball, someone simply put a gentle bear hug on Shaq and sent him to the line. I'd previously warned Shaq that Dunleavy was likely to do something like this, and Shaq was very good behind it all. He still got frustrated, but he no longer got angry. Shaq also accepted the fact that the only way he could change the sequence of events was to convert his free throws. His mantra became, "Make them pay." Shaq ended up making twenty-one of forty free throws, and even though our lead shrunk to nine, we eventually won by 109–94. The last quarter took over an hour to complete.

I think the Hack-a-Shaq methodology can be effective if it's used selectively, maybe three or four times a game. But the Trail Blazers hurt themselves in game one because the constant fouling restricted them to playing half-court basketball, and they soon lost their offensive rhythm.

When Wilt Chamberlain was in the league, he was also a horrible free-throw shooter, so the NBA simply changed the rules to accommodate him: instead of being awarded two free throws, a player was given three chances to make two. But free-throw shooting is just another part of the game that has to be mastered, so I'd hate to see the rules changed to accommodate Shaq.

I do know this, however. The rules of the game are designed to prevent the team committing a foul from reaping any benefits. My suggestion is that the ludicrously deliberate foul should be treated like all deliberate fouls are in the last two minutes of the game—one free throw taken by any player designated by the offended team, plus possession.

Of course Shaq is more intent than ever on improving his percentage, because Hack-a-Shaq is downright embarrassing. But this is what we tell him: an NBA team averages from eighty to eighty-five possessions per game, and also averages 1.1 or 1.2 points per possession. So all Shaq needs to do is consistently make one of two free throws, and all the hullabaloo will end.

In game two Pippen went straight at Glen Rice, posting up, driving to the basket, challenging our interior defense, and scoring twelve big points in the first quarter. Late in the quarter, Pippen took a fall and dislocated two fingers on his left hand. From there on he only scored five points, but he'd already provided the energy to catapult the Blazers into a double-figure lead. Rasheed Wallace took over when Pippen was injured, and in addition to hurting us in the low post, he also knocked down four three-pointers.

Portland ended up shooting twenty-five free throws in the first half. Everything we did was a foul, and the Blazers just kept taking it to us. At the half, Shaq, Kobe, Harper, Horry, and Rice all were saddled with three fouls each. The refs in game two had previously worked the New York/Miami series, which had been unusually physical and tightly officiated, and I think the refs' call-every-touch mindset had carried over. And with Kobe in constant foul trouble, we hadn't been able to maneuver the matchups so that he could post up Stoudamire. Anyway, the Blazers feasted off Pippen's early run, and we never got back into the game, losing 106–77.

After a practice session in Portland prior to game three, we had a team meeting. "I think it's time to put Kobe on Pippen," I said. "You've got to avoid early fouls, Kobe, but at the same time you've got to prevent Pippen from taking the ball to the basket. We've got to really dedicate ourselves to containing Pippen."

Then John Salley, sitting in his usual seat in the back row, said this: "I know Phil's not going to say this and Harp doesn't want to say this, either, but Scottie Pippen... you've got to beat up on him. That's what we did in Detroit. Just knock him down at every opportunity and make him have to think twice about trying to penetrate."

My response was that we couldn't afford to have Shaq committing unnecessary fouls. Besides, following in the footsteps of the Pistons Bad Boys was not the nature of our ball club. We just had to stay in front of Pippen and make it difficult for him to freely move about.

Then Kobe stepped up and said something disrespectful about Pippen. "No," I said. "That's not the way we approach situations like this. We just have to knuckle down and take away Pippen's instinctive moves. If you don't respect your opponent, then you'll never play at your best."

The next two games were in Portland: Kobe did an admirable job on Pippen; Harp and Fisher were able to keep Stoudamire out of the lane; and we won the first game by 93–91, and the second by 103–91. The only bad news was that Kobe suffered a slightly sprained ankle in game three that would hamper him for the duration. Even so, heading back home with a 3–1 lead, we knew we had to close out the series ASAP because the Blazers were such a dangerous team. But we felt good about the way we were playing: we had a feel for Portland and were sure we'd be able to put them out of their misery.

That's not the way it happened. The Blazers were incredible in game five, and we were the ones who were miserable. Sabonis came up big, Wallace was unstoppable, and Stoudamire got everybody involved right away. And just as I'd feared, it was Pippen who really put a charge into the Blazers. He had to pick his spots because of his injured fingers, but when he thought the time was right, he absolutely blistered us.

Dunleavy also made a good move by using Detlef Schrempf to make the entry pass into Wallace. Schrempf was a smooth operator, and his efficient passes took the adventure out of what had sometimes been an iffy situation for them. We had to play uphill all game long, and the final score was 98–88.

Portland certainly deserved all the credit for resurrecting the series. It's certainly difficult to win three games in a row against such an excellent ball club, but I also believe that my guys relaxed a little too much. Too many of them thought the series was already a done deal and that the Blazers would just roll over. They anticipated that the game itself would get their chops up, so they weren't mentally or emotionally prepared. In the play-offs, however, you can't expect your opponent to lose a game—you've got to go out there and win it. Losing game five really hurt.

So we talked it over, and everybody agreed that we'd finally learned our lesson. Blah, blah, and blah. Now the task was to avoid a seventh game by beating the Blazers up in Portland for the third time—a difficult task because Portland was really clicking, and they'd certainly be ready for us.

What was happening was that our defense was suddenly failing us. Both Wallace and Smith were killing us inside. Kobe's ankle was aching and, being a half-step slow, he'd been in constant foul trouble. He tried to keep himself in the game by playing soft, and he was getting burned. When we did hump up our defense, we'd get overwhelmed on the offensive boards, and Portland's second shots were devastating. Also, Shaq was having trouble staying in touch with Sabonis, and the big guy was picking us apart with his pinpoint passes. Even worse, Shaq wasn't actively defending all the spots he was responsible for, nor was he playing hard enough. I don't know whether he was trying to conserve energy or stay out of foul trouble, but if Shaq wasn't doing the job, then our defense was too full of holes. And Portland sure had the ammunition to take full advantage.

Like Phoenix, Portland wanted to get the ball to their dominant players in isolation situations. The Blazers' ultimate goal was for one of those players to find his own way to the basket or get fouled. Short of that, he could usually compromise the defense and force a double-team, then kick the ball out to an open man for a free shot at three points. It's difficult to contain good scorers one-on-one because the referees referee the defensive player.

There's nothing wrong with this kind of basketball. It is a system, except that you don't use all of your players all of the time—and iso-lation-type basketball also puts a lot of pressure on guys to make shots. Strange to say, but ultimately the Blazers' biggest problem was also their greatest strength: They simply had too many potent scorers—Wallace, Smith, Stoudamire, Pippen, Schrempf, and Wells. The Knicks play a similar system, and their choices are simpler—Allan Houston or Latrell Sprewell. Indiana goes to either Jalen Rose or Reggie Miller. But whose number does Dunleavy call in the clutch? Who's Portland's go-to guy when the game's on the line? No one in particular, and this creates a bit of uncertainty just when a team has to feel positive about what it has to do and who has to do it.

We were having our troubles on offense, especially in the first quarters. Because A. C. and Harp were subpar shooters, Portland was ganging up on Shaq with quick triple-teams, so we weren't getting too many shots from inside the lane. We seemed to be down by ten points before the six minute time-out. Having to play catchup can be exhausting.

Dunleavy's emphasis was always on defense, so whenever Kobe shook loose in the middle of a pinch-post action, he'd be double-teamed by Pippen and Wallace. Our answer was to space the floor with an open offense, forcing the double-teamers to come a longer distance to get to the ball. This open-floor structure was something that we kept in the bank and saved for the play-offs, and it worked very well for us.

In addition to quickly sending defenders to crowd Shaq, Dunleavy had another strategy to try to neutralize him: the Blazers would pressure the passer so that the ball would have to be lobbed into Shaq. A direct unimpeded pass would be like, boom, the ball's there and the defense has to scurry to double-down. A lob pass is lofted into the air for about two or three seconds, so by the time Shaq caught the ball, he was already surrounded.

We did have another trump trick up our sleeve, however: what we call switch cuts. Here, we form the triangle on the strong side, then reverse the ball. Now the weak-side forward moves into the low post, and the strong-side wing runs the baseline corner-to-corner, which gives us another triangle on the opposite side of the court. Meanwhile Shaq stays put, and he winds up isolated on what's now the weak side. One more swing pass, and the ball can be dropped to him in the paint. This time, the help defense is too far away to get to Shaq in time to keep him out of the middle. I also dusted off a back pick off a two-guard front that created everything from open shots for Rice to basket cuts for Horry and driving lanes for Kobe. In fact, Kobe got his points (thirty-three), but we were never in the game.

So we went back up to Portland for game six, and once again Stoudamire ran amok, and we had to play from behind. Meanwhile Kobe's ankle was sore, and Harper was burned out from playing too many minutes. We couldn't get any breakaway baskets and had to struggle just to find acceptable shots.

Our general game plan was to stay in touch with a team, wear them down with Shaq in the middle, then turn up our defense in the fourth quarter, when the opponents' outside shooters are tired and more likely to misfire. Ten points was stretching the limit but was usually an acceptable early deficit for us—a small enough margin so we could make effective adjustments at halftime.

But we were flat in game six, and they were hell-bent on destruction. At the half, we were down by fifteen, and there was a doom-and-gloom attitude in the locker room. Then Rick Fox started grousing. "Here we go again," he said. "Everybody's got a blank look on their face. So what are we going to do about it? Are we going to let the referees dictate the terms of the game? Are we going to be passive and get blown out again? Or are we going to stand up on our own feet? Are we going to provide support for each other?"

Tex Winter leaned over to me and said, "Phil, you'd better tell him to shut up."

"No," I said. "Somebody's got to say these things."

Because Rick was a holdover from the Lakers' play-off woes of the past three years, he could see the same patterns being repeated, and he wasn't going to accept them. At the same time, in my position as a newcomer, I could afford to let the veterans be the team's conscience.

Then I addressed the team: "We should all be taking to heart what Rick just said. Everybody's got to find a way to get emotional about the ball game. One guy, no matter how good he is, can't do it alone."

I was hoping that, given a loss, we could at least make the Blazers work hard and expend some energy. Perhaps we'd even be able to create a small spark of self-doubt. We did manage to scratch at Portland's lead to make the final score (103–93) somewhat respectable, but I didn't feel that we'd pushed them enough.

Just about our only demonstrative act in game six in Portland was that somebody got physical with Pippen. Shaq came over as Scottie approached the hoop and knocked him ass-over-teakettle. Scottie hit the floor pretty hard and Shaq got a flagrant foul.

We watched the game tape on the flight back to Los Angeles and were able to zero in on three of the Blazers' plays that continued to confound us. One was the forty-two drop, which was usually a post-up for Bonzie Wells or Steve Smith. The second was a play that we hadn't solved all series long—a cross-pick to bring Wallace to the right box. This particular sequence could also become a down pick, a screen/roll, or a power triangle, and was something Dunleavy inherited from Pat Riley when he played for the Lakers. Their calls were "live ball," where the guard dribbled out the small forward, who went across the lane to cross pick for Wallace; and "dead ball," in which the guard passed to the small forward and set the cross-pick himself. The refs were calling fouls every time we tried to jam the picker or time-delay Wallace with a brush bump. What we worked on before game seven was riding Wallace over the top of the pick and not letting him go baseline.

Smith was also eating us alive on a high screen/roll situation. He shoots so well going left that we wanted to push him right and live with him going over the top, but we were losing control of him. The remedy was for Shaq to aggressively switch out on Smith and take our chances with a forward switching onto Sabonis.

We were definitely at risk in a seventh game against a team that apparently had our number. But I also felt that while the Blazers had had to play totally balls out for two straight games, we still had some emotional resources available.

This would be the fifth game seven that I'd coached—the Bulls lost to Detroit in my rookie year, beat the Knicks in the semifinals on our way to a repeat championship, lost to the Knicks in the semifinals in 1995 when Michael was playing baseball, and defeated

Indiana in 1998. There's something electric, and at the same time almost nostalgic, about preparing for a seventh game. You keep thinking, Maybe this is the last drive to the gym, maybe this is my last practice session. Will I be playing basketball next week? Or golf? There's an aura of finality that haunts everything you do.

I remember going through a whole deal with the Bulls' players about how to approach a seventh game. Even worse than actually losing is the fear of losing. We can lose. We will lose. We won't lose. But what if we do lose? Your mind goes around and around.

The reality is that winning is a function of hard work, skill, and belief in what you're doing. If you can trust all of these things, then everything will work itself out. Worry and fear just make you frazzled and unsettled. And the truth is that win or lose, life still goes on.

We had a good practice session the day before the game, then, as usual, I assembled the team in our film room. But before going over the game tapes, I had another agenda in mind. I'd come in early that morning to write something special on our game board: the Noble Eightfold Path.

Let me preface all this by reiterating that I was raised in a Christian home by Pentecostal ministers. While I was growing up, Christianity was the touchstone of my life, and Christian principles constituted my first and last thoughts every day. Near the end of my playing career I was attracted to Buddhism because I'd become disenchanted with some of the otherwordly aspects of Christianity— the afterlife, the cycle of sinning and redemption. Buddhism contained elements that seemed more immediate and more pragmatic. It concerned what I was doing in my life right here and now. Eventually I was able to find a personal synthesis, and I now identify myself as a Zen Christian. If the essence of Buddhism is compassion, and the essence of Christianity is love, then the two are certainly compatible. Nor is Buddhism a religion—it's actually a nontheistic philosophy. So the connection really works for me, and I tried to share it with my players.

The Noble Eightfold Path that Buddha taught was a way to find release from the suffering that necessarily exists in this (fallen) world of samsara:

1. Right understanding
2. Right thought
3. Right speech
4. Right action
5. Right livelihood
6. Right effort
7. Right mindfulness
8. Right concentration

I presented these to my players as a guide to help explain from a different perspective what we were trying to accomplish on and off the court. Each of us has to understand our own personal role and the role of the entire team. We have to think about these roles and be verbally supportive of our teammates and ourselves.

Let's say the team goes down the court with the ball, and player A passes the ball to player B, who is bumped and misses a shot, but player C was wide open and didn't get the ball. If player B blames himself for the miss or blames the referee for not calling the foul, his mind will be cluttered, and he can't and won't "play" the next sequence at the defensive end. Or another very likely scenario might happen: Player C might be hurt that he was overlooked and blame player A for not giving him the ball or might yell at player B for missing the shot. So as a result of having another agenda, player B might carry the play mentally for two or three trips up and down the court, creating a difficult situation for himself, his teammates, and his coach. This happens all the time. We're all susceptible to not paying attention to the moment because of being too hasty, or of living in the past. Right thought means being in the moment as much as humanly possible. Right action means playing every play, every quarter, every game to its fullest—that's my goal for the team. Winning is only the secondary effect of right thinking and right action.

As far as right livelihood is concerned, I told them that some people make money from gambling, or drugs, or prostitution, or a number of other ways destructive to individuals and to society at large. Our livelihood as professional athletes and coaches is not destructive unless we're too concerned with things like selling sneakers to kids who can't afford them. If we're just using whatever status we have to create personal wealth, if we're not giving anything back to our communities, then all we're really doing is creating poverty.

The sixth, seventh, and eighth principles are quite obvious, particularly in their relation to basketball: right effort has to do with unselfishness and working to benefit the team. Right mindfulness is about playing with precision, making the correct pass, the correct cuts, and so on. Right concentration emphasizes the importance of focus, the one quality that gives a player the capacity to be in the flow.

I pointed out that they have to be conscious of everything they do. They can't recklessly party after a ball game, thinking that there's no connection between partying and basketball. Everything is connected, and the oneness of all things is what keeps you going in the right direction. It's this very connection that can provide strength and energy in a crisis.

It was a message they needed to hear, and they were able to hear it clearly.

Well, our guys came out and played inspired basketball in the first half. We were able to exert some degree of control over Portland's three troublesome plays. We'd managed to establish a small lead early in the second half, when Portland suddenly hit a hot streak. Whereas a team is happy to score 1.2 points for every possession, they registered 18 points in seven trips down the floor. Smith hit a thirty-foot three-pointer. Scottie connected on a beautiful turnaround jumper just in front of our bench to beat the shot clock. And we were down by 16 and fading fast.

I called a time-out late in the third quarter to bark at them about playing hard. But I must admit that I thought we might be dead in the water. In recent years, the Lakers had a history of collapsing in the play-offs, and perhaps history was about to repeat itself.

When the game resumed, we went to screen/rolls for Kobe, who hit some big shots, as well as some counteractions for Shaq. Brian Shaw canned some crucial threes, made a nifty pass to Shaq for a score, and then stole a rebound out of Grant's hands. And most importantly, we started playing defense like gangbusters. That's when Smith and Wallace went cold, and Portland was scoreless in thirteen consecutive possessions.

Then there was that wonderful pass Kobe threw to Shaq, who went two feet above the rim to catch the ball and slam it home. That one play was a symbol of how far these two young men had come in connecting with each other.

For most of the season, Kobe had been primarily concerned with putting his own personal stamp on a ball game by creating a moment that highlighted his skill and his style. And for much of the season this had been an irritant for his teammates. The question was, could Kobe find the kind of satisfaction he needed without jeopardizing the team's chances of winning? There was pressure on me too. How much of Kobe's showmanship could I tolerate without killing his spirit? The turning point had come after that game against Cleveland in Los Angeles when Shaq had stood up in a team meeting and called Kobe on the carpet. Once the problem had been exposed, we had come together and found a mutual level of acceptability. Kobe could do *this*. But he couldn't do *that*.

And the dramatic pass to Shaq also symbolized how far Kobe himself had come. He could be the engine for our offense. He could break down a defense within the context of our system and make the play for Shaq to finish.

Portland did make another run at us. Wallace hit a thirty-five-foot three-ball to close our lead to three points. And then came a crucial play when Smith drove to the basket, and there was some obvious contact between him and Shaq without a foul being called. The way we saw the play was that Horry had already deflected Smith's shot before the contact, and that's why the refs didn't penalize Shaq.

The final score was 89–84, and even though the Lakers were unquestionably Shaq's team, Kobe led us in points (25), rebounds (11), and assists (7)—quite a clutch performance for a young man who'd normally be a college senior.

Our defense had been the determining factor, but the Trail Blazers had also arrived at the end of their tether. Their emotional and physical exertion in games five and six had indeed taken its toll. In fact, after the game was over I had a chance to talk to Scottie, and he agreed. "We were completely worn out, Phil," he said. "We played the last half of the fourth quarter on shaky legs." So it wasn't a question of Portland choking or anything of that nature.

Another problem that came back to haunt Portland was the fact that they needed to put the ball into the hands of somebody who could take them home. The Bulls always had Michael, who could take them over the top by digging down and finding something, anything, to take them there.

Rasheed Wallace was a young twenty-five-year-old who probably needs another couple of years to fully mature. He's one of the most talented players in the league, and when he grows into his game, he'll be able to find a way to bring his team to the pinnacle.

What other influences were at work to so dramatically turn the game around? We made some hustle plays, hit some three-pointers, and cut our deficit to under ten points. That's just about when the notoriously laid-back L.A. crowd got inspired and were able to feed us a lot of energy. I'd also like to think that the guys finally started believing in themselves. But who knows? Maybe it was just divine intervention.

There was only one more team standing between us and a championship—the Indiana Pacers.

The media had been claiming all season long that whoever came out of the West would be champs, so we were trumpeted as being the overwhelming favorites. As far as my staff and I were concerned, however, we had a load of respect for the Pacers, and we knew the series would be a dogfight.

That said, we also felt that the Indiana team that the Bulls had defeated in the Eastern Conference finals in 1998 was a better ball club. The biggest difference was the absence of Antonio Davis, who was a wonderful defender and powerhouse rebounder. Also, back then Chris Mullin was two years younger. Mullin had since been replaced by Jalen Rose, who was a more dynamic scorer, but there's no substitute for experience. Mullin was a clever, unselfish player, and the Pacers had much better ball movement when he was playing and in his prime.

Larry Bird had been a rookie coach in 1998, and since then he had certainly developed a more forceful personality on the bench. Bird was going to make the decisions, play the game the way he wanted it played, and override any of his players' dissatisfactions through the sheer force of his will. When the Pacers lost to the Knicks in the 1999 Eastern Conference finals, it was clear that Bird was highly critical of his players. He hadn't been able to mask his disgust as the offending players came out of the game and approached the bench. Even this year, I thought that Larry might not have really liked all the guys on his team. I wondered how much he enjoyed coaching someone like Jalen Rose, who was constantly breaking plays and going off on his own. And how did Bird feel about Reggie Miller, a hell of a competitor with great heart, but a guy who's always looking for the nearest defender to jump into or flop over so that he can get to the foul line? When Larry was with the Celtics, he would shout at his teammates whenever they messed up or took shortcuts, and he'd order them over to where they were supposed to be. He was almost like a coach on the floor. This year, Bird controlled the Pacers' offense more than he'd done in the past by making calls on virtually every half-court possession.

Another mark of Bird's increasing maturity as a coach was that under his tutelage his players have shown a dramatic improvement. Bird was able to imbue guys like Austin Croshere, Jalen Rose, and even Dale Davis with the self-confidence each of them needed to step up their games.

I also liked the way that Bird involved his assistant coaches—Dick Harter on defense and Rick Carlisle on offense. Bird wasn't afraid to take their advice and in some cases actually defer to them. This showed me that Bird's ego was never at stake, that he was only interested in winning.

While I have the utmost respect for Larry, we have no personal relationship whatsoever. This is the standard operating procedure in the NBA, but there are some notable exceptions. There are many coaches, for example, who have a shared history of being college or NBA assistants under the same head coach, or of going to the same school, or of working the same summer camps. Don Nelson has his group of acolytes, including Del Harris and George Karl. Larry Brown's most noteworthy disciples include Allan Gentry, Bill Blair, and John Calipari. These guys will play golf during the summer, and make sure to touch base on a regular basis.

I'm not a golfer, and I really don't socialize with many people. It's my lifestyle more than anything else—the constant traveling, and the lack of any set routine. And in the off season, I make a beeline to my home in Montana. There's also a generation gap between old-timers like me and the younger coaches who're coming into the league in increasing numbers, guys like Doc Rivers, Byron Scott, and Scott Skiles, who don't remember JFK being assassinated.

Even before the season began, Bird announced that this was going to be his last year on the bench. Of course the media tends to simplify everything, so the finals were seen as pitting me against Larry Bird. It's only natural that a lot of people wanted to see Larry go out with a championship. I can certainly understand that. But what happened in some quarters was that I somehow became the fall guy. The natural cycle is that the media build people up and then tear them down. Some of them simply had had enough of all the adulatory stuff that's been written about me over the years—the Zen stuff, the Native American paraphernalia, the mumbo-jumbo about the Triangle. It was time for the wheel to turn again, and that's fine with me.

If the play-offs last two months, there are maybe three or four days during that period where I'm not required to stand in front of the media with microphones and cameras shoved into my face. They're at every practice and every shootaround, and I also have to be available to the media before and after every game. I try to be patient, yet so much public attention can't help generating a certain amount of stress. And the media people are under their own pressure to come up with a fresh angle every day, so even the most lighthearted comments are exaggerated into something serious and even sinister, and every expression of confidence in my team is interpreted as a sign of arrogance. That's the media's reality. My reality is that I have to do my job the best way I know how. And when yesterday's newspaper is in the garbage can, when last night's SportsCenter is forgotten, all that's left is the game. For sure, I'm sensitive about how I'm portrayed in the media, but at the same time, I can't afford to care. The game is the thing.

Anyway, the Pacers' journey to the finals hadn't been an easy one. Like us, they'd been pushed to five games in their first series. The Milwaukee Bucks had hurt Indiana with high screen/rolls, especially when seven-foot-four Rik Smits was on the floor and had to play defense twenty-five feet from the basket. The Pacers had needed a last-second three-pointer by Travis Best in the deciding game to put the Bucks away.

Indiana's series against the Philadelphia 76ers had been extremely physical. Reggie Miller was suspended for one game for getting into a battle with Gary Geiger (who had to sit out two games). But the Pacers were able to stand toe-to-toe with Philadelphia and knock them down in six games.

The Eastern Conference finals had been a replay of 1999— Indiana versus the Knicks. In 1999 the Pacers never really adjusted to the Knicks' screen/rolls, but this season was a different story. Another difference was the absence (in 1999) and the presence (in 2000) of Patrick Ewing. Of course Ewing can still get his points, but he's slow to rotate on defense, and he's also slow to the balls that come off the boards. The Knicks are so much quicker without Ewing, and that's the key against the Pacers. This year, the Pacers successfully dealt with the Knicks' screen/rolls, took advantage of Ewing's relative immobility, and won the series in six games.

For the championship series, the format was changed. We retained the home-court advantage, but instead of a 2-2-2-1 setup, it was 2-3-2. This meant that it was imperative for us to win the first two games in Los Angeles. A split would mean that Indiana could theoretically end the series without our returning home. (In truth, however, no homestanding team ever sweeps the middle three games.) We'd split our two regular-season games, and it was the Pacers who'd terminated our sixteen-game winning streak, so we knew there was nothing we could take for granted.

Indiana was the best shooting team in the league and could come at you with a multitude of weapons: Miller, of course, either in isolations or running around a maze of picks; Rose, a great one-on-one player with a quick left-handed release; Mark Jackson, who liked to postup smaller guards; Croshere, a three-point shooter and hard-nosed driver;

Travis Best, the quickest of the Pacers and an explosive shotmaker; Smits, an excellent jump shooter with good moves in the paint, whose function was to jump-start the offense; Sam Perkins, whose three-point accuracy presented a problem for Shaq; and even Dale Davis, who had become a threat to score with his back to the basket.

Our game plan to start the series was to give the Pacers a heavy dose of Shaquille O'Neal. And that's exactly what happened. Shaq's size and speed dominated game one; we got the early lead and maintained it throughout. There was one other factor, though, which contributed to our early breakout.

The game began at six o'clock local time, which can be a tricky situation for someone who's not familiar with the traffic patterns in Los Angeles, where the freeways start getting clogged at about three-thirty. In addition, the Democratic National Convention was due here in August, so several of the major arteries were being repaired. Since the Pacers were staying in Santa Monica, their only route to the Staples Arena was Interstate 10, which at that hour was as crowded as a parking lot. As a result, instead of arriving at the arena two hours before game time, they showed up an hour before the tip-off. They just had time enough to get taped and hustle out onto the court. This disruption of the Pacers' normal pregame routine had as much to do with their poor start as anything we did. Why else would a great shooter like Reggie Miller wind up going 1–16 from the field?

The final count was 104–87, with Shaq contributing forty-three points and nineteen rebounds. I was certainly relieved to have the first one in the bag. At the same time, we'd started every other series with a convincing win, so I wasn't too impressed. As with Sacramento, Phoenix, and Portland, the Pacers would make their adjustments, and we'd have to find other ways to win.

We were in fairly good shape as the second game was under way, with Shaq still in firm command of the paint. Then, nine minutes into the first quarter, Kobe came down on Rose's foot and turned his ankle. It was obviously a major-league sprain, the kind that can bother a player for months. But the task at hand was to find some way to win the game. Shaq was Shaq (forty points, twenty-four rebounds, four assists, and three blocked shots), while both Harper (twenty-one points, six assists) and Rice (twenty-one points, including five or six three-pointers) stepped up to fill the void. We overcame a minor Hack-a-Shaq attack (he shot 18–39 FTs), as well as strong performances from Rose, Miller, and Croshere (who combined for seventy-five points) to prevail by 111–104.

Okay, we'd survived without Kobe, and were more than likely going to be without him for game three, the first of the three-game set in Indiana. Our mindset was that we only needed to win one of those three games and the series was over, because the Pacers weren't likely to beat us twice in L.A. Indiana had matched us for the NBA's best home record at 36–5, but they weren't a very good road team (20–21).

The Pacers left L.A. right after the ball game, but we stayed home overnight. Then because of a WNBA game we had to adjust our departing flight so that we could practice at the Conseco Fieldhouse. It had gotten to the point where the WNBA season was infringing on the NBA play-offs.

I've always had good feelings about Indianapolis. The bus driver who drove us from the hotel to the new fieldhouse was just about my age, fifty, and we both waxed nostalgic about the old Pacers team in the defunct American Basketball Association. In fact, on our way to the fieldhouse we had to drive past the fairgrounds where the Pacers used to play. When I was playing with the Knicks, we'd once come to town to play an exhibition game against the Pacers, who were the ABA's reigning champs. With players like Freddie Lewis, Bob Netolicky, Billy Keller, and Rick Mount, the Pacers had given us a tough ball game. The citizens of Indianapolis had taken the Pacers and the ABA to their hearts, and a strong sense of shared community still survived.

For me, that's what sports is all about. Whether it's the World Cup in soccer or the Albany Patroons in the CBA, bringing people together in a common spirit ultimately transcends wins and losses.

When we finally arrived at the fieldhouse, Kobe couldn't rise up on his toes without creating some pain. He told me that he wanted to play anyway, but I decided to give him another three days' rest.

Besides, my players were primed to win without Kobe—not because of any personal animus toward him but just to pick up a teammate, and also end the series before the Pacers heated up.

Indiana came out with tremendous energy and had us down by eight at the quarter. Since there was a Sunday-to-Wednesday wait-around for the next game, Bird played Rose and Miller the entire first half, and the two of them shot the lights out. Besides featuring Shaq, our main emphasis was trying to get Glen Rice going. We crept back to a five-point deficit midway through the third quarter, but then the bottom fell out. The Pacers started raining threes, and almost before we knew it we were down by seventeen.

There were two minutes left in the third quarter when I decided to put some of our tougher guys into the game—Horry, Fox, and Fisher. I didn't care if Jackson posted the much smaller Fisher and backed him to the basket. And, lo and behold, we got back into the game. Indiana's margin had been reduced to four points, with just under two minutes to go, when Horry tossed up a three that would have brought it down to one—but the shot missed. From then on we had to commit fouls, and the Pacers closed us out by 100–91.

I was happy with our effort. The only glitch was that Glen didn't have a very good game, shooting only 3–9. Fox was playing so well that Glen wound up playing only twenty-seven minutes. Even though he spent more minutes than he wanted to on the bench, Glen was very supportive of the guys on the court.

The trouble came after the game, when Glen's wife, Christy, complained to the media. She said that the only thing the Lakers cared about was winning, and that my sitting him for most of the fourth quarter might have justified Glen's going after me the way that Latrell Sprewell had gone after P. J. Carlesimo—except that her husband wasn't that kind of person. She said that I'd never liked Glen, and that I'd been upset when we couldn't trade him for Scottie Pippen.

It was a sad affair all around, especially since Glen and I had already talked it over. Scottie had played the Triangle for nine years and his presence in L.A. would have helped the other guys learn the system quicker and more efficiently. Another factor in the Lakers trying to deal for Pippen was that Glen was in the free-agent year of his contract, while Scottie was signed for another five years. Glen totally understood what was happening, and he had no beef. The guys on the team knew that we'd worked hard to create a positive sense about ourselves, and we weren't going to take a step backward because of some comments in a newspaper. Credit Glen for supporting his wife but not publicly defending what she'd said.

The day after game three, I was doing yet another stint in front of the TV cameras, and some guy popped off this question: "How do you feel about the fans here in Indiana?" My answer was that the Pacers fans were decent, fair-minded people who were really into basketball—even if Indiana lost, they'd come over and tell us that we'd played well—but the fans in Sacramento and Portland made more noise. In Portland, there was a group of a dozen or so guys who'd stand behind our bench and shout insults at us all game long. I also told the reporter that when I left the court in Sacramento and Portland, my ears were ringing, but that wasn't the case in Indiana.

Just before game four started, a skewed version of my quote showed up on the Jumbo-Tron, to the effect that the fans were better in Sacramento and Portland. This wasn't an accurate representation of what I'd actually said, but the fans were very riled up.

To top it off, one of Harper's characteristically humorous quotes was also posted: "This is a nice building with a lot of room in the rafters for championship banners. I didn't notice any of them hanging up there, and there sure isn't going to be one put up there this year."

All of the hoopla stoked the Pacers fans into a frenzy. I'd learned long ago not to take any of the fans' emotional outbursts in a personal way. The only thing I was worried about was my players being able to hear me during time-outs.

So we went into game four with the crowd berserk and with Kobe ready to play. There were seventeen lead changes throughout, and the game was just a terrific example of NBA action. The Pacers were very comfortable playing in their building and were starting to play the way they wanted to play—shooting threes, swarming the offensive boards, out-quicking us to loose balls, and beating us with their early offense. Even when we did succeed in slowing the Pacers to a walk and making them run their half-court sets, Smits and Miller were well-nigh unstoppable.

I was hoping that Glen would rebound from all the controversy and have a good game, but he was only 3–8 from the field and had three turnovers. Shaq was routinely awesome, Harper had a great floor game, and Horry was sensational. The biggest surprise was Kobe, who finished the game with twenty-eight points without ever going to the free-throw line.

As the game raced to the wire, the Pacers had a chance to win it because Horry turned the ball over with the score knotted in the last few seconds. When Indiana inbounded the ball, our strategy was to switch on every crossing—which we did, only to find Shaq guarding Travis Best twenty feet from the basket. Earlier in the game, Shaq had blasted Best to the floor while trying to block the little man's shot and was called for a flagrant foul. Best had taken a hard fall and jammed his left shoulder. It was evident that even as Best tried maneuvering around Shaq, seeking to launch the game-winning shot, his left shoulder was bothering him. As a result, Best's shot was an airball, and we actually wound up getting the last shot—a long hook by Shaq that also went awry.

Overtime. And Shaq fouled out within the first minute. It was up to Kobe to carry us home, and the young man proceeded to score eight of the team's total of sixteen overtime points.

We had a three-point lead near the end of the extra period, and the Pacers were poised to inbounds the ball when the referees made an unusual call—a foul on Rick Fox while the ball was still out of bounds. Miller made the resulting free throw, and our lead was clipped to two. The replay was never shown on TV, but in going over the game tape, we could see that Rose had jammed Fox into Perkins to create the contact. The call might have cost us the ball game, but when Reggie Miller missed a three-pointer at the buzzer, the game was ours, 120–118.

Bird had gone for the win, which was something that I wouldn't have done. Let's say that Miller was at best a 45 percent three-point shooter. I'd anticipate that with the game on the line he would've been at least a 55 percent shooter had he been looking to score only two (to say nothing of the possibility of drawing a foul). Plus, with Shaq out, and the likelihood of forcing Kobe to play another five minutes on his injured ankle, I would have gone for two and taken my chances in another overtime. On the other hand, Perkins had hit a three-pointer to tie the game at the end of regulation, and with only 3.4 seconds remaining, the chances are that a three wouldn't have drawn as much of a defensive crowd as a two.

After the final buzzer Shaq went onto the court to find Kobe and give him a big hug. It was a beautiful sight for me to behold. What had once been a situation that had divided the team was now totally healed.

After the game, the media wanted me to compare Kobe with Michael. I did say that Kobe was probably a better player at age twenty-one than Michael had been. The kicker, however, was that at age twenty-one, Kobe had been playing in the NBA for four years, while Michael was just a rookie. Yes, Kobe had taken advantage of his opportunity, but I didn't consider his overtime performance to be anything more than a good start for his career. I had coached Michael in 115 play-off games, and he'd had 90 transcendent games.

Of course the media's angle was that since we were ahead 3–1, and since Kobe was healthy, he would play like Michael Jordan again, and there was no doubt that we'd close the book on the series in game five. The reality was that Indiana was tough as nails at home. And besides, we had too many distractions to get our heads clear enough to keep playing at the same high level.

First off, our hotel accommodations in Indianapolis weren't very satisfactory. We were in a Sheraton located on the beltway fifteen miles out of town. There were too many kids hanging around the hotel, and the players had no privacy. Also, without a car there were no places to get a meal after the ball games. My practice has always been to allow my players to bring their family to all of the road games in the finals. But since the hotel was bad news, I'd arranged for us to fly to L.A., win or lose, immediately after game five. This was a logistical nightmare because we had to pack our bags before leaving for the game. We traveled to the arena in a convoy of three buses, and the guys had to worry about taking care of Momma, Baby, and maybe even Grandpa and

Grandma. It was too much of a hullabaloo for us to properly prepare for the game, and that showed up not long after the opening tip-off.

Glen Rice hit one of two free throws to stake us to a 1–0 lead, and that was the high point of the game for us. From there, the Pacers bombed us into oblivion with three-pointers. Rose was 3–3 from beyond the three-point line, and Miller was 2–2. All told, the Pacers shot an incredible 15–20 from the field for the first period! Then things really got bad—midway through the second quarter, Indiana reeled off eight straight points and took a 54–35 lead.

Kobe had one of those atrocious games that could easily destroy a young ballplayer's self-confidence for life. He missed open jumpers, layups, and put-backs. The only shots he didn't miss were free throws, and that's because he didn't take any. Here's a kid that drives hard to the hoop and *gets* to the foul line, but so far in four games he'd only shot a total of two free throws.

The Pacers, of course, came out sky-high and played a smart, energetic game. Within one minute of play at the end of the third quarter and the beginning of the fourth, they tallied eleven points. They even scored a total of four four-point plays—three when a three-point shooter was fouled in the act and the basket was good, and one on a three-point shot by Miller and a technical on Fisher. Even though the Pacers were the third-worst rebounding team in the league, they also pounded us to death on the boards.

(Statistics can be misleading, and nothing is more misleading than a team's offensive rebounding numbers. Bad-shooting teams invariably get more opportunities to rebound their own misses. Conversely, good-shooting teams like Indiana have fewer opportunities. This said, I firmly believe that championship teams usually find a way to produce second-chance shots. The Bulls were a team that always had a high field-goal percentage, yet we were perennially one of the leading offensive rebounding teams in the league. This was because one of the advantages of the Triangle is that it produces optimum angles and lanes for rebounders to follow shots to the boards.)

The final score was 120–87, a thirty-three-point loss!

Because we were traveling with our families, we couldn't use our customized plane, so we'd chartered a standard 757 instead.

Unfortunately, the plane had only fourteen first-class seats, which were reserved for the players, while everyone else was in coach. We left Indianapolis at one a.m. for a five-hour flight. The video machine was broken, so we couldn't watch the game tape. It was an hellacious trip. I was jammed into a small seat and unable to sleep at all.

How could a team with championship ambitions play such a horrible game? Thirty-three points? By far our worst performance of the season. Sure, we'd come away from Indianapolis with the one victory I'd wanted, but still... There was no way the Pacers would shoot as well in L.A., but still... Thirty-three points? Was this the most embarrassing loss of my entire coaching career?

We landed at five in the morning, and I arranged to meet with my coaching staff twelve hours later. We had to find a way to control the Pacers' scoring.

After reviewing the film of game five, we decided to change our defensive assignments. Harper was switched from Jackson to Miller, Kobe from Miller/Rose to Jackson, Rice from Miller to Rose. We thought this alignment would put more pressure on the basketball. Harp had the experience to bother Miller and not be sucked into cheap fouls. And we needed to get Rice fired up about jailin' Jalen.

Up till that point, we'd had Shaq start every game either guarding Smits or, because Indiana went to Smits right off the bat in hopes of pinning early fouls on Shaq, Dale Davis. We decided to put A. C. on Smits and front him. The Pacers generally had trouble making the lob pass over a fronting defense, and Smits wasn't comfortable having to catch the ball while turning blindly to the basket.

Aside from the individual matchups, Indiana had been murdering us with their version of one of the basic NBA offenses—the single-double. If a team couldn't defend the single-double, they'd never win a game. Our philosophy required a defender to tailgate a player as he snaked through the picks. The big men were then supposed to step out and bang the cutter to prevent him from curling sharply to the basket. But Rose and Miller were too tricky—popping, flattening out, faking a curl, then stepping back—and were escaping our control. The only answer we had was to start switching, even if that meant winding up with Horry or A. C. on either Miller or Rose.

Another reason why we'd had so much trouble with their single-double was that we hadn't been challenging the pickers enough to get a foul call. The Pacers were infamous for setting moving screens—sliding their feet, using their hips and/or arms to move into the defender's path. On tape, we'd seen the Pacers commit at least three or four illegal picks per game in the Indiana–New York series, and the refs were just as reluctant to make the calls in our series.

With the referees' sanction, Reggie Miller was also having a field day. There was one sequence in game five where Miller literally ran into Horry (who was guarding Croshere), then flopped like he was the foulee. And the referees bought it.

As we went over and over the most recent game tape, I became more and more incensed. We just couldn't have the Pacers beating us so easily on both ends of the court. There was a total sense of urgency as we compiled our game plan for game six.

Leaving the film room, we came across Shaq on the court practicing his free throws. He'd been 1–6 in game six and had aborted whatever early rallies we'd almost managed to string together. Talking about how contagious poor free-throw shooting is: Glen Rice shot 87 percent in the regular season, but was merely 4–7 in the infamous game five.

When we reconvened for practice on Sunday, we concentrated on containing Indiana's single-double. Kobe's ankle was sore, and ordinarily he would've been resting it and getting treatment, but we asked him to tape up and walk through our new defensive schemes.

We also worked with Shaq on how we wanted him to guard Smits, keeping him out of the middle and forcing him to turn baseline for his fadeaway jumper. In the last two games, Smits had averaged over a point a minute. True, there were a couple of times when Shaq had cleanly blocked Smits's jump hooks but had been whistled for fouls. It was just bad officiating. After both of those calls, however, Shaq had backed off and played too passively. We reinforced the principle that if Shaq continued to be aggressive, then the referees would change the way they called the game.

I must confess, though, that despite myself I gained a lot of respect for the referees during this season. The previous summer,

word had come down from the top commanding the refs to dephys-
icalize the game. Defenders were no longer allowed to impede the
progress of a cutter. This is a ridiculous concept that basically pro-
hibits defense. The referees were handed a loaded gun, and if they
fired a shot every time a defender tried to protect the lane, then
defense would be dead and NBA teams would average 160 points a
game.

Another thing that the coaching staff gleaned from the last game
tape was that we were settling too often for jump shots. In game six
we needed to drive the ball to the basket and put pressure on the
Pacers' interior defense.

We emphasized that once again we were in a position to avoid a
game seven. This was *the* game. We had to get down and get busy,
and it all had to start with our defense.

Reggie Miller came out and said that the pressure was all on the
Lakers. The Pacers were playing with confidence, and the onus was
on us to play well enough to beat them. I thought Reggie had it backward. If we lost game six, we still had another chance to win in our
building. If they lost, they were toast.

So—pump up the ball, turn on the lights, and here we go again.

The Pacers were indeed playing with confidence, and they
jumped out ahead. We did a much better job of solving their single-
double, but Miller and Rose were on fire. Smits rarely plays well on
the road, and he had a subpar game (1–8 from the field). The biggest
surprise, however, was Dale Davis. He wiped the offensive boards
clean and hit a few turnaround jumpers that not even Shaq could
catch up with. Croshere was another strong force in the game. We'd
resolved to keep him out of the lane and live with his outside shooting—then the sucker hit three three-pointers on us.

But we battled back. Shaq owned the paint, and Glen connected
several times from long range. We were up by one when Mark
Jackson flung up a turnaround three-pointer from half-court that
split the net. That improbable shot put us down 26–24 at the first
quarter break.

And I thought, man, the Pacers were riding a big wave, and we were
going to have to endure it until their momentum broke. Surely they

couldn't continue shooting the lights out in our building. But they did. With Rose, Miller, Davis, and Croshere firing away, Indiana won the second quarter by a point and had us down 56–53 at the half.

All season long the third quarter had been a productive time for us. We could make our adjustments at halftime, refocus our energy, and get our chops up. But the Pacers kept making their three-pointers. Perkins hit two, Jackson one, and even Derrick McKey, a defensive specialist, hit one. (For the game, Indiana shot 12–25 from three-ball range.)

Meanwhile, Shaq kept pounding away inside, but Kobe was having trouble locating the hoop. Fortunately, Derek Fisher, Rick Fox, and Robert Horry gave us big numbers off the bench. After three quarters, the Pacers had forged ahead by 84–79.

One of the statistics that we kept track of was the quarter scores. At the break, I told the guys that all we had to do was win the fourth quarter. One good quarter out of four would be enough.

Furthermore, I fully expected that Indiana would undergo the same type of emotional and physical letdown that Portland had suffered at the end of game seven. The Pacers did have a long bench, but not as long as Portland's. Perkins was thirty-nine years old, and it was a grunt for him to take a beating guarding Shaq at one end, and then be sliding out to the three-point line on offense. Croshere played well, but his minutes (twenty-seven) were limited by foul trouble. And with his left shoulder still painful, Best was not at his best.

I also made several important adjustments to start the fourth quarter. I knew that defending the screen/roll was one of Indiana's weaknesses. The Pacers' philosophy was to blitz the screen/roll and aggressively abandon the screener to double-team the ball. This would result in one of their big men (Smits or Davis) chasing a guard or small forward thirty feet from the basket. Any kind of counteraction would find their middle exposed and their big men too far away to help. We used screen/rolls in the overtime of game four, but hadn't shown it to them since then. Showing your best weapon too early gives your opponent a chance to get used to the action and make their own adjustments.

Our wrinkle was to send a guard to the corner as though we were forming a strong-side triangle. Then we set up a wing screen/roll situation (which we call a "fist-chest") with someone like Harper or Kobe handling the ball, and Horry or Fox setting the screen. When the screener's defender jumped out to pressure the ball, someone had to rotate to cover Horry or Fox, since they're both dangerous three-point shooters. So now the Pacers had three men moving away from the basket, and when we counteracted the ball back across the grain, we could make an easy pass into the guard in the corner and then another one into Shaq. In the process, either Shaq was left to be defended one-on-one (an overwhelming advantage for us), or else one of our three-point shooters would have an open look.

We ran the fist-chest six times in the last nine minutes of the game, and there were several big plays for us down the stretch: Shaw blocking Rose's shot from behind, which got us an easy bucket in the subsequent fast break; Fox hitting a three-pointer, unchallenged by Miller; Miller badly missing a wide-open three-ball; Horry making a three on a counteraction; Shaq stuffing home a miss by Kobe; Shaw driving hard right to the hoop, then deliberately tossing the ball high off the backboard so that Shaq could make an easy catch and a dunk—a situational play that we call "The Shaw-Shaq Redemption."

With about a minute left to go, about twenty-five security cops showed up to rope off the court. If either Bird or I wanted to make a substitution, the new player would've had to climb over the rope to access the court. It was quite a hubbub. Neither the bench players nor the coaches knew where we were supposed to be, so most of us stepped over the rope and hovered on the edge of the court while the game counted down.

The last pivotal play happened with thirty-five seconds remaining and the Pacers behind, 112–109. That's when Miller pulled up for a quick off-balance shot from thirty feet. It was a poor decision on his part. We grabbed the rebound and finally put them away when Kobe made a pair of free throws with thirteen seconds left.

We'd scored thirty-seven points in the fourth quarter and won the game 116–111.

The Lakers were the champs!

It was the ninth time for me—two as a player with the Knicks, and six times coaching the Bulls—and each final buzzer of each final game was a totally unique and utterly unmitigated thrill!

In the early stages of the on-court celebration I sought out Larry Bird and told him that he'd done a superior job. His team had showed great courage and had everything to be proud of. We'd won the series; they hadn't lost it. Then I wished him luck on whatever path he chose.

(I have no inside information concerning Bird's future plans. He'll bide his time, but now that Rick Pitino has left Boston, I would not be surprised to see Larry take over the Celtics.)

In the locker room, I tried to stay out of the way. I even managed to avoid getting doused with champagne. It was difficult to personally connect with my players because the media is king, and the guys were being hustled from one TV camera to the next. We usually form a circle after every game, but even that was violated. So I just gave up, went into the coaches' office, and shared a toast with my staff. I thanked them all for their work and their support. Then it was my turn to face the media.

Some of the local Los Angelenos were fearful that a Lakers championship might trigger riots in the streets. In Chicago there'd been a couple of times when some celebrations got out of hand. Windows were broken, cars were overturned, several people were hurt, and there'd been a definite undertone of rebelling against authority. But I didn't believe that the same kind of situation existed in L.A. I thought that there might be some kind of energy release akin to a spring break. Of course, there was a to-do in the Staples parking lot, a few cars burned, and a few storefronts were trashed. It was just a group of kids running wild, and I think the entire situation was overblown by the media.

I didn't try to leave the arena until three hours after the game. There's a beautiful club there that's probably more comfortable than anyplace else available in the surrounding area. So that's where the organization's initial celebration took place.

More than anything, I really got a kick out of watching how some of the guys reacted to winning their first championship. The young players—Travis Knight, Devean George, Derek Fisher, John Celestand, and Kobe Bryant—were overwhelmed with joy and believed they were destined to be champs happily forever after. The elder statesmen—Rick Fox, Glen Rice, and Shaquille O'Neal—were somewhat more subdued, knowing how rare was the prize they'd just won.

Three weeks later I was back in Montana, where I had time to decompress, reflect on the season, and evaluate the progress (or lack thereof) of the players within our system.

The Lakers' championship reinforced what I'd known for a long time—paying attention to basics is the key to success. The most fundamental aspect of the Triangle offense is the ability of the players to quickly and effectively pass the ball. A lot of NBA coaches don't want to take the time to teach passing, but we were willing to work on it all season long. Even so, up until the end we had several guys who had trouble making the right pass at the right time. What worked in our favor was the fact that Shaq could really go get the ball.

Horry, Fox, Shaq, and Travis Knight made the biggest improvements in this area. Even though Fisher was not a natural playmaker, his decisions in three-on-two and two-on-one fast-break situations improved. Salley was always a good passer, except for his tendency to try to throw a home-run pass. Kobe's problem was getting the ball out of his hand quick enough when he saw an open man—scorers generally have sticky fingers. Glen became adept at dropping passes into Shaq, but not at making snappy perimeter passes. Shaw was always one of our better passers, and Harp certainly knew all the appropriate angles. Harp's only problem was executing passes with his left hand.

Proper footwork is another key to our offense. It's crucial in setting up a defender, in receiving and protecting the ball (especially on the wing), and generally in allowing time for our spacing to develop. We teach four different varieties of footwork—two for inside-foot pivots and two for outside-foot pivots. These are: rear turns, baseline pivots, front turns, and inside reverse pivots. (The steps are reversed on the opposite side of the floor, so all told there are eight variations.) Again, these universally applicable skills were once taught by college coaches, but the only footwork moves still taught are the drop step and the baseline reverse pivot that Jack Sikma popularized. But I consider these to be mere survival techniques.

We were still working on our footwork in the Indiana series, concentrating mostly on pinch-post moves, and also the proper steps that would facilitate swinging the ball around the perimeter.

I thought that Shaq could be a devastating force receiving the ball near the foul line at the pinch post. His footwork is certainly deft enough for him to easily drive around guys like Ewing, Sabonis, and Smits. The advantage Shaq would gain is that it's virtually impossible to double-team someone at the high post. But Shaq's not very comfortable playing so far away from the basket, and he was also afraid of getting a charging foul.

Rick Fox probably made the biggest advance in terms of his footwork. He learned several rear-turn moves that were absolutely legal but that the referees frequently interpreted as traveling. We had guys routinely called for offensive fouls when they used a reverse pivot to legally screen an opponent. It just bewilders me that the referees neither recognize nor honor good footwork.

With only a sometimes grasp of the basics, it's no wonder that the Lakers often had difficulty with our offensive flow. Our most chronic problem was trying to format the Triangle out of a fast-break situation. One night we'd have it all figured out, then the next night we were totally stymied. For several players the offense never became instinctive.

I was more than pleased with how well Fox, Horry, and Fisher came to understand the Triangle. Brian Shaw accelerated the ball in good fashion, yet he sometimes got us out of control because his spacing was off. When he was responsible for initiating the offense, Brian would often wander toward the middle of the court so that our sideline triangle would be cockeyed.

Glen had a penchant for running the floor and then looking for a quick post-up. The trouble was that there wasn't much time for Shaq to find his spot in the pivot. Because Glen's instincts proved to be hard to retrain, he sometimes strung us out a little.

Robert Horry developed a wonderful comprehension of the Triangle. More often than not, though, he'd get frustrated when he executed properly and no one else did. Horry's attitude was, "Okay, I'm going to go through with this the right way even if the rest of you guys are shortcutting." But I liked that attitude because Robert made his errant teammates toe the line.

Kobe's habit was to chase the ball and not stay at home. He wasn't willing to wait for the ball to come to him, and his impatience sometimes destroyed our spacing.

A. C. was really good in the offense. His only problem was that Shaq became annoyed when A. C.'s defender sat on his doorstep. Shaq wanted A. C. to bail out off the corner so he'd be isolated in the pivot, but when A. C. left his position too soon, it was much easier for the defense to double Shaq. It was difficult to convince this team that shortcuts don't win championships.

As the season wore on, I studied some of the game tapes from the 1998–99 season, and I came to understand what the Lakers' offense used to be. Basically, the game plan had been to rush the ball into the forecourt, make a play, and take a quick shot. The players' attitude was this: "I'm going to come at you dead-on, and you can't stop me." If nothing came of that headlong approach, then they'd just reverse the ball and try the same thing from the other side. It was an immature, macho philosophy. No wonder the holdover players had such a hard time with the Triangle. And knowing where they came from, I could more readily understand why their attention span was so brief.

At the start of the season, the guys had barely been able to watch five minutes of a game tape without getting so restless that they couldn't concentrate. Slowly, however, I was able to build up their endurance so that by the play-offs they were able to view entire ball games with full attention. Similarly, I initially introduced them to three-minute periods of meditation and gradually stretched them out to ten minutes. After a while, they were even willing to participate in yoga sessions. The constant practice of awareness and concentration certainly made the guys easier to coach.

All of these so-called extras were so vital to our success; we were far from being the most talented team in the league. Indiana, Portland, Phoenix, Sacramento, and New York were all ball clubs whose top eight or nine players had more talent than we had in our regular rotation.

We won for several reasons: because our fundamentals were sound. Because Shaq was so dominant, and Kobe was so creative. But we also won because we developed a certain confidence in our ability to win. This confidence enabled us to go off on several major and minor winning streaks, which in turn generated more confidence. In addition, our defense was able to survive other teams' hot streaks. With our defense emerging as a rallying point, we had many opportunities to recover from large deficits and go on to win ball games that might easily have been lost. It's crucial for a team with championship hopes to have a highly developed comeback ability. All of these qualities more than made up for our talent deficiencies.

Why were we capable of developing these particular qualities? Because we had players of solid character, guys dedicated to playing hard game after game. Guys like A. C. Green, who loved to compete, who, at age thirty-six, averaged twenty-four hard-assed minutes per game. A. C. was usually matched up against players who were bigger, stronger, quicker, and younger, so he was forced to absorb a great deal of physical punishment. But his competitive spirit never wavered.

Ron Harper played more minutes than I wanted him to play, and he was forever complaining about his various aches and pains. But Harp found a way to play hard every time he stepped on the court.

Rick Fox and Derek Fisher also showed me their warriors' hearts and never took a night off. John Salley didn't play many minutes, but he worked hard in practice and encouraged his teammates to do the same.

Some of the guys had to save themselves in practice sessions. Horry had a bad knee, and Rice had tendinitis. Shaq was also plagued with some tendinitis, but he wasn't used to working hard either. At the same time, Shaq knew that he had to play forty minutes every game, so he was compelled to lighten up in practice. Shaq was very driven to win a championship, and he learned in a hurry that the only way to accomplish that goal was to bust his butt every minute of every game.

Kobe probably practiced and played with more energy than anybody else. Our two rookies, Devean George and John Celestand, had to upgrade their intensity level to the point where they were able to push the veteran in practice. All during the regular season our quest was to bring ourselves up to that furious yet controlled competitive level necessary for us to succeed in the play-offs.

After we won the title, I was frequently asked about my personal goals—"Is there anything that you feel you haven't achieved?" "Now that you've won without MJ, is there anything left to achieve?" Of course there is! I'd like to coach a full season without disrupting my personal life or health. I still get a technical or two each year. I still overextend myself in an effort to please too many people at the expense of my loved ones.

At the same time, many basketball pundits have tried to diminish the job I did with the Lakers. There's a line from a Kipling poem that I like to tell my players: "The strength of the pack is the wolf, and the strength of the wolf is the pack." Whether or not you have Michael Jordan or Shaquille O'Neal on your team, a good leader needs to see the truth of this concept. All I can say is that I'm grateful to have been given the opportunity to coach such great players—and I'm glad that together we went the distance.

And what about me? What kind of a season did I really have? Charley insists that the best seasons I've ever had as a coach were my first championship season with the Bulls in 1991, the 1993–94 season without Michael, and last year with the Lakers. Given that different teams call for different responses, and not to denigrate any of my teams, I'd have to agree with Charley.

More than any of my previous teams, the Lakers needed me to be patient. Yes, I told my players, I know that learning the offense is going to be a long and difficult undertaking. You might not be truly comfortable with it until the play-offs, but that's okay. We're going to lose some games because of our confusion, but we're never going to panic. Notwithstanding all of the preseason trade rumors about Scottie Pippen, I had to reassure everybody that I believed we could win a championship with the players we already had onboard.

Nor was I as demanding of them as I'd been with other teams. I tried to maintain a light touch throughout, and I took pains to keep my composure on the bench—not to get unduly emotional when officials missed some calls, and not to freak out when players messed up.

My patience and composure extended into my personal life as well. When I first moved out to Los Angeles, I had anticipated that I'd be out and about more than I'd been in Chicago or New York. I'd be strolling on the beach every day and generally become more available to the public. But that's not the way my life worked out.

I live in a small community near the beach in which I can move around without being hassled too much. There's a neighborhood pub where I can enjoy a beer and a cigar and shoot the breeze with the locals, a café for my breakfasts, a deli for take-out lunches, and a post office. Otherwise, I'm driving my car to practice, to ball games downtown, or to an after-game meal at a restaurant. My knee bothered me all season long, and I simply don't have the overall physical vigor that I did when I was younger. If my workaday life in L.A. hasn't turned out to be what I'd expected, nevertheless I have thoroughly enjoyed being here and working here.

Living in such a wide-open city as Los Angeles has made it difficult to create a sense of community within the team. We are all so separated geographically that our personal lives tend to be separated too. My teams in Chicago had a much deeper sense of community.

Another factor in L.A. has been that so many of the guys are either single or spending the season away from their wives and their children. There isn't a feminine presence at hand—wives calling each other to check on sick kids, to arrange shopping adventures, and just to socialize when the team is out of town. Men aren't supposed to take an interest in each other's personal problems, especially in the male world of professional sports. I profoundly hope that someday, as our cultural consciousness continues to expand, men will be able to feel more intimate with each other.

Despite all the roadblocks, we were able to work out our own unique sense of community. I understand that I'm not always a very open person myself. Like everybody else, I have plenty of personal problems, but I don't like to wear them on my sleeve. And yet there's still a way to demonstrate my sincere interest in my players. That's exactly what my purpose is in giving the players books as Christmas presents. My aim is to make a gift that says to another human being, "I think I know who you are, I respect who you are, and I think I know what interests you." The gift and the intention behind it are what matters. Whether the player will pick up the book and look at it or read it in ten days, ten months, or ten years, he'll register the fact that there's something that's been shared between us.

Somewhere down the road, when our NBA days are done, our paths might cross, and we'll have good feelings about each other. I know that whenever I come across any of my old Knicks' teammates and any of the guys who played for me in Chicago, we still feel a common bond.

Hopefully, our understanding of the power of community will extend beyond our own rather insulated little groups. Perhaps that same realization will manifest somewhere else in the players' lives—as parents, as friends, as community leaders.

One of the most beautiful things about basketball is that developing this sense of community will eventually lead to success on the court. In the long run, nothing's more important than the evolution of consciousness. Winning championships is the greatest feeling in the world, but it passes. In even the best-case scenario, it is just a by-product. What doesn't pass is the opportunity it offers each individual player for personal growth and evolving consciousness. After a great win, Tex tells the team, "Remember, you are only successful for that moment when you have completed a successful task."

FIFTEEN

WHO'S GOT NEXT?

PHIL AND CHARLEY

CHARLEY: So the question is this: What is there about this game that compels us both to so totally devote our lives to it?

PHIL: For me, a lot of it has to do with sensory modes. Touch, hearing, sight, smell. The contact between the sweaty bodies. The footwork and the spins that make up the dance. The squeak of sneakers on a wooden floor. I could be blindfolded and know by the smell that I'm inside a basketball gym.

I can vividly remember that anxious feeling whenever I was late to a pickup game and the guys were already playing. As I hurried toward the gym, I'd hear the unmistakable rhythm of a basketball being dribbled, then came the long silence after the ball was shot and was spinning toward the goal. Did it swish? Did it bounce off the rim and miss?

Even the smell of winter still triggers basketball memories from my North Dakota childhood days. It would have to be really cold, so that the snow was tightly packed, and we'd play outside wearing gloves that had the fingers cut off. We'd also have to overinflate the ball because rubber balls didn't bounce high enough in cold air. All of these sense memories are part of who I am.

I was brought up in a small community where basketball was considered to be a legitimate vehicle that could safely carry me into the larger world. Right after we won the high school state championship, the mayor of Williston took me downtown to a clothing store and bought me my first suit, size XXL, so that I'd be well dressed when I went off to college.

Of course, you grew up in a big city, Charley, so the game must have been very different for you.

CHARLEY: At first, playing ball was an excuse to get away from my father, so there was something forbidden about it. This feeling was further reinforced by the fact that the neighborhood basketball court was in the schoolyard of P.S. 4 and surrounded by a cyclone fence that must have been at least twenty-five feet high. I was such a big, klutzy kid that I couldn't climb the fence, so I'd stand outside and watch the other guys play. Hooking up with the black guys and Bill the ex-Globetrotter was what changed everything around for me. After that, the basketball court was still a refuge, but in a much more positive sense. There was a ready-made brotherhood within the white lines. It was a place where a big kid like me could hide in the crowd. After a while, it became a sacred space.

PHIL: Yeah, the camaraderie was a boon to me, too. Especially on the road trips. Starting when I was about thirteen and playing for the Four-H team, we'd make weekend trips to places like Bismarck. There'd be four boys together in a hotel room, and it was always a ton of fun. By the time I was fifteen, I was already a road warrior.

CHARLEY: I didn't go on an overnight road trip until I was out of college and playing in the Eastern League. In high school we traveled to away games on the subway. At Hunter, a big road trip was to go play Fairfield or Bridgeport up in Connecticut. Or to New Jersey to play Rider College or Fairleigh Dickinson.

PHIL: I'm sure you played well against Fairly Ridiculous.

CHARLEY: Absolutely. We'd get two dollars for meal money and stop in some burger emporium on the way home.

PHIL: The young kids growing up these days have an entirely different experience. They play AAU ball from the time they're thirteen or fourteen, so they're being recruited at an early age, bribed with free sneakers and sweat suits, and flown all over the country to play in tournaments. Then they jump into the NBA when they're like eighteen years old without serving a long enough apprenticeship.

CHARLEY: Being recruited for AAU teams, then high school, then colleges, then being recruited by agents, it's no wonder that so many of these kids become so narcissistic and so cynical at such an early age. Their motivation is totally skewed.

PHIL: When I first started playing, I was motivated by one thing: winning. It wasn't just the participation or the friendships. It was about proving myself over and over again. When I was at the University of North Dakota, I developed another reason for playing: breaking the school's scoring record. But every time I stepped on a court, there was also a risk that the team would lose, I'd play poorly, and I'd become an object of ridicule. I guess there was an under current of fear that kept me playing so hard. The more success I had, the more enjoyable I found it. My love of the game was something that developed gradually over time.

CHARLEY: Throughout high school and college, I took every game to be a personal challenge. At Hunter, especially, I got the ball in the pivot, and everybody stood around and watched me try to score. If I scored enough points, we'd win. If I didn't, we'd lose. It wasn't until I got older, in my forties actually, that I discovered that playing basketball can be a transcendent experience. Not until after I'd lost a step, or two or five, and I couldn't overpower anybody who wasn't as decrepit as I was.

I think the time we spent together with the Patroons had a lot to do with my basketball evolution. Just being so immersed in the game. Getting pulled into your search for the right system. Experimenting with various offenses. Seeing what playing the game correctly demanded from both the players and the coaches. That was the first time I'd ever been exposed to authentic coaching.

From there it was easy to find my way on my own. Tapping into the flow of a game, with everybody communicating and playing the role that suits them best—the whole being greater than the sum of its parts. It's like what Bill Russell describes in his book *Second Wind*, where you just play in the flow and the score doesn't matter. You can reach a certain level where instead of seeing the game as five good guys versus five bad guys, you perceive it as ten guys playing the same game. Then the buzzer sounds, and you have to look up at the scoreboard to find out who won the game.

That kind of thing happened to me several times as a player, and even a couple of times as a coach. It's more difficult for a coach to get there, because even though you're emotionally and psychically involved in the game, you're still on the sidelines. But it's happened often enough for me to know that consciousness is what the game is all about. If you can get into that space, it doesn't matter what the scoreboard says. You're always a winner.

PHIL: A basketball team should work together like the five fingers on a hand. The thumb is more powerful than the pinkie, but the pinkie provides balance. And all the fingers move instinctively in conjunction to solve the problem.

CHARLEY: The problem at hand?

PHIL: In the late seventies Neal Walk was a teammate of mine on the Knicks, and he had what was identified back then as a hippie consciousness. "Why do we have to keep score?" he wanted to know. "Why can't basketball be played for the sheer enjoyment of the spectacle, of the athletic grace of the players. They don't keep score in ballet."

CHARLEY: That's because nobody plays defense in ballet.

PHIL: Neal had the right idea, though, that basketball in its highest expression is an art form.

CHARLEY: And as such, it's also a spiritual experience.

PHIL: There it is, the S word. Basketball is a game of moment-to-moment action, and this is where I'm able to bring Zen into the picture. Practicing any kind of Zen or Buddhist meditation is attempting to bring yourself back to the moment. One breath to the next breath. As you meditate, all kinds of thoughts are going to come pouring into your mind. You've got to go to the dentist that afternoon. The rent bill is due today. What did your partner mean yesterday when she said...? But you stay focused on your breath because the breath is the only thing that's real and present in the moment, while your thoughts are just biochemical energy flashing around inside your brain that have no inherent reality. In basketball it's playing one play, then playing the next play. If you're thinking about how long it's been since you took a shot, or what move you're going to make the next time the ball comes to you, or how that last foul on you was such a bad call, then your mind gets in the way of the game.

Players learn to love the game when they can get into the moment, the here and now, and lose themselves in it. Suddenly they're just breathing and playing basketball and it's all natural and it's all exactly what it's supposed to be. There's no conflict with their teammates, and the door's wide open in front of them.

CHARLEY: And that's what I think is the ultimate value of the Triangle. It facilitates and systematizes the possibility of basketball players getting into this sacred space.

PHIL: Remember this, though: I tout my system because I believe in it. But the Triangle is only one system, and there are many others that can work just as well.

CHARLEY: Still, it's no accident that you've won seven championships.

PHIL: Yes, that's true.

CHARLEY: So where's the game heading, Phil? Is the Triangle forever? Or merely an aberration?

PHIL: Let me put it this way—I think that the game itself is truer than its rewards. Tex and I often talk about how the inherent qualities of the game itself will eventually bring out the right values. Selfishness can only get a player so far. No matter how talented a player might be, there's always someone else who's just as talented. So the only way to win is to share the ball. Otherwise, this gimme, gimme attitude will eat you up, one way or the other. It may not happen until you're fifty, but it's bound to happen. You can't be a taker and expect to live happily ever after.

But I believe that the young kids coming into the league with selfish attitudes—kids like Allen Iverson—will eventually mature. Face it, Charley, they have the same selfish outlook that the two of us had when we were their age. You didn't catch on until you were past forty, right? I didn't get it until I was thirty-two and my skills had seriously eroded. Shaq got it last year when he was only twenty-eight. I believe that maturation is a natural and inevitable process.

CHARLEY: When Tex retires, when you're spending your winters holed up in Montana, who's going to keep the torch burning?

PHIL: Of course, Tim Floyd is running the Triangle in Chicago, but I don't know how long he's going to be able to hold out with so many young kids on his team. When and if Jimmy Cleamons gets another shot, he'll do a good job with the Triangle. Quinn Buckner has the right idea, if not the depth of experience. Several guys who played for me are dedicated advocates of the Triangle. Craig Hodges ran it when he coached a women's team in the ABL. Steve Kerr; John Salley, for sure; B. J. Armstrong—all of these guys would be wonderful coaches if that's what they want to do. John Paxson is another outstanding candidate.

And as for the Lakers, we're clearing the slate of the last season and beginning the defense of our title this week. Now the only difference will be when the team is introduced before a game. It's the NBA Champion Los Angeles Lakers—and we have a reputation to uphold.

CHARLEY: So the Triangle lives.

PHIL: Amen to that.

ARM-BAR. Flexing arm and holding in in front of chest so that forearm is parallel to the floor. Primarily a defensive tactic used in a variety of ways, most of them violent.

AUTOMATIC RELEASES. Prearranged movement toward the player with the ball by a frontcourt player (usually power forward or center) to provide an alternative pass whenever ballhandlers are being pressured or even doubleteamed near the midcourt line. Not necessarily designed to facilitate an attack on the basket.

BACK PICK. See Figure 8. Offensive player moves up behind a teammate's defender in order to block the defender's path as the teammate cuts to the basket and receives a pass.

BACKCOURT: Area on the basketball court before one crosses the midcourt line. Also can refer to the guard position.

BACKDOOR STEP. On offense, faking a movement toward the ball then cutting sharply behind the defender toward the basket.

BALL REVERSAL. Passing the ball from one side of the offensive zone to the other.

BLIND PIG. An automatic move to relieve pressure on guards before half-court offense can be initiated. If the guard is being tightly defended as he dribbles the ball up court, the weak-side wing will move to the high-post area to receive a pass. The wing will then return the ball to the guard after he has created space between himself and his defender and is in a better position to begin the offensive set—or else initiate an aggressive attack on the basket.

(*Note*: This is Tex's term. Imagine his chagrin when told that "blind pig" was a term that jazz musicians in 1930s and 1940s used for a marijuana cigarette!)

BLINDSIDE PICK. An offensive maneuver whereby a player sets an unexpected pick on the blindside of defensive player in motion. Usually very effective and very painful.

BLOCKS (RIGHT BLOCK/LEFT BLOCK). See Figure 1. Area near the basket just outside the foul lane (low-post area). Often marked by small squares along the foul lane marker. Left or right side is determined when facing the basket.

BOX OFFENSE. See Figure 5. Two wings positioned on opposite blocks. Two big men positioned on opposite elbows. Guard with ball at top of key. A wide variety of screens possible—big men picking down lane for wings, picking diagonally for wings, wings cross-picking for each other, then pickee getting doublepick from big men. Screen and roll options also available.

BOX SCORE. Statistical results of ball game as printed in newspaper. Includes quarter-by-quarter point totals for each team, individual statistics such as field goals attempted and made, free throws attempted and made, rebounds (offensive and defensive), assists, steals, blocked shots, turnovers, personal fouls, total points, technical fouls. Also total attendance at game, and names of referees.

BOXING OUT. Last act of defense: placing your body in between an offensive player and the basket while a shot is in the air. This is to prevent offensive rebounds. A lost art in the NBA, where players tend to rely on brute strength and leaping ability to get rebounds.

BUTTON HOOK. When an offensive player moves away from the player with the ball then makes a sharp curl back toward him.

CENTER RUB. Center acting as blocking post, but a more passive act than a screen, and used primarily to clear an area for a teammate.

CONTAIN DEFENSE. Maintaining a position between the offensive player and the basket.

CORKSCREW JUMPER. Acrobatic shot common in the NBA where player starts his shooting motion with back to basket, then spins and ends up facing hoop as he releases the shot. Often called "turnaround jumper."

CROSS PICK. See Figure 8. Player C has the ball in corner, with B positioned in strong-side low post, and A in weak-side low post. B moves across foul lane and sets pick for A, who moves into strong-side low post position to receive pass from C.

DOUBLE PICK. See Figure 8. Two offensive players placed in tandem so that a teammate (usually without the ball) can maneuver his defender into or around them, hopefully creating an open area where he can receive the ball for an unimpeded shot.

DOWN-SCREEN. See Figure 8. A screen set by an offensive player moving from (or above) the foul line to somewhere near the baseline.

DRIBBLE WEAVE. A motion where a player will dribble toward a teammate. When the two cross, the player with the ball has the option of passing the ball off to his teammate or continuing with his dribble.

DRIVER-SLASHER. A player who moves sharply hoopwards either with (driver) or without (slasher) the ball. This is what poor shooters do to get easier shots.

ELBOW. See Figure 1. Corners where the foul line joins either of the foul lane markers.

FAST BREAK. Usually occurs after a missed shot, when the rebounding (defensive) team moves the ball up the court as quickly as possible in order to score before their opponents have a chance to set up their defense.

FILLING A LANE. In a fast break situation, lanes are pathways to the basket. Ideally, wings should occupy lanes five to ten feet from each sideline and even or just ahead of the ballhandler who should in the middle lane. Big men trail the action. By properly filling the lanes, the fast-breaking team maximizes its options, making the fast break more difficult to defend.

FIST-CHEST. Lakers' sign for certain pick/roll plays. Hand signals are used for every possible offensive set and play because of crowd noise.

FLEX OFFENSE. See Figure 3. A basic motion offense. Wing (3) stationed along baseline on left, Other wing (2) stationed opposite along right baseline. One big man (5) stationed on left block. Other big man (4) stationed opposite on right block. Guard (1) with ball at top of key. (This is a 1-4 alignment, or set.) Guard dribbles five or six feet to either side (let's say he goes right). Opposite big man (5) moves to elbow to receive pass. Wing 2 cuts along baseline using 4's screen, while 1 moves down the lane to set screen for 4. 4 then moves up to elbow and receives pass from 5. 3 cuts along baseline using 2's screen, while 5 moves downlane to set screen for 2, who moves up to elbow to receive pass from 4. Etcetera.

FOUL LANE. See Figure 1. Rectangular area that extends from the foul line to the baseline directly under the basket. Also called the 3-second lane.

FOUL LINE EXTENDED. See Figure 1. An imaginary line extending the foul line to both sidelines. Used to identify optimum position of wings.

FRONTCOURT. See Figure 1. The half of the basketball court containing the basket at which your team is shooting. Also called the offensive zone. The term "frontcourt" can also refer to the center and forward positions.

FRONTING DEFENSE. Defending a player in the low post by maintaining a position between that player and the ball.

GIVE-AND-GO. Basic offensive play wherein A passes laterally to B, then cuts sharply to basket, hopefully to receive a return pass and shoot a layup.

HIGH POST. See Figure 1. Area at or just above the free-throw line.

ISOLATION PLAYS. An offensive situation where a player is able to work on his defender one-on-one. NBA players are so talented offensively that when left to operate in "iso" situations doubleteams are just about mandatory.

LAG PASS. A pass made from one guard to another guard who's positioned farther away from the basket. This facilitates reverse action.

LINE OF DEPLOYMENT. Set-up that positions player in the low post on a direct line between the ball and the basket.

LOW POST. See Figure 1. Area close to the basket just outside of the foul lane.

MOTION OFFENSE. *See* FLEX. Offensive scheme where players are in constant motion. Generic movement is passing, picking away from the ball resulting in teammates' cutting toward the ball. When Doug Moe coached the Denver Nuggets, his commands for a motion offense were: "Just keep moving and don't run into each other."

OFFENSIVE ZONE. *See* FRONTCOURT.

ONE-GUARD FRONT. An offensive set where a solitary guard is responsible for dribbling the ball into the frontcourt and then initiating the halfcourt offense.

PICK. Often used interchangeably with screen. Sometimes used to identify screen made on the weak side.

PINCH POST. Area on weak side at edge of free-throw line.

PINCH-POST MOVES. Facing, and then attacking, the basket from the pinch post.

PIVOT PLAY. What happens when a player receives the ball close to basket and tries to maneuver himself into a good shot.

PIVOTMAN. A player who, on offense tends to play close to basket with his back to the basket. Usually (but not exclusively) big men, like George Mikan, Kareem Abdul-Jabbar, Shaq.

POST-FILL FORWARD TRIANGLE. See Figure 2. Center fills strong-side triangle in low-post position.

POST-UP. To assume the low-post position.

REBOUND CUT. Move toward basket to set a screen, then continue to basket for rebound.

REVERSE ACTION. Quickly moving the ball from one side of the offensive zone to the other, hoping to catch defensive players overcommitted to strong-side action.

RIP SCREENS. See Figure 8. Guard cuts off high-post screen by big man, but instead of continuing to the basket, reverses field and sets back screen on the big man's defender. A risky business for a small man. One of John Stockton's favorite ploys.

SCREEN. One player assumes a stationary position while ballhandler maneuvers so that his own defender is run into screener. Usually, the screener's defender and the ballhandler's defender will "switch," with each covering the other's man. Since the screener is usually much bigger than the ballhandler, this often creates a mismatch in which the smaller, quicker ballhandler is defended by a bigger, slower player.

SCREEN AND ROLL. See Figure 8. After a screen is set (see above), the screener cuts to the basket.

SIDELINE TRIANGLE. See Figure 2. The basic Triangle formation—usually has ball handler (1) positioned about ten feet from sideline and perhaps twenty feet from baseline, a wing near the foul line extended (3), and a big man near the strong-side block (5).

SINGLE-DOUBLE. See Figure 4. An offense that features a double pick in one low-post position and a single pick in the other. Offensive player runs (without the ball) a variety of possible routes around these picks.

SOLO CUT. Wing man and post man work together on the strong side in a pass and cut two-man game.

SPEED CUT. A controlled, full speed dash to the basket in an attempt to outrun the defender to the basket or down court.

STATION-TO-STATION. A term referring to a slow, deliberate halfcourt offense.

STEP HOOK. In low-post position with back to basket, take one dribble, one long step, then shoot hook shot. The lefty step hook was PJ's bread and butter, which he often accomplished while throwing his right elbow into his defender's face.

STRONG SIDE. Draw an imaginary line from the midcourt circle to the basket creating two sides to the offensive zone. The strong side is the side that at any given time contains the basketball.

SWITCH CUTS. A maneuver used when a defensive team is switching coverage off a single screen, forcing the screener's defender to pick up the first cutter, thereby creating an unguarded space for the screener.

THREE-TWO PRO SET. One-guard front, two opposite wings above foul line extended, center on strong-side low post, power forward either on weak-side low post or weak-side elbow.

TIME-DELAY. A defender putting his body (or parts thereof) in path of a cutting offensive player to either slow up the cut or make the cutter alter his path.

TRANSITION DEFENSE. When Team A misses a shot that is rebounded by Team B, Team A must instantly switch from offense to defense to prevent easy fast-break scores by Team B.

TWO-GUARD FRONT. Ball is brought into frontcourt, and offense is initiated, by either of two guards working in tandem.

TWO-ONE-TWO SET. Two-guard front, with wings in opposite corners, and center at high post.

WEAK SIDE. The side of the offensive zone opposite to the strong side, i.e., where the basketball isn't.

WINGS. Small forwards and big guards who normally operate at the foul line extended or away from the basket along either baseline.

WING-CROSSING TRANSITION PATTERN. A sequence in fast-break offense where two wings run the court parallel to (and ten feet or so away from) the sidelines, then cross under the basket. This allows one of the wings to quickly post up before the defense can adjust.

ZONE DEFENSE. Where defenders guard specific areas of court in instead specific men. Zones come in many configurations, most commonly 2-1-2 (guards at each elbow, center in middle of the foul lane, forwards at each block) and 1-3-1 (which is vulnerable to active big men since only one defender is near basket). Zones are illegal in the NBA, though most teams employ them at some point.

ZONE PRESS. Defensive process by which the player with the ball is doubleteamed (usually, but not exclusively, in the backcourt) when on certain areas on the court— generally in corners or along sidelines, to cut down on maneuverability of ballhandler. Other defenders not near the ball play a zone defense.

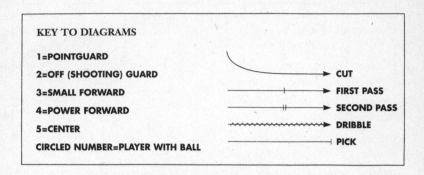

KEY TO DIAGRAMS

1=POINTGUARD

2=OFF (SHOOTING) GUARD

3=SMALL FORWARD

4=POWER FORWARD

5=CENTER

CIRCLED NUMBER=PLAYER WITH BALL

CUT

FIRST PASS

SECOND PASS

DRIBBLE

PICK

Figure 1—The Offensive Zone (Frontcourt)

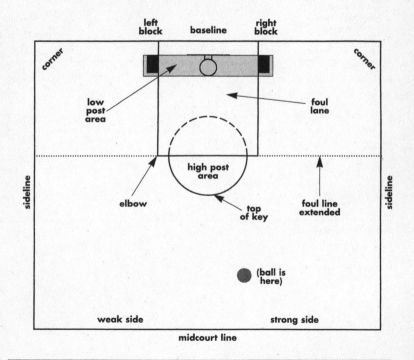

Figure 2—Basic Ways to Fill the Triangle

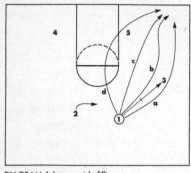

DIAGRAM 1 (strong-side fill)

On #1 pass from (1) to 3
a. guard outside cut
b. guard slice cut
c. guard blur screen cut
d. guard basket cut

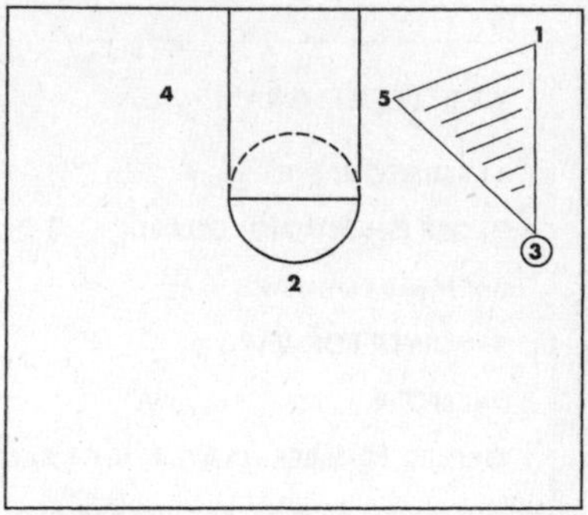

DIAGRAM 1A (positions filled)

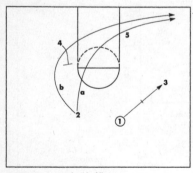

DIAGRAM 2 (weak-side fill)

On #1 pass from (1) to 3
a. guard 2 basket cut
b. wing 4 back picks 2 to corner

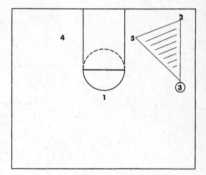

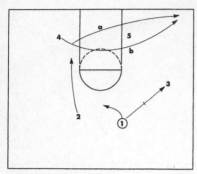

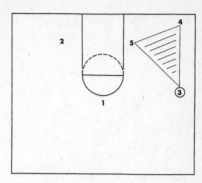

DIAGRAM 3 (weak-side fill)

On #1 pass from (1) to 3
a. 4 baseline cut to corner
b. 4 over top cut to corner

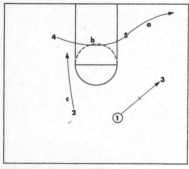

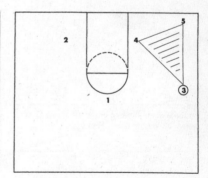

DIAGRAM 4 (strong-side fill)

On #1 pass from (1) to 3
a. post fills corner
b. 4 cuts to vacant post
c. 2 cuts to weakside wing spot

Figure 3—The Flex Offense

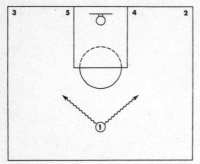

1 declares side.

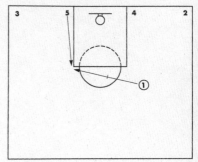

Weak-side big man (5) comes to pinch post to receive pass.

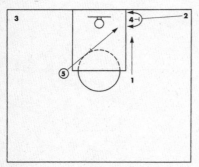

Opposite wing (2) cuts to basket off of pick. 1st option is to pass to cutter. If not open...

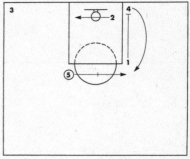

1 sets pick for 4, who cuts to high post to receive pass from 5.

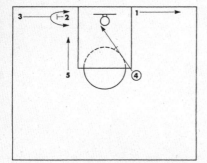

Opposite wing (3) cuts to basket off of 2's pick. 1st option is to pass to cutter. If not open...

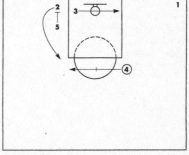

5 sets pick for 2, who cuts out to receive pass from 4. Should result in an open shot for 2.

Figure 4—Single-Double—one possible option

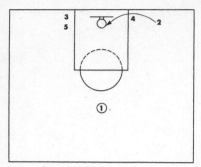

2 cuts underneath basket, then...

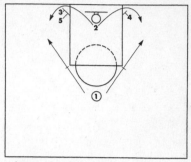

2 chooses side: either single pick by 4 or double
pick by 3 and 5, or...

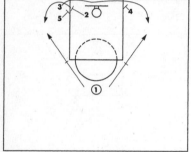

2 picks for 3 then curls out. 3 cuts off 2's pick, then
4's pick.

Figure 5—The "Box" Offense—one possible option

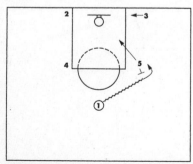

High screen-roll. 1 either shoots or passes to
cutting 5 or...

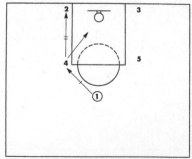

Pass to 4. 4 passes to 2 in low post. 2 either shoots
or passes to cutting 4.

Figure 6—Sam Barry's Center Opposite

Point guard passes to wing then fills corner.

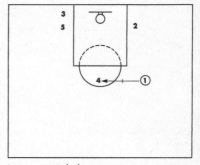

Strong-side triangle is formed when 4 cuts across middle.

Figure 7—The Hawk Series

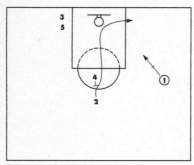

2 cuts off high post screen. If open, 1 passes to 2. If not...

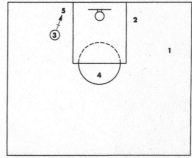

1 passes to 4 in high post.

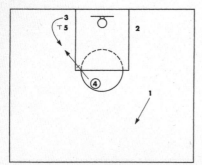

3 curls out off 5's screen. 4 passes to 3 for open shot, or...

3 passes to 5, who is now being covered by 3's defender in low post.

Figure 8—Various Picks and Screens

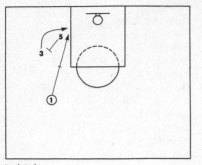

Back Pick

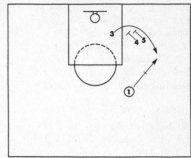

Double Pick

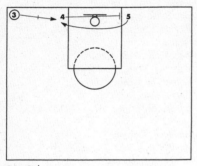

Cross Pick

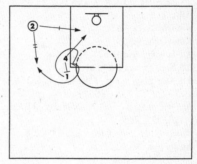

Rip Screen

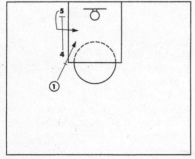

Down-Screen

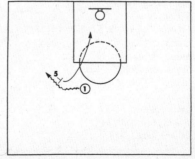

Screen and Roll

Key to abbreviations: ABA (American Basketball Association), CBA (Continental Basketball Association), CR (Charley Rosen), NBA (National Basketball Association), PJ (Phil Jackson), and Shaq (Shaquille O'Neal)

AAU teams, 28, 287
Abdul-Jabbar, Kareem, 197, 231
Adelman, Rick, 206, 210, 236, 237, 238, 244
Ainge, Danny, 240
Akron Goodyears, 28
Albany Patroons, 14–15, 16, 60–66, 71, 100–101, 130, 139, 265
Albeck, Stan, 77, 130
Albert, Marv, 58
Albert, Steve, 59
All-Rookie team, 44
All-Star game, 195–201
All-Star players, 15, 112, 125, 126, 156, 167, 170, 202, 225
American Basketball Association (ABA), 50, 225, 265
American History X (movie), 237–238
Anderson, Nick, 237
Anderson, Shannon, 179
Anthony, Greg, 176, 247, 248–249
Armato, Leonard, 182
Armstrong, B. J., 202, 290
Armstrong, Hank, 90
Arthur, Don, 59
Atlanta Hawks, 49, 51, 173, 181, 214
Auerbach, Red, 85
Augmon, Stacey, 247
Augustana College, 121
"Babe" (PJ's first coach and mentor), 20
Bach, Johnny, 72, 78–79, 80, 83, 131, 133, 148, 150, 214
Ballard, Greg, 154

Baltimore Bullets, 12, 129
    See also Washington Bullets
Bannister, Ken, 83
Barkley, Charles, 161, 179–180
Barnett, Dick, 44
Barney Polan's Game (Rosen), 84
Barry, Jon, 206, 237, 239
Barry, Rick, 37, 225–226
Barry, Sam, 110, 121, 122, 135
Basin League, 27–28
basketball rules
    international, 75
    original, 233–234
Basset, Tim, 54, 59
Battie, Tony, 169
Bay State Bombardiers, 66
Baylor, Elgin, 123, 231
Beard, Butch, 51
Bee, Clair, 128
Bellamy, Walt, 43, 44, 46
Benjamin, Benoit, 168
Berry, Sam, 160
Bertka, Bill, 146, 147, 183–184, 215, 232
Beshore, Del, 66
Best, Travis, 262, 263, 268, 274
"Beyond Basketball" (class), 84
Bibby, Henry, 47, 92
Bill (played basketball with CR), 32, 286
Billings, Montana, 58
Bird, Larry, 50, 82, 260–261, 262, 265, 268, 275–276
Black, John, 201
Blair, Bill, 261
Blazers (NBA team). See Portland Trail Blazers
Block, John, 43
Boeheim, Jim, 72
Bombardiers (CBA team). See Bay State Bombardiers

Boston Celtics, 76, 79, 146, 153,
168–169, 204, 208–209, 261, 276
Bowman, Nate, 44
"box" offense, 16, 87, 100
Boynes, Winford, 56
Boys State, 27
Bradley, Bill, 13, 37, 44, 45, 47, 49, 62,
140
Bradley, Shawn, 158
Brand, Eldon, 161, 182
Brandon, Terrell, 214
Brogan, Louie, 27
Brooklyn College, 35–36
Brown, Dale, 128
Brown, Herb, 72
Brown, Hubie, 57, 80, 214
Brown, Larry, 37, 59, 72, 210, 261
Brown, Tico, 86, 87, 88
Brown University, 79
Bryant, Emmette, 43, 44
Bryant, Joe, 189–190
Bryant, Kobe
    against 76ers, 203, 211
    against Grizzlies, 206, 210
    against Hornets, 202
    against Kings, 206, 209–210, 238
    against Knicks, 211
    against Pacers, 264, 265, 267, 268,
        270, 271, 272, 274, 275
    against Spurs, 213, 215–216
    against Suns, 243
    against SuperSonics, 188, 213
    against Timberwolves, 214
    against Trail Blazers, 185–186, 190,
        248, 250, 251, 252, 253, 254,
        258–259
    against Warriors, 185
    against Wizards, 207
    creativity, 279
    injuries, 173, 174, 181, 183
    interaction with teammates,
        189–190, 201, 205, 244, 259
    and media, 169
    passing, 277
    PJ's assessment of, 167–168, 170,
        186, 187, 189–190, 207, 269

    in practice, 280
    reaction to championship, 276
    and Ruben Patterson, 163
    and Shaq, 178, 189–190, 259, 269
    suspended, 211
    and Triangle offense, 185, 227,
        278–279
Buckner, Quinn, 153–156, 157, 290
Bucks (NBA team). See Milwaukee
    Bucks
Buechler, Jud, 147, 152
Bullets (NBA team). See Baltimore
    Bullets; Washington Bullets
Bulls (NBA team). See Chicago Bulls
Burden, Ticky, 50
Burks, Luther, 100
Buss, Jerry, 149, 170
California State University-Long
    Beach, 128
Calipari, John, 138, 261
Callahan, Duke, 91
Camby, Marcus, 139
Campbell, Elden, 202
Canisius College, 58
Carlesimo, P. J., 72, 266
Carlisle, Rick, 261
Carlson, Buddy, 23
Carril, Pete, 232, 236
Carter, Vince, 182
Cartwright, Bill, 103, 105–106, 108,
    109–110, 137, 160, 166
Cassell, Sam, 157, 158
Cato, Kelvin, 179
Cavaliers (NBA team). See Cleveland
    Cavaliers
Cavalry (CBA team). See Oklahoma
    City Cavalry
Cedar Rapids Silver Bullets, 94–95
Celestand, John, 276, 280
Celtics (NBA team). See Boston Celtics
"center opposite" offense, 110, 121,
    122, 160
Central Missouri State University, 160
Chamberlain, Wilt, 37, 125, 231, 249
Chambers, Ray, 138
Charlotte Hornets, 167, 202

Checketts, Dave, 138–139, 199
Chicago Bulls
    after PJ, 137–138
    against Lakers, 202
    compared to Lakers, 216
    compared to Trail Blazers, 259–260
    ethnic make-up, 152
    PJ as assistant coach, 77–82,
        103–104, 109, 132–133
    PJ as head coach, 11, 82, 83–84, 104–
        116, 137, 191–192, 197–198, 214
    recruiting, 201–202
    Tex Winter as assistant coach,
        128–135
    Tim Floyd as coach, 160–162,
        181–182
Childs, Chris, 211
City College of New York (CCNY), 33,
    34
Clark, Jimmy, 225
Cleamons, Jim, 51, 104, 146, 147, 148,
    156–159, 223, 228, 290
Cleveland Cavaliers, 51, 62, 146, 156,
    188–189, 191–192, 204, 229
Clippers (NBA team). See Los Angeles
    Clippers
CNN, 155
Coaches All-Star game, 128
Cockroach Basketball League, The
    (Rosen), 84
Cofield, Fred, 90
Collins, Doug
    All-Star coach, 196
    color commentator, 142
    head coach of Bulls, 77, 80–82, 103,
        104, 131–133
    and Johnny Bach, 79
    offense, 80, 108
    player for Illinois State, 30
Compton Junior College, 121
Condors (ABA team), 126
Continental Basketball Association
    (CBA)
    All-Star game, 61
    changes, 83
    coaches, 91, 213–214

franchises, 58, 85–86
indignities, 88–89
and LA Summer League, 132
nicknames, 14
players' physical welfare, 88
referees, 90–91, 92, 115, 230
road game travel rules, 63–64
salaries, 65
and teamwork, 64–65
Copeland, Hollis, 61
Coquis (CBA team). See Puerto Rico
    Coquis
Costello, Larry, 160
Cousy, Bob, 156
Cowens, Dave, 82
Crawford, Joey, 115–116
Croshere, Austin, 261, 263, 264, 272,
    273, 274
Cunningham, Billy, 81
Daia (CR's fiancée), 145
Dallas Mavericks, 153–155, 156, 166,
    177, 178–179, 186, 214–215
Dalmau, Raymond, 73
Daugherty, Brad, 200
David, Kornel, 160
Davis, Antonio, 260
Davis, Dale, 261, 263, 271, 273, 274
DeBusschere, Dave, 46, 47, 48
Delany, Bob, 115
Delk, Tony, 206, 237, 239
Denver Nuggets, 148, 155, 181, 195,
    206–207, 241
DePaul University, 29, 129
Detroit Pistons, 196, 197, 198,
    207–208, 250–251, 255
Detroit Spirits, 61, 86
    See also Savannah Spirits
Divac, Vlade, 210, 225, 236, 239
Donovan, Eddie, 39, 40, 44
Drexler, Clyde, 161
Dukes, Alvin "Bo," 86, 87
Dumas, Tony, 157
Duncan, Tim, 161, 186, 199, 201, 216,
    240
Dunleavy, Mike, 227–228, 244, 247,
    248, 249, 251, 253, 255

Eastern Conference finals, 48, 191, 260, 263
Eastern League, 37, 48, 286
Egan, Johnny, 127
Elliot, Bob, 53
Elliot, Sean, 193–194
Erving, Julius, 12
ESPN, 58, 128, 143, 155, 262
Ewing, Patrick, 112–113, 197, 198, 211, 263, 278
Final Four, 123, 127–128
Finkel, Henry, 43
Finley, Michael, 157, 158
Fisher, Derek
  against Pacers, 266, 270, 274
  against Spurs, 213
  against Trail Blazers, 191, 249, 250
  character, 168, 280
  injuries, 214
  passing, 277
  PJ's assessment of, 167, 168, 175, 207
  reaction to championship, 276
  and teammates, 244
  and Triangle offense, 278
Fitch, Bill, 26, 27, 28, 29, 42, 85, 105, 146
Fitzsimmons, Cotton, 124
Flathead Valley Community College, 59
Fleischer, Mike, 34–36
Fleishman, Jerry, 37
flex offense, 16, 63, 73, 76, 83, 87, 100, 101
Floyd, Tim, 160–161, 181, 290
Ford, Chris, 208
Fordham University, 79
Forte, Joe, 180
4-H (Health, Hands, Heart, and Hearth), 20–21, 286
Fox, Rick
  against Grizzlies, 210
  against Pacers, 266, 268, 274, 275
  against Suns, 209, 242, 245
  against Trail Blazers, 254
  character, 280
  as college player, 208

footwork, 278
passing, 277
PJ's assessment of, 167
plays for Celtics, 208–209
in practice, 120
reaction to championship, 276
role on Lakers team, 164, 183
technical fouls, 245
and Triangle offense, 278
Frank, Jerry, 94, 97, 99
Frazier, Walt, 27, 28, 43, 44, 49, 62
Gardner, Jack, 122, 123
Garner, Gary, 160
Garnett, Kevin, 199, 214
Garretson, Darell, 90, 114–115
Garretson, Ronnie, 115
Gatling, Chris, 158
Geiger, Gary, 263
Geiger, Matt, 210–211
Gentry, Allan, 261
George, Devean, 164, 167, 244, 245, 276, 280
Georgetown Gallop, 112–113, 198
Georgetown University, 76
Gertch, D., 224
Gervin, George, 156
Gianelli, John, 49
Gladiator (movie), 244
God, Man and Basketball Jones (Rosen), 156
Golden State Warriors, 79, 185, 206, 208, 211, 212
  See also Philadelphia Warriors
Gondrezick, Glen, 51
Goodyears (AAU team). See Akron Goodyears
Grace Dodge Vocational High School (N.Y.), 33
Grand Fork Central High School (N.D.), 25
Grant, Brian, 190–191, 247, 249, 258
Grant, Horace, 105, 108, 109, 134, 224
Grateful Dead, 13, 48–49
Green, A. C.
  against Kings, 209, 236, 238, 239
  against Pacers, 271

against Spurs, 213
against Suns, 242
against Trail Blazers, 253
competitive nature, 280
with Mavericks, 157, 158
PJ's assessment of, 166–167, 183,
    187, 207
and Triangle offense, 223, 279
Grizzlies (NBA team), 175, 210
Grunfeld, Ernie, 138–139, 199
Gugliatta, Tom, 240
Hack-a-Shaq, 177, 182, 245, 249–250,
    264
Hall of Fame, 48, 121, 125, 161, 201
Hamblen, Frank, 137, 146, 147–148
Hannum, Alex, 121, 126, 159–160
Hardaway, Penny, 167, 211, 240, 241,
    242, 243
Harper, Derek, 167, 168
Harper, Ron ("Harp")
    acquired by Lakers, 168
    against Pacers, 264, 267, 271, 274
    against Spurs, 213
    against Suns, 211, 242
    against SuperSonics, 188
    against Timberwolves, 214
    against Trail Blazers, 176, 248, 250,
        251, 253, 254
    against Wizards, 207
    character, 280
    passing, 174, 277
    PJ's assessment of, 175, 187
    in practice, 120
    and teammates, 189, 244
    and Triangle offense, 230–231
Harris, Del, 72, 148, 168, 215,
    225–226, 261
Harrison, Phil, 216
Harter, Dick, 261
Have Jump Shot Will Travel (Rosen), 48
Hawk series, 52, 76, 80, 214
Hawkins, Connie, 37
Hawks. See Atlanta Hawks; Hunter
    College Hawks
Hawn, Goldie, 230
Hayes, Elvin, 125–127

Healthcenter, 177, 223–224, 226, 231
Heat (NBA team). See Miami Heat
Henderson, Reggie, 87
Hennessy, Joe, 76
Henry, Carl, 90
Heyman, Art, 37
Heywood, Spencer, 51
Hill, Grant, 161, 201
Hobbit, The (Tolkien), 14
Hodges, Craig, 290
Holzman, Red
    coach in Puerto Rico, 72
    coach of Knicks, 38, 44–47, 68, 105
    compared to Kevin Loughery, 52
    death, 199
    offense, 61, 105, 133
    practice sessions, 44, 150
    recruits PJ for Knicks, 30, 39–40,
        42, 43
    retirement, 50
Hornets (NBA team), 167, 202
Horry, Robert
    against Cavaliers, 204
    against Kings, 209, 230
    against Pacers, 266, 267, 268, 271,
        272, 274, 275
    against Spurs, 213
    against Suns, 212, 242, 243
    against Trail Blazers, 205, 248, 250,
        253, 259
    injuries, 187, 277
    passing, 277
    personal life, 193, 195
    PJ's assessment of, 167, 171–172,
        183, 207
    in practice, 120
    and Triangle offense, 278
Hotchkiss, Don, 20–21
House of Moses All-Stars, The (Rosen),
    84
Houston, Allan, 252
Houston Rockets, 161
    against Lakers, 179–180, 192–193,
        194, 204
    coached by Tex Winter, 125–127,
        132

and Frank Hamblen, 148
and Rick Barry, 225–226
and Robert Horry, 167, 171
and Shaq, 191
trades Scottie Pippen, 175
See also San Diego Rockets
Hughes, Alfrederick, 90
Hummer, John, 12
Hunter College Hawks, 33–37, 48, 286
Huntington Park High School (Calif.), 120
Iba, Hank, 79, 81, 128
Illinois State University, 30
Imhoff, Darrell, 122
Indiana Pacers
    against Bulls, 130–131, 255, 260
    against 76ers, 210
    against Lakers, 188, 206, 260–276
    against Shaq, 191
    fans, 267
    offense, 252–253
Indiana University, 16, 17, 153, 154
Iowa State University, 160
Irish, Ned, 40
Irvine, George, 208
Iverson, Allen, 203, 211, 290
Jablonksi, F. (police officer), 98
Jackson, Ben (PJ's son), 57, 143
Jackson, Brooke (PJ's daughter), 144, 145, 201
Jackson, Charles (PJ's father), 19–20, 22, 25, 26, 142
Jackson, Charley (PJ's son), 57, 62, 143
Jackson, Chelsea (PJ's daughter), 49, 144, 145, 201
Jackson, Chuck (PJ's brother), 25
Jackson, Elizabeth (PJ's daughter), 201
Jackson, Elizabeth (PJ's mother), 19, 22, 25, 26, 142, 195
Jackson, Jimmy, 154, 158
Jackson, Joan (PJ's sister), 24
Jackson, Joe (PJ's brother), 25, 56
Jackson, June (PJ's wife), 53, 57, 60, 62, 139–140, 140–141, 142, 144, 196
Jackson, Mark, 263, 266, 271, 273
Jackson, Nate, 52

Jackson, Phil
    assistant coach of Bulls, 77–82, 132–133
    assistant coach of Nets, 14, 53–59
    attends Bobby Knight's clinic, 16–18
    on basketball, 15–16, 285–290
    builds Montana house, 56, 58
    coaches in Puerto Rico, 71–75, 77
    as color commentator, 46, 58, 59
    drafted by New York Knicks, 39–43
    dress style, 14, 77–78
    eating habits, 226
    head coach of Albany Patroons, 14–18, 60–66, 76–77, 78
    head coach of Chicago Bulls, 82, 104–116, 137, 191–192
    head coach of Lakers, 11, 145–152, 159, 163–217, 235–283
    injuries, 45–47, 65, 171, 182
    marriage, 139–140, 140–141, 144
    and media, 149=150, 195, 196, 198, 201–203, 221, 226, 246, 262, 267
    as motivational speaker, 137, 141–142
    and music, 170
    and Native American paraphernalia, 223, 262
    nicknames, 22, 27, 199
    in NY to negotiate contract with Knicks, 39–42
    office, 223–224
    perceived as hippie, 14, 93, 130
    personal life, 281–282
    physique, 13, 20, 21, 23, 25, 68, 172
    plays for New Jersey Nets, 52–53, 56
    plays for New York Knicks, 43–52, 132, 141
    plays for University of North Dakota, 27–30
    plays for Williston High School, 21–26
    plays in 4-H basketball league, 20–21
    plays one on one against CR, 67–70
    profiled by CR in Sport, 12–14

recruited by college basketball
    coaches, 25–26
and religion, 19, 22–23, 64, 185, 256
taste in music, 13, 64, 145
and team leadership, 28–30
technical fouls, 88, 180, 281
in various sports, 20, 23–24, 27–28
and Zen Buddhism, 20, 256–258,
    262, 289
Jacobson, Sam, 164
Javie, Steve, 115
Jazz (NBA team). See New Orleans
    Jazz; Utah Jazz
Johnson, George, 53, 54, 55, 57
Johnson, Kannard, 90
Johnson, Magic, 50, 189–190, 197, 200,
    231
Johnson, Neil, 41
Jones, Eddie, 202
Jones, K. C., 122
Jones, Mark, 66
Jones, Sam, 72
Jordan, Eddie, 56
Jordan, Michael
    against Cavaliers, 191–192
    against Pistons, 110
    competitive drive, 108–109
    free throws, 111, 192
    injuries, 130, 212
    and Kobe Bryant, 201, 269
    playing time, 130–131
    and referees, 197–198
    and teammates, 80, 82, 122, 152,
        191–192, 259–260, 281
    and Triangle offense, 105–106,
        108–109, 133–134, 157, 169, 232
Kansas State University, 122, 123, 124,
    129, 232
Karl, George, 61–62, 100, 261
Keller, Billy, 265
Kelley, Rick, 56, 57
Kerr, Steve, 122, 147, 152, 194, 227,
    290
Kidd, Jason, 154, 157, 201, 240, 241,
    242, 243, 244
Kilborn, Craig "Bibs," 89

Killilea, John, 77
King, Bernard, 52, 53, 55, 56
Kings (NBA team). See Sacramento
    Kings
Kinney, Jim, 96
Knicks (NBA team). See New York
    Knicks
Knight, Bobby, 16–18, 150, 153, 154
Knight, Toby, 51, 62
Knight, Travis, 168–169, 173, 183, 203,
    216, 244, 276, 277
Komives, Howard "Butch," 44, 45, 46
Krause, Jerry
    approaches PJ with job offer, 226
    compared to Jerry West, 148
    and CR, 93
    eating habits, 226
    general manager of Bulls, 128–131,
        133, 134, 142, 160, 161, 202
    offers PJ Bulls head coaching job,
        103–104
Krause, Kevin, 94–95
Kukoc, Toni, 152, 160–161, 203
Kundla, John, 26
Kupchak, Mitch, 148, 170
Lakers (NBA team). See Los Angeles
    Lakers
Lampley, Jim, 90
Lancaster Lightning, 61
Lantz, Stu, 125
Lapchick, Joe, 81
Larsen, Robb, 85, 89
LaRue, Rusty, 160
LaRusso, Rudy, 43
Leamons, Abe, 99
Leonard, John, 61
Lester, Ronnie, 148
Lewis, Freddie, 265
Lightning (CBA team). See Rockford
    Lightning
Locke, Tates, 56
Lombardi, Vince, 14
Longley, Luc, 152, 166, 240, 241, 242,
    247
Los Angeles, Calif., 149, 151–152,
    222–223, 264

Los Angeles Clippers, 206, 241
Los Angeles Lakers
  1999-2000 season, 163–217
  2000-2001 season, 291
  championship series against Pacers,
    260–276
  coached by Bill Sharman, 214
  coached by Del Harris, 215
  coached by John Kundla, 26
  coached by Pat Riley, 197, 255
  coached by PJ, 11, 145–152, 159,
    163–217, 235–283
  contact PJ's agent, 142–143
  fans, 223, 225, 229, 232, 260, 276
  and media, 149, 169–170, 181, 239,
    240, 246, 276
  PJ's assessment of, 277–283
  play-off series against Kings, 236–240
  play-off series against Suns, 240–246
  play-off series against Trail Blazers,
    246–260
  and Tex Winter, 119–120
Los Angeles Summer League, 104, 132,
  133, 159
Loughery, Kevin, 14, 52–55, 56–57, 58,
  81, 115, 129
Louisiana State University, 128
Louisiana Tech University, 29
Love, Stan, 12
Loyola Marymount University, 132
Lucas, Jerry, 44, 47, 48
Lue, Tyronn, 167, 178
MacKinnon, Bob, 56, 57, 58
MacPherson, Ralph, 61
Magic. See Johnson, Magic; Orlando
  Magic
Malone, Karl, 112, 175, 183, 200, 201
Mannion, Pace, 90, 92
Maravich, Pete, 156, 231
Marbury, Stephon, 204
Marion, Sean, 240, 241
Marquette University, 122–123
Martin, Derek, 210
Martin, Slater, 156
Mashburn, Jamal, 154
Mason, Anthony, 197, 207

Mast, Diane, 145
Mast, Eddie, 38, 62, 84, 145
Mathis, Mike, 112
Mauer, Kenny, 230
Maverick (Jackson and Rosen), 48, 49,
  130
Mavericks (NBA team). See Dallas
  Mavericks
McAdoo, Bob, 50, 51
McClain, Dwayne, 92
McCloud, George, 158
McCracken, Paul, 127
McCray, Scooter, 90
McDaniel, Xavier, 197
McGuire, Dickie, 43, 44, 52, 103
McKey, Derrick, 273–274
McKinney, Billy, 127
McKinney, Jack, 197
McMahon, Jack, 126
McManus, Howard, 33
McMillen, Tom, 50–51
Meadowlands arena, 58, 138
Mealy, Cliff, 125
Meanwell, Walter, 121
meditation, 279, 289
Meminger, Dean, 47, 49, 60, 61
Meyer, Loren, 157
Meyer, Ray, 129
Miami Heat, 198, 199, 206, 208, 250
Mile Above the Run, A (Rosen), 49
Miller, Andre, 204
Miller, Reggie
  against Lakers, 264, 265, 267, 268,
    269, 271, 273, 275
  playing style, 261
  and referees, 112, 272
  role with Pacers, 252–253, 263
  suspended, 263
  three-point shots, 268, 270
Milwaukee Bucks, 53, 79, 110, 148,
  160, 187, 192, 262–263
Minnesota Timberwolves, 103, 188,
  195, 204, 210, 213–214, 246
Mobridge, South Dakota, 27–28
Moe, Doug, 72
Money, Eric, 54, 56

Monroe, Earl, 49, 51
Montross, Eric, 158
Moore, Lowes, 64, 66
Motta, Dick, 156, 157
Motumbo, Dikembe, 112–113
Mount, Rick, 265
Mourning, Alonzo, 112–113, 199
Mullaney, Joe, 56
Mullin, Chris, 260
Mumford, George, 244
Murphy, Calvin, 125
Murray, G. (police officer), 96–99
Musburger, Todd, 142–143
Musselman, Bill, 76, 88, 94
Musselman, Eric, 94–95
Myers, Pete, 90
Naismith, Ian, 233, 234
Naismith, James, 233
National Association of Basketball
    Coaches, 127–128
National Basketball Association (NBA),
    155–156, 161
  autograph requirements, 173
  broadcasters, 58
  coaches, 55, 56, 76, 146, 155, 261–262
  double-teaming, 57, 113
  dress code, 14
  franchise, 59
  free-throw rules, 249–250
  general managers, 128–129
  and LA Summer League, 132
  lifestyle, 78
  and media, 48, 150–151, 169–170
  and military obligations, 45
  offense plays, 52
  players, 109, 287
  predraft camp, 77
  referees, 90, 111–116, 167, 176–177,
    198, 230
  roommates on the road, 62
  roster size, 50
  Rules Committee, 113
  scouts, 30, 64, 77
  superstar players, 12
  time-outs, 75
Natt, Calvin, 56

NBA Entertainment, 206
NBA Productions, 144
NCAA (National Collegiate Athletic
    Association), 58, 59, 72, 128
  championship, 34, 122, 153
  Coach of the Year, 123
  Small College Division Tournament,
    27, 28, 29–30, 39
  tournaments, 128, 208
Nelson, Don ("Nellie"), 53, 157–158,
    159, 177, 200, 207, 215, 261
Netolicky, Bob, 265
Nets (ABA team). See New York Nets
New Jersey Nets, 14, 52–59, 130,
    138–139, 158, 183, 184–185, 204
New Orleans Jazz, 147
    See also Utah Jazz
New York Knicks, 49–52, 252, 255
  1967-1968 season, 43–45
  1968-1969 season, 45–46
  1969-1970 season, 46
  1973-1974 season, 48
  against Lakers, 42–43, 197, 198, 208,
    209, 210, 211
  against Pacers, 260, 263, 265
  approach PJ, 103, 104, 138–139, 199
  coached by Don Nelson, 207
  draft PJ, 39–43
New York Nets, 225
Newell, Pete, 122, 125
Newell, Tom, 154
Newlin, Mike, 56, 125
Nissalke, Tom, 90, 135
Noble Eightfold Path, 256–258
North Carolina State University, 76
North Central Intercollegiate Athletic
    Conference, 27
North Dakota State University, 26
Northern Idaho Community College, 59
Northwestern University, 127, 129
Norton, Ed, 237–238
Nuggets (NBA team). See Denver
    Nuggets
Nunn, Ronnie, 115
Oakley, Charles, 103, 139, 197
O'Bannon, Ed, 158

O'Hara, Joe, 101
Oilers (AAU team). *See* Phillips 66
    Oilers
Oklahoma City Cavalry, 83, 99–100
Oklahoma City University, 99
Olajuwon, Hakeem, 161, 179, 180
Olympic Games, 72, 79
Omega Institute, 84, 145
O'Neal, Jermaine, 176, 227, 247
O'Neal, Shaquille ("Shaq")
    against Bulls, 182, 241
    against Cavaliers, 189, 204, 229
    against Clippers, 206
    against 76ers, 210
    against Heat, 208
    against Jazz, 191
    against Kings, 206, 210, 236, 237,
        238, 239, 244
    against Knicks, 208, 211
    against Mavericks, 178–179
    against Nuggets, 181
    against Orlando Magic, 203
    against Pacers, 263, 264, 266, 267,
        268, 271, 272, 273, 274, 275
    against Rockets, 179–180
    against Spurs, 142, 216
    against Suns, 181, 211–212,
        241–242, 243, 244
    against SuperSonics, 188
    against Timberwolves, 214
    against Trail Blazers, 176–177, 205,
        248, 249, 250, 251, 252, 253, 254,
        255, 258, 259
    against Warriors, 212
    and Benoit Benjamin, 168
    captain of Lakers, 189, 191–192,
        221–222
    dominance, 279
    double-teaming, 142, 166, 177,
        183–184, 186, 191, 204, 214, 227,
        247, 253, 278
    as football player, 225
    footwork, 278
    free throws, 178, 179, 182, 187, 188,
        205, 224, 238, 240, 246, 249–250,
        264, 272

    injuries, 211, 212, 213, 277
    and Kobe Bryant, 189–190, 259, 269
    and media, 169
    with Orlando Magic, 202–203
    passing, 277
    personal life, 193, 195
    personality, 166, 170, 178–179, 182,
        192, 277, 290
    physique, 182, 199, 247
    on PJ, 229–230
    PJ's assessment of, 170, 281
    playing time, 149, 191
    in practice, 120, 173
    reaction to championship, 276
    self-confidence, 191–192, 207
    stepfather, 216
    and teammates, 169–170, 191, 244
    technical fouls, 176–177, 179
    and Triangle offense, 165–166,
        174–175, 183–184, 186–187, 205,
        217, 227, 230, 232, 253, 277, 278,
        279
Oregon College, 160
Oregon State University, 121
Orlando Magic, 134, 146, 165, 174,
    201–203
Pacers (NBA team). *See* Indiana Pacers
Pacific Division, 193
Pack, Robert, 158
Paige, Satchel, 28
Patroons (CBA team). *See* Albany
    Patroons
Patterson, Ray, 125, 127
Patterson, Ruben, 163–164, 188
Paultz, Billy, 12, 226
Paxson, John, 105, 106, 109, 110, 146,
    291
Payton, Gary, 188, 201
Pederson, Bob, 21, 23, 25, 26
Pederson, Paul, 27
Penn State University, 79
Pensacola Tornadoes, 88
Perkins, Sam, 263, 268, 273, 274
Perot, Ross, 158
Philadelphia 76ers, 110, 160, 189, 203,
    210–211, 263

Philadelphia Warriors, 160
  See also Golden State Warriors
Phillips 66 Oilers, 28
Phoenix Suns, 44, 57, 157, 181, 197,
  208, 209, 211–212, 240–246, 252
Pinholster, Horst, 79
pinwheel offense, 79
Pippen, Scottie
  against Lakers, 175–176, 186, 205,
    246, 249, 250–251, 252, 253, 255,
    258, 259
  against Pistons, 198
  and Jerry Krause, 134
  Lakers try to acquire, 167, 266, 281
  plays for Bulls, 105–106, 109, 110,
    152
  plays for Trail Blazers, 175–176,
    186, 227, 247–248
  and Triangle offense, 105–106, 109,
    175, 190, 228
Piscataway, New Jersey, 52, 58–59
Pistons (NBA team). *See* Detroit
  Pistons
Pitino, Rick, 77, 168–169, 276
Pittsburgh Condors, 126
Polan, Jay, 90, 94
Pornish, Pete, 24
Portland Trail Blazers
  against Lakers, 175–177, 183,
    185–186, 190–191, 204–205,
    246–260, 274
  fans, 267
  and referees, 244
  and Triangle offense, 227–228
Posey, James, 181
practice sessions, 15, 44, 57, 150, 157,
  158, 163–164
Presley, Dominick, 83
Price, Mark, 200
Princeton University, 232, 236
Puerto Rico Coquis, 66, 71
Puerto Rico Superior League, 71–75,
  77
racism, 59–60, 87, 125, 223
Rambadt, Steve, 86
Rambis, Kurt, 168

Ramsey, Jack, 56, 160
Rapid City Thrillers, 94
  See also Tampa Bay Thrillers
Raptors (NBA team). *See* Toronto
  Raptors
Reed, Willis, 42–43, 47, 48, 50, 51–52
Reeves, Khalid, 158
referees
  and A. C. Green, 167
  CBA, 90–91, 92, 115, 230
  college, 113
  and CR, 83, 90–91, 92, 96
  and Dean Smith, 208
  doubtful calls, 55
  and footwork, 278
  in Lakers-Kings series, 238, 239, 244
  in Lakers-Pacers series, 271–272
  in Lakers-Suns series, 244, 245
  in Lakers-Trail Blazers series, 250,
    252, 255, 259
  in Lakers-Wizards game, 207
  and Mike Dunleavy, 244
  NBA, 90, 111–116, 167, 176–177,
    198, 230
  as necessary evil, 15, 90–91
  and palming the ball, 231
  and PJ, 88, 180
  in Puerto Rico, 73
  and Vlade Divac, 225
Reid, J. R., 202
Reinsdorf, Jerry, 104, 128, 130,
  137–138, 162
Rellford, Richard, 90
Rice, Christy, 266
Rice, Glen
  against Heat, 208
  against Jazz, 175
  against Knicks, 211
  against Nets, 185
  against Nuggets, 181
  against Pacers, 264, 266, 267, 269,
    271, 272, 273
  against Suns, 243
  against SuperSonics, 188, 213
  against Trail Blazers, 176, 250, 253
  against Wizards, 207

on defense, 187
illnesses and injuries, 210, 277
and media, 169
passing, 277
PJ's assessment of, 170–171, 172, 175
in practice, 173
reaction to championship, 276
and teammates, 169–170, 244
traded to Lakers, 202
and Triangle offense, 110–111, 167, 174, 186, 278
Rice University, 59
Richmond, Mitch, 207
Rider, Isaiah, 227
Rider College, 35
Riley, Pat, 85, 153, 172, 197–199, 230, 255
Rivers, Doc, 146, 201, 203, 262
Robertson, Oscar, 37, 156, 189–190
Robertson, Scotty, 29
Robinson, Cliff, 56, 57, 209, 240, 241, 242, 245
Robinson, David, 186, 200, 216, 240
Rockets. See Houston Rockets; San Diego Rockets
Rockford Lightning, 61, 83, 89–92, 94–100
Rodgers, Jimmy, 29, 93, 146, 214
Rodman, Dennis, 111, 115–116, 152, 200
Rogers, Rodney, 240, 241, 242, 243
role players, 15, 156, 161
Roman, Ed, 34
Rooks, Sean, 166
Roosevelt High School (West Bronx, N.Y.), 33
Rose, Jalen, 252, 260, 261, 263, 264, 265, 268, 269, 271, 273, 275
Rosen, Alexandra (CR's daughter), 87
Rosen, Charley
  accredited trainer, 63–64, 88
  arrested, 83, 96–99
  assistant coach of Patroons, 15–18, 62–66, 76, 85, 88
  attends Bobby Knight's clinic, 16–18

on basketball, 15–16, 35–38, 285–289
basketball injuries, 34–35, 38
considered for Bulls coaching job, 83–84, 93
and father, 31, 33–34, 92, 286
graduate school, 37–38, 85
head coach of Lightning, 61, 89–92, 94–100
head coach of Patroons, 100–101
head coach of Spirits, 83, 85–89
life after leaving Patroons, 83–84
marriage, 92, 145
nickname, 64
observes Patroons game, 61
physique, 33, 68, 286
plays one on one against PJ, 67–70
taste in music, 48–49, 64
technical fouls, 90–91, 96
in various sports, 31–32
as writer, 12–14, 48–49, 84, 92–93, 101, 145–146
Rosen, Darrell (CR's son), 49, 87
Rosen, Susan (CR's wife), 49, 64, 87, 91, 92, 101
Rossini, Lou, 72
Rugby High School Panthers (N.D.), 24
Rupp, Adolph, 128
Russell, Bill, 81–82, 122, 125, 288
Russell, Cazzie, 37, 43–44, 45, 61, 91
Russo, Tony, 33
Rutgers University, 52
Ruth, Babe, 126
Sabonis, Arvydas, 177, 205, 247, 248, 249, 250, 252, 255, 278
Sacramento Kings, 148, 156, 186, 206, 207, 209–210, 236–240, 242, 267
Salley, John
  against Rockets, 180
  against SuperSonics, 213
  against Trail Blazers, 250
  character, 185, 280
  passing, 168, 277
  PJ's assessment of, 168, 203
  and Triangle offense, 231, 290

San Antonio Spurs
    against Knicks, 139
    against Lakers, 142, 186, 191,
        193–194, 212–213, 215–216
    against Suns, 240–241
    lockout season, 212–213
San Diego Rockets, 125, 126, 147–148
    See also Houston Rockets
Saunders, Flip, 213–214
Sanders, Jeff, 100, 101
Sanders, Satch, 56
Savannah Spirits, 83, 85–89
    See also Detroit Spirits
Schalow, Jack, 66
Schneiderman, Mr. (owner of used
    clothing store), 33–34
Schrempf, Detlef, 247, 251, 252
Schueler, Mike, 59
Schweitz, John, 90
Scott, Byron, 262
Seattle SuperSonics, 100, 164, 185,
    188, 210, 213, 226
Second Wind (health club), 59, 60
Second Wind (Russell), 288
Sellers, Brad, 131
seventh game, 255–256
76ers (NBA team). *See* Philadelphia
    76ers
Shannon, Howard, 232
Sharman, Bill, 121, 160, 214
Shaw, Brian, 174, 206–207, 243, 244,
    258, 275, 277, 278
Shelton, Lonnie, 51
Shue, Gene, 81
Sikma, Jack, 277
Silas, Paul, 82
Silver Bullets (CBA team). *See* Cedar
    Rapids Silver Bullets
Sixers (NBA team). *See* Philadelphia
    76ers
Sizzlers (CBA team). *See* Tampa Bay
    Sizzlers
Skiles, Scott, 240, 241, 242, 244, 262
Sloan, Jerry, 82, 174
Smith, Dean, 108, 208
Smith, Leon, 155

Smith, Steve, 176, 246–247, 248, 249,
    252, 255, 258, 259
Smits, Rik, 262, 263, 267, 271, 272,
    273, 274, 278
Sonics (NBA team). *See* Seattle
    SuperSonics
"Soul Brothers, The" (article by CR),
    12–14
Southeast Missouri State University,
    160
Southern Illinois University, 27, 28
Southwest Los Angeles Community
    Center, 177–178
Spirits. *See* Detroit Spirits; Savannah
    Spirits
Sport (magazine), 12, 126, 227
SportsCenter (ESPN), 262
Sprewell, Latrell, 139, 252, 266
Spriggs, Larry, 61
Spurs (NBA team). *See* San Antonio
    Spurs
St. Jean, Gary, 115
St. John's University, 59
Staples Arena, 151, 175, 206, 210, 264
Staples Center, 177, 180, 183, 226, 276
Starks, John, 139, 197, 198
Stojakovic, Predrag, 206, 237, 239
Stoudamire, Damon, 205, 247, 248,
    249, 250, 251, 252, 253
Strickland, Eric, 179
Sullivan, Tom, 73–74
Summer League (Los Angeles), 104,
    132, 133, 159
Sund, Rick, 154, 157
Suns (NBA team). *See* Phoenix Suns
Superior League, 71–75, 77
SuperSonics (NBA team). *See* Seattle
    SuperSonics
Syracuse Nationals, 159–160
Syracuse University, 147
Tampa Bay Sizzlers, 88
Tampa Bay Thrillers, 76
    See also Rapid City Thrillers
Texans (CBA team). *See* Wichita Falls
    Texans
Theokis, Charlie, 55

Thomas, Isiah, 200
Thompson, Jackie, 33
Thrillers (CBA team). *See* Rapid City
    Thrillers; Tampa Bay Thrillers
Timberwolves (NBA team). *See*
    Minnesota Timberwolves
Tomjanovich, Rudy, 82, 125, 161, 179
Tormohlen, Gene, 148
Tornadoes (CBA team). *See* Pensacola
    Tornadoes
Toronto Raptors, 182–183
Trail Blazers (NBA team). *See* Portland
    Trail Blazers
Treasure State Community College, 59
Triangle offense
    CR on, 289–291
    and guards, 204
    mechanics, 105–108
    philosophy of, 129, 152
    PJ on, 289–291
    players on, 230–231
    and Trail Blazers, 227–228
    use by Bulls, 81, 108–111, 130, 131,
        132, 133–134, 160–162, 181, 224,
        230, 270, 290
    use by Jazz, 227
    use by Lakers, 163–166, 183–184,
        185, 205, 217, 230–231, 277, 278
    against Kings, 239, 240
    against Rockets, 180
    against Spurs, 213
    against Suns, 181, 242
    against Trail Blazers, 190, 253
    in LA Summer League, 104
    use by Mavericks, 153–159, 223
    use by Patroons, 100–101
    use by Rockets, 179, 227
    use by University of North Dakota,
        29
    variations, 159–160
Triple-Post Offense, The (Winter), 100,
    123–124, 154, 197
Tulsa Fast Breakers, 92
Turner, Elston, 90
University of California at Los Angeles
    (UCLA), 59, 110, 123, 128, 157

University of California-Santa Barbara
    (UCSB), 170, 172–173
University of Colorado, 144
University of Iowa, 95
University of Kansas, 208
University of Kentucky, 122
University of Minnesota, 26
University of North Carolina, 76, 108,
    208
University of North Dakota, 13, 26,
    146, 287
University of Southern California, 121,
    122, 182
University of Washington, 124–125
University of Wisconsin, 121
Unseld, Wes, 125
Utah Jazz, 112, 174, 175, 183, 191,
    194, 195, 212, 246
    See also New Orleans Jazz
Van Arsdale, Dick, 43–44, 45
van Breda Kolff, Jan, 54, 56
Van Eman, Lanny, 131, 132
Van Exel, Nick, 181
Van Gundy, Jeff, 115, 138–139,
    196–197, 198–199
Vancouver Grizzlies, 175, 210
Vega, Alex, 73–74
Villanova University, 76
Virginia Tech, 232
Vitti, Gary, 187
Wake Forest University, 241
Walk, Neal, 288–289
Walker, Jimmy, 125, 127
Walker, Samaki, 216
Wallace, Rasheed, 183, 205, 227, 246,
    247, 248, 249, 251, 252, 253, 254,
    258, 259, 260
Warriors (NBA team). *See* Golden
    State Warriors; Philadelphia
    Warriors
Washington Bullets, 156
    See also Baltimore Bullets
Washington Wizards, 173, 186, 207
Webber, Chris, 209, 210, 236, 237, 238,
    239, 240
Wellington, Texas, 120

Wells, Bonzie, 247, 249, 255
West, James, 58
West, Jerry, 85, 148, 149, 156, 169,
    170, 177, 231
Western Conference, 191, 195, 205,
    215, 246–260
Westhead, Paul, 72, 190, 197
Wetzel, John, 232
Whittaker, George, 94–96, 97, 98
Wichita Falls Texans, 91, 100
Wildcatters (CBA team). *See* Wyoming
    Wildcatters
Williams, Jason, 206, 210, 236–237,
    238, 239
Williams, Ray ("Ray-Ray"), 51
Williams, Vanessa, 245
Williamson, Corliss, 237
Williamson, John ("Super John"), 52,
    54, 55, 56
Williston High School (N.D.),
    21–26
Wingfield, Dontonio, 227
Wingo, Harthorne, 62
Winter, Ernest, 120
Winter, Mona Francis, 120
Winter, Nancy, 124, 128
Winter, Tex, 119–135
    approached by Mavericks, 154
    assistant coach of Bulls, 78, 80, 82,
        108, 109, 137, 146, 154, 161

on basketball and values, 290
coaches in Puerto Rico, 72
eating habits, 226, 231–232
footwork, 156
and Jimmy Cleamons, 157
and LA Summer League, 104
with Lakers, 119–120, 146, 147, 172,
    174, 178, 209, 246, 254
on Pete Maravich, 231
on PJ and Triangle, 229
with Rockets, 179
Seven Principles of Sound Offense,
    106–107, 172
on success, 283
teaches clinics, 29
two-guard front, 110
use of Triangle by various teams,
    160
Winter, Theo, 120
Wittman, Randy, 154
Wizards (NBA team). *See* Washington
    Wizards
Wohl, Dave, 54–55
Wood, David, 90
Wooden, John, 128
Woolpert, Phil, 122
Woolrich, Jim, 160
Wright, Brad, 90
Wyoming Wildcatters, 66, 71, 91
yoga, 279